Mergers and Acquisitions

Mergers and Acquisitions

A.P. Dash
Professor
Finance & Strategy
Power Management Institute, Noida
(NTPC Ltd.)

TECHSAR™
NEW DELHI

Published by
I.K. International Pvt. Ltd.
4435-36/7, Ansari Road, Daryaganj
New Delhi–110 002 (India)
E-mail: info@ikinternational.com
Website: www.ikbooks.com

ISBN 978-93-80578-15-6

Reprint 2023

Published by Krishan Makhijani for I.K. International Pvt. Ltd. 4435-36/7, Ansari Road, Daryaganj, New Delhi–110 002.

Dedicated
to
my wife
Dipti

Preface

Starting from megamergers to megabucks, the world has witnessed dramatic changes in corporate restructuring. Every day we come across incidences of mergers and acquisitions (M&A) somewhere in the world, which create ripples in the corporate circles. Fuelled by capital-rich Private Equity funds and Hedge funds, the field of mergers and acquisitions has assumed great significance. M&A, of late, has redefined the way we look at business and conduct business. It has reshaped the landscape of business to an extent that every corporate strategy is intricately interwoven with certain M&A activity. In the last two decades, we have seen countless companies, like General Electric, going for aggressively acquiring other companies- big or small – and in the process, built revenues, brand equity and won market share.

This book is an honest attempt to capture the entire spectrum of M&A activity and share the contours of the implementation process. From valuation to integration, the book is sure to help managers think through what such a strategic move would mean to the organisation. The book attempts to provide working knowledge and skill of underlying concepts, contractual obligations, tax impact and legal background of M&A. Precisely, the book is written to show business managers and financial executives which kind of corporate restructuring can be worked out in the organisation and how best to analyse, design and implement M&A deals.

The book can be classified into four basic frameworks. The first three chapters may be clubbed into the conceptual framework, where conceptual issues and economic consequences of M&A are discussed in detail. Critical issues like valuation and due diligence, which forms an integral part of any M&A, are examined with great care to emphasise the framework for pre-merger issues. The legal framework borders on areas like regulatory issues, tax impact, cross-border legal complications, transfer pricing and deal structuring. It is worth mentioning that the structuring of the deals has changed a lot in the recent years under the weight of hundreds of legal precedents, accounting rules and regulatory impositions. The last framework encompasses strategic issues of merger management leading to creation of value to the organisation. Attempt has also been made to find out why mergers fail and how to make them successful. To have a logical conclusion, towards the end, great corporate cases have been presented with high level of clarity and openness to reinforce the learning in earlier chapters. In fact, the cases are the USP of the book.

M&A is no easy path to riches. Despite major failures in M&A, those who make them work, pull the right trigger in exercising great care and restraint in the development of M&A deal. The purchase and sell of a business enterprise is one of the most complex transactions one can undertake. It can be a make or break decision for major corporations. While an error in a typical M&A deal may create havoc leading to a colossal loss, a well structured deal may unleash great value for the corporation. In the book, an attempt has been made to show both sides of the same coin and bring out an objective and dispassionate analysis of the entire M&A process.

A.P. Dash

Contents

1

Cross-Border Mergers and Takeovers: A Recent Trend

Competitiveness in the national arena is now forcing business to go global. The days of regional differentiation are over. Old strategies that professed "Small is Beautiful" or offered lessons on how companies could "survive in a niche" are no longer viable. Yes it is true that there are still micro-cosmos that thrive at the small business level and there is a new generation of savvy entrepreneurs who will develop and continue to fuel healthy business in the shadows of corporate juggernauts well into the future. One of the most important situations that they eventually face is the key to their survival: acquire or be acquired. In other words the only optimal size is big, grow bigger than last year, grow larger and faster than the competitors. Stagnation or slow growth is a sure recipe for disaster.

Globalization is a strong force that enables industrial consolidation. During the Asian economic crisis in 1997 and 1998, global organizations such as International Monetary Fund, The World Bank and the WTO assisted and encouraged countries including Thailand, South Korea and Indonesia to restructure their financial institutions and open up their economies by reducing trade barriers. A direct result of these policies was that global financial services companies began to acquire and buy equity stakes in financial service players in each of these economies. From 1998 to 2000, Thailand experienced a wave of acquisition activity. Globalization has had a number of drivers including advances in information and communication technology, advances in travel, the reduction of barriers to trade and the growth of overseas markets that could no longer be ignored. What characterizes the current business environment is that we now see all industries are potentially global, and see all industries taking part in the game.

GLOBAL STRATEGIES AND M&A

In a sense, world has become a global village. Mergers and Acquisitions are no longer restricted by borders or geography anymore, because technology and the passion to grow, has made everything possible. There was time when M & A activities were very less in India, unlike USA, which had waves of M & A activities throughout its history. But in the last decade, even India has witnessed a tremendous shift in its gear and the growth for hunger has given a thrust, largely seen around 2000 when 1344 M & A deals were struck.

An ambitious organization would like to grow fast and develop strategies for it. While formulating a strategy, be it any kind, an organization needs to consider few very crucial things - right from the strategy formation to how can it be successfully implemented. The organization needs people who will strategies based on the need for growth and who will keep in mind not only the long term implications but also the short term objectives of the organization which needs to be achieved as well. There are many different school of thoughts that propound different strategies which an organization should use.

Boston Consulting Group emphasizes on three concepts, firstly, the experience curve which represents volume-cost relationship. According to this concept, the larger the cumulative output the firm achieves, the lower cost it incurs. Thus, it suggests an early entry and price policies to develop volume. Second concept is about the product life cycle. This includes the phases a product goes through in its life, i.e. right from developing it to maturity and decline of its profits. Based on this, the last concept of portfolio balance suggests that total corporate cash inflows will roughly balance total corporate investment. But the issue with BCG approach is that it is not fit for every type of organization.

Another school of thought is the **Porter Approach**. Michel Porter discusses his approach in 3 steps

- Step 1
  Select an attractive industry
- Step 2
  Develop competitive advantage through cost leadership
- Step 3
  Develop attractive value chains

But again this approach is very subjective in nature, as for every organization the approach will be viewed in a different light and would bear different results. For an organization to decide which strategy to use and when, requires in depth knowledge and study of the environment, changes which are prevalent in the industry, market, SWOT of the organization and the synergy achieved etc.

Another new approach is the **Blue Ocean Strategy.** This strategy gives a systematic approach to making the competition irrelevant. Blue ocean strategy has six principles basically dealing with how to reconstruct market boundaries, focus on the big picture, reach beyond existing demand, get the strategic sequence right, overcome organizational hurdles, and build execution into strategy. This is a very revolutionary new way of thinking that the organization should now worry about how to tap newer markets than to worry about how to exist in the same market where their rivals have already established themselves.

There are various types of strategies that an organization uses but it depends whether the organization is going for internal or external growth. External growth is favorable when certain goals and objectives are achieved earlier, cost of building and starting from the scratch requires loads of time which can be saved, tax advantages and other opportunities are available. On the other hand, internal growth is favorable when the above stated advantages are less or minimal in nature. Also at times it is more economical. But, it seems like from the trends seen, an organization which wants to grow M

& A activity opens up a brighter horizon. For instance, the Ispat steel co. has become one of the world's largest steel companies because of the long series of successful acquisition. Also, Lakshami Mittal considers the Mergers and Acquisition to be the best way to grow business and an effective way too. But then there are many other businessmen who feel that acquisitions are certainly very good way to add a product line or distribution channel that would be too costly to build from scratch. But they don't replace the internal growth or alliances. Assets go up the elevator at night and down in the morning. They usually like to build internally when they feel confident that they have the product and process knowledge to capitalize on an opportunity quickly. The same thought somewhat is echoed by David Komwasky of Meryll Lynch, who says that one must not go for an acquisition just for the sake of it. These various thoughts give rise to the need of knowing mergers and acquisition up close and studying them to understand when they can be used to make better gains for the organization.

Once an organization knows the need of the hour, the next step comes of formulating a strategy. Formulation of strategy is one of the most crucial and decisive step for an organization, as one wrong decision might end up making loads of trouble for them. Strategic formulation is thus, a combination of three main processes which are as follows:

- Performing a situation analysis, self-evaluation and competitor analysis: both internal and external; both micro-environmental and macro-environmental.
- Concurrent with this assessment, objectives are set. These objectives should be parallel to a time-line; some are in the short-term and others on the long-term. This involves crafting vision statements (long term view of a possible future), mission statements (the role that the organization gives itself in society), overall corporate objectives (both financial and strategic), strategic business unit objectives (both financial and strategic), and tactical objectives.
- These objectives should, in the light of the situation analysis, suggest a strategic plan. The plan provides the details of how to achieve these objectives.

Last but not the least, every M&A decision need to be framed in tune with the overall corporate strategy and emanate from the mission and vision.

There is a variety of drivers and motivating factors at play in the M&A world. Apart from personal glory (or greed), M&A deals are often driven by many justifiable market consolidation, expansion or corporate diversification motives. And, of course, ever present as an inspirational force in M&A is the old reliable financial, generally tax related motivation. Expansion is one of the primary reasons to cross the borders as the national limits fail to provide growth opportunities. One has to look outside its boundaries and play out in the global arena to seek new opportunities and scale new heights. With the habit of creating an empire it becomes difficult for these entrepreneurs to stay within its limits. The simple fact is that most key players in many markets have already extracted a significant proportion of the available value from the domestic resources. They have improved profitability through better cost management and through efficiency gains realized after domestic consolidation.

Another reason is to gain monopoly, the company which has been acquired by the acquirer is always a company which is trembling financially but had something to offer the acquiring company. It may be the market share or intellectual capital or other reasons but one thing that the acquirer looks is for is the untapped resources to be exploited which can lead the company a step higher in the ladder of success. Globalization is a key to help in the rapidity of the M&A as it is globalization that integrates world economies together and many nations have opened themselves, the countries have made laws and regulations that attract new companies to come into the country and make it easy for the companies to easily perform their operation of M&A.

There are also new forces in play that make cross-border expansion more feasible and capable of creating value. For example, international deregulation is removing old barriers. Institutional investors are taking a more global perspective. Customer profiles across markets are becoming more homogeneous.

Cross-border takeover bids are complex transactions that may involve the handling of a significant number of legal entities, listed or not, and which are often governed by local rules (company law, market regulations, self regulations, etc.). Not only a foreign bidder might be disadvantaged or impeded by a potential lack of information, but also some legal incompatibilities might appear in the merger process resulting in a deadlock, even though the bid would be 'friendly'. This legal uncertainty may constitute a significant execution risk and act as a barrier to cross-border consolidation.

In some cases, legal structures are not only complex but also prevent, *de jure* or *de facto*, some institutions to be taken over or even merge (in the context of a friendly bid) with institutions of a different type. Such restrictions are not specific to cross-border mergers, but could provide part of the explanation of the low level of cross-border M&As, since consolidation is possible within a group of similar institutions (at a domestic level) whereas it is not possible with other types of institutions (which makes any cross-border merger almost impossible).

Specific domestic tax breaks may favour specific, non-harmonized products or services, with the result that every institution has to provide this service or product if it wants to remain competitive. In such a situation, a merger between two entities located in that domestic market may yield synergies of scale, whereas it will be more difficult to exploit comparable synergies for a foreign institution taking over a domestic one, while not being entitled to the tax break in their home state.

The impact of taxation on dividends may influence the shareholders' acceptance of a cross-border merger. Even though a seat transfer or a quotation in another stock market might be justified for economic reasons, groups of shareholders could be opposed to such an operation if it implies higher non-refundable withholding tax, and thus lower returns on their investments.

What are the challenges in cross-border mergers and acquisitions?

"Marriage of two lame ducks will not give birth to a race horse."

But the biggest challenge to a cross-border merger and takeover are the **cultural issues.** According to KPMG study, "83% of all the mergers and acquisitions failed to produce any benefit for the shareholders and over half actually destroyed value". Interviews of over 100 senior executives involved in these 700 deals over a two-year period revealed that the overwhelming cause of failure is the people and the cultural differences. Difficulties encountered in mergers and acquisitions are amplified in cross-cultural situations, when companies involved are from two or more different countries. Up to the point in the transaction, where the papers are signed, the merger and acquisition business is predominantly financial valuing of the assets, determining the price and due diligence. Before the ink is dry, however, this financially driven deal becomes a human transaction filled with emotions and trauma and survival behaviour, the non-linear, often the irrational world of human beings in the midst of changes. In the case of international mergers and acquisition, the complexity of these processes is often compounded by the differences in national cultures. People living and working in different countries react to the same situation or events in a very different manner. Therefore, a company involved in an international merger or acquisition needs to consider these differences right from the design stage if it is to succeed.

Individual preoccupation on "How is it all going to impact me?" weakens the commitment to the job at hand. This in turn translates people looking in for work in other companies. Often a firm in midst of transition loses its own talent, strengthening the competition. In countries where people identify largely with groups; people tend to look for support within their group. Employees' reluctance within the target company of a cross-border deal might also pose a threat to the successful outcome of the transaction. Indeed, employees may not accept to be managed from another country. A public opposition to the project may influence analysts' assessment.

Given that cross-border mergers are complex and need to overcome a number of execution risks (as evidenced in this document), there might be an impact on shareholders' and analysts' apprehension of failure risk when it comes to cross-border mergers. Consumers may mistrust foreign entities, meaning that all parameters being equal, a

Table 1.1: Cross-border mergers and acquisitions

Year	Sales	Purchases
2000	1219	910
2001	1037	2195
2002	1698	270
2003	949	1362
2004	1760	863
2005	4210	2649
Total	10873	8249

Source: UNCTAD World Investment Report, 2006.

local incumbent may have an advantage over a competitor identified as foreign. This explains why foreign institutions often prefer to keep a local brand. The companies will have to keep in mind that cross border mergers are not only business proposals but a corporate marriage of both the entities which require deeper and insightful solutions.

Cross-border M&A is always fraught with high risk. But in spite of the risk, more number of companies have shown greater propensity to go for M&A. Instead of setting up new business and starting a new company from scratch, taking over companies with lock, stock and barrel was a preferred way, as statistics suggests, of expanding business in new countries.

Mergers have consequences for the structure, behaviour and performance of the industries where it takes place. The major effect on structure is the degree of concentration and barriers to entry. Mergers increase the degree of concentration due to changes in the number and size distribution of firms. In case the economies of scale are available to more than two firms, there may be competition and it will promote efficiency. Otherwise, there is a possibility of using potential market power advantages. In cases where economies of scale are realized through mergers, this will act as an entry barrier to others. Mergers may strengthen product differentiation due to intangible assets such as patents.

Product differentiation also leads to change in behaviour of the merger. The larger firm with its resources can resort to non-price forms of competition. Sometimes, it may resort to predatory pricing against competitors. To understand the increasing trend towards cross-border M&As, one has to know the historical precedence of such activities. During the last century, there have been various rationale for M&As. Such activities have been more prevalent in the US and the UK. However, in recent years, there is a trend in other countries also to resort to mergers and acquisitions. The nature of changes occuring in Europe and Asia is as follows:

Europe In the 1980s, mergers and acquisitions were perceived as *financial engineering* and were discredited. This was because most of the deals were leveraged deals. In the 1990s, mergers and acquisitions were in the form of making logical industrial deals which were appealing to shareholders. The increase in M&A activities in Europe is due to deregulation of previously protected industries. Companies are encouraged to restructure. Much of M&A activity is a function of the emergence of global competition industries such as those in pharmaceuticals, as well as deregulation of telecommunications. Now, the companies are driven by industry on a world-wide basis.

Asia There is a growth of mergers and acquisitions among Asian-Pacific companies. This is due to continued high economic growth in Asia and the need for corporations to grow and compete in the global economy. In addition, traditional family-owned businesses are now more willing to sell assets to third parties. The younger generation is much more willing to part with family-built assets.

2

Introduction to Mergers and Acquisitions

In today's global business environment, companies need to grow to survive, and one of the best ways to grow is by merging with some other company or acquiring other companies. Massive, multibillion-dollar corporations are becoming the norm, leaving an entrepreneur to wonder whether a merger ought to be in his or her plans, too.

When a small business owner chooses to merge with or sell out to another company, it is sometimes called "harvesting" the small business. In this situation, the transaction is intended to release the value locked up in the small business for the benefit of its owners and investors. The impetus for a small business owner to pursue a sale or merger may involve asset planning, a need to diversify his or her investments, an inability to finance growth independently, or a simple need for change. In addition, some small businesses find that the best way to grow and compete against larger firms is to merge with or acquire other small businesses.

In principle, the decision to merge with or acquire another firm is a capital budgeting decision much like any other. But mergers differ from ordinary investment decisions in at least five ways. First, the value of a merger may depend on such things as strategic fits that are difficult to measure. Second, the accounting, tax, and legal aspects of a merger can be complex. Third, mergers often involve issues of corporate control and are a means of replacing existing management. Fourth, mergers obviously affect the value of the firm, but they also affect the relative value of the stocks and bonds. Finally, mergers are often "unfriendly."

The key principle behind buying a company is to create shareholder value over and above that of the sum of the two companies. Two companies together are more valuable than two separate companies. The rationale is particularly alluring to companies when times are tough. Strong companies will act to buy other companies to create a more competitive, cost-efficient company. The companies will come together hoping to gain a greater market share or to achieve greater efficiency. Because of these potential benefits, target companies will often agree to be purchased when they know they cannot survive alone.

DISTINCTION BETWEEN MERGER AND ACQUISITION

Although they are often uttered in the same breath, the terms merger and acquisition mean slightly different things. When one company takes over another and clearly establishes itself as the new owner, the purchase is called an acquisition. From a legal point of view, the target company ceases to exist, the buyer "swallows" the business and the buyer's stock continues to be traded. In the pure sense of the term, a merger happens when two firms, often of about the same size, agree to go forward as a single new company rather than remain separately owned and operated. This kind of action is more precisely referred to as a "merger of equals." Both companies' stocks are surrendered and new company stock is issued in its place.

For example, both Daimler-Benz and Chrysler ceased to exist when the two firms merged, and a new company, DaimlerChrysler, was created. In practice, however, actual mergers of equals don't happen very often. Usually, one company will buy another and, as part of the deal's terms, simply allow the acquired firm to proclaim that the action is a merger of equals, even if it's technically an acquisition. Being bought out often carries negative connotations, therefore, by describing the deal as a merger, deal makers and top managers try to make the takeover more palatable.

A purchase deal will also be called a merger when both CEOs agree that joining together is in the best interest of both of their companies. But when the deal is unfriendly—that is, when the target company does not want to be purchased—it is always regarded as an acquisition. Whether a purchase is considered a merger or an acquisition really depends on whether the purchase is friendly or hostile and how it is announced. In other words, the real difference lies in how the purchase is communicated to and received by the target company's board of directors, employees and shareholders.

Merger or amalgamation may take two forms:

- Merger through absorption
- Merger through consolidation

Absorption

17 shares of Tata Chemicals Ltd., TCL, (market value per share being Rs. 114) for every 100 shares of Tata Fertilisers Ltd.,TFL, held by the shareholders is a combination of two or more companies into an existing company(an absorption). All companies except one lose their identity in a merger through absorption. An example of this type of merger is the absorption of Tata Fertilisers Ltd. (TFL) by Tata Chemicals Ltd. (TCL). TCL, the acquiring company (a buyer), survived after merger while TFL, the acquired company (a seller), ceased to exist. TFL transferred its assets, liabilities and shares to TCL. Under the scheme of merger, TFL shareholders were offered.

Consolidation

Consolidation is a combination of two or more companies into a new company. In this form of merger, all companies are legally dissolved and a new entity is created. In consolidation, the acquired company transfers its assets, liabilities and shares to the acquiring company for cash for exchange of shares. In a narrow sense, the terms amalgamation and consolidation are sometimes used interchangeably. An example of consolidation is the merger or amalgamation of Hindustan Computers Ltd., Hindustan Instruments Ltd., Indian Software Company Ltd., and Indian

Reprographics Ltd. in 1986 to an entirely new company called HCL Ltd.

Acquisition

A fundamental characteristic of merger (either through absorption or consolidation) is that the acquiring company (existing or new), takes over the ownership of other companies and combines their operations with its own operations. An acquisition may be defined as an act of acquiring effective control by one company over assets or management of another company without any combination of companies. Thus, in an acquisition, two or more companies may remain independent, separate legal entity, but there may be change in the control of companies.

Takeover

A takeover may also be defined as obtaining of control over the management of a company by another. An acquisition or take-over does not necessarily entail full, legal control. A company can have effective control over another company by holding minority ownership. Under the Monopolies and Restrictive Trade Practice Act, takeover means acquisition of not less than 25 per cent of the voting power in a company. Section 372 of the Companies Act defines the limit of a company's investment in the shares of another company. If a company wants to invest in more than 10 per cent of the subscribed capital of another company, it has to be approved in the shareholders general meeting and also by the central government. The investment in shares of other companies in excess of 10 per cent of the subscribed capital can result into their takeover.

Takeover vs. acquisition

Sometimes, a distinction between takeover and acquisition is made for obvious reasons. The term takeover is understood to resemble hostility. When an acquisition is a 'forced' or 'unwilling' acquisition, it is called a takeover. In an unwilling acquisition, the management of "target" company would oppose a move of being taken over. When the management of "target" company mutually and willingly agree for the takeover, it is called acquisition or friendly takeover. An example of acquisition is the acquisition of controlling interest (45 per cent shares) of Universal Luggage Manufacturing Company Ltd. by Blow Plast Ltd. Similarly, Mahindra and Mahindra Ltd. a leading manufacturer of jeeps and tractors acquired 26 per cent equity stake in Allwyn Nissan Ltd. Yet another example is the acquisition of 28 per cent equity of International Data Management (IDM) by HCL Ltd. In recent years, due to the liberalization of financial sector as well as opening up of the economy for foreign investors, a number of hostile takeovers could be witnessed in India. Examples include takeover of Shaw Wallace, Dunlop, Mather and Platt and Hindustan Dorr Oliver by Chhabrias, Ashok Leyland by Hindujas and ICIM, Harrison Malayalam and Spencers by Goenkas. Both Hindujas and Chhabrias are non-resident Indians (NRIs).

Holding Company

A company can obtain the status of holding company by acquiring shares of other companies. A holding company is a company which holds more than half of the nominal value of the equity capital of another company called a subsidiary company, or controls the composition of its Board of Directors. Both holding and subsidiary companies retain their separate legal entities and maintain their separate books of accounts. Unlike some countries, like the USA, or UK, in India, it is not legally required to consolidate accounts of holding and subsidiary companies.

Motives and Benefits of Mergers

Why do mergers take place? It is believed that mergers and acquisitions are strategic decisions leading to the maximization of a company's growth by enhancing its production and marketing operations. They have become popular in the recent times because of the enhanced competition, breaking of trade barriers, free flow of capital across countries and globalization of business as a number of economies are being deregulated and integrated with other economies. A number of reasons are attributed for the occurrence of mergers and acquisitions. For example, it is suggested that mergers and acquisition are intended to:

- Limit competition
- Utilize under-utilised market power

- Overcome the problem of slow growth and profitability in one's own industry
- Achiever diversification
- Gain economies of scale and increase income with proportionately less investment
- Establish a transnational bridgehead without excessive start-up costs to gain access to foreign market
- Utilize under-utilised resources—human and physical and managerial skills
- Displace existing management
- Circumvent government regulations
- Reap speculative gains attendant upon new security issue or change in P/E ratio
- Create an image of aggressiveness and strategies opportunism, empire building and to amass vast economic powers of the company.

Are there any real benefits of merger? A number of benefits or mergers are claimed. All of them are not real benefits. Based on the empirical evidence and the experience of certain companies, the most common motives and advantages of mergers and acquisitions are explained below:

- Maintaining or accelerating a company's growth, particularly when the internal growth is constrained due to paucity of resources;
- Enhancing profitability, through cost reduction resulting from economies of scale, operating efficiency and synergy;
- Diversifying the risk of the company, particularly when it acquires those businesses whose income streams are not correlated.
- Reducing tax liability because of the provision of setting-off accumulated losses and unabsorbed depreciation of one company against the profits of another.
- Limiting the severity of competition by increasing the company's market power.

Accelerated Growth

Growth is essential for sustaining the viability, dynamism and value-enhancing capability of a company. A growth-oriented company is not only able to attract the most talented executives but it would also be able to retain them. Growing operations provide challenges and excitement to the executives as well as opportunities for their job enrichment and rapid career development. This helps to increase managerial efficiency. Other things being the same, growth leads to higher profits and increase in the shareholders' value. A company can achieve its growth objective by:

- Expanding its existing markets
- Entering in new markets

A company may expand and/or diversify its markets internally or externally. If the company cannot grow internally due to lack of physical and managerial resources, it can grow externally by combining its operations with other companies through mergers and acquisitions. Mergers and acquisitions may help to accelerate the pace of a company's growth in a convenient and inexpensive manner.

Internal growth requires that the company should develop its operating facilities—manufacturing, research, marketing etc. Internal development of facilities for growth also requires time. Thus, lack or inadequacy of resources and time needed for internal development constrains a company's pace of growth. The company can acquire production facilities as well as other resources from outside through mergers and acquisitions. Specially, for entering in new products/markets, the company may lack technical skills and may require special marketing skills and/or a wide distribution network to access different segments of markets. The company can acquire existing company or companies with requisite infrastructure and skills and grow quickly.

Mergers and acquisitions, however, involve cost. External growth could be expensive if the company pays an excessive price of merger. Benefits should exceed the cost of acquisition for realizing a growth which adds value to shareholders. In practice, it has been found that the management of a number of acquiring companies paid an excessive price for acquisition to satisfy their urge for high growth and larger size of their companies. It is necessary that price may be carefully determined and negotiated so that merger enhances the value of shareholders.

Enhanced Profitability

The combination of two or more companies may result in more than the average profitability due to cost reduction and efficient utilization of resources. This may happen because of the following reasons:

- Economies of scale
- Operating economies
- Synergy

Economies of scale

Economies of scale arise when increase in the volume of productions leads to a reduction in the cost of production per unit. Merger may help to expand volume of production without a corresponding increase in fixed costs. Thus, fixed costs are distributed over a large volume of production causing the unit cost of production to decline. Economies of scale may also rise from other indivisibilities such as production facilities, management functions and management resources and systems. This happens because a given function, facility or resource is utilized for a larger scale of operation. For example, a given mix of plant and machinery can produce scale economies when its capacity utilization is increased. Economies will be maximized when it is optimally utilized. Similarly, economies in the use of the marketing function can be achieved by covering wider markets and customers using a given sales force and promotion and advertising efforts. Economies of scale may also be obtained from the optimum utilization of management resource and systems of planning, budgeting, reporting and control. A company established management systems by employing enough qualified professionals irrespective of its size. A combined firm with a large size can make the optimum use of the management resource and systems resulting in economies of scale.

Operating economies

In addition to economies of scale, a combination of two or more firms may result into cost reduction due to operating economies.

A combined firm may avoid or reduce overlapping functions and facilities. It can consolidate its management functions such as manufacturing, marketing, R&D and reduce operating costs. For example, a combined firm may eliminate duplicate channels of distribution, or create a centralized training centre, or introduce an integrated planning and control system.

In a vertical merger, a firm may either combine with its suppliers of input (backward integration) and/or with its customers (forward integration). Such merger facilities better coordination and administration of the different stages of business operations—purchasing, manufacturing, and marketing—eliminate the need for bargaining (with suppliers and/or customers), and minimizing uncertainty of supply of inputs and demand for product and saves costs of communication.

An example of a merger resulting in operating economies is the merger of Sundaram Clayton Ltd. (SCL) with TVS-Suzuki Ltd. (TSL). By this merger, TSL became the second largest producer of two-wheelers after Bajaj. The main motivation for the takeover was TSL's need to tide over its different market situation through increased volume of production. It needed a large manufacturing base to reduce its production costs. Large amount of funds would have been required for creating additional production capacity. SCL also needed to upgrade its technology and increase its production. SCL's and TSL's plants were closely located which added to their advantages. The combined company has also been enabled to share the common R&D facilities. Yet another example of a horizontal merger motivated by the desire for rationalization of operations is the takeover of Universal Luggage by Blow Plast. The intended objectives were elimination of fierce price war and reduction of marketing staff.

Synergy

Synergy implies a situation where the combined firm is more valuable than the sum of the individual combining firms. It is defined as 'two plus two equal to five' (2+2 = 5) phenomenon. Synergy refers to benefits other than those related to economies of scale. Operating economies are one form of synergy benefits. But apart from operating economies, synergy may also arise from enhanced managerial competitive creativity, innovativeness, R&D and market coverage capacity due to the complementarity of resources and skills and a widened horizon of opportunities.

Diversification of Risk

Diversification implies growth through the combination of firms in unrelated businesses. Such mergers are called conglomerate mergers. It is difficult to justify conglomerate merger on the ground of economies as it does not help to strengthen horizontal or vertical linkages. It is argued that it can result into reduction of total risk through substantial reduction of cyclicality of operations. Total risk will be reduced if the operations of the combining firms are negatively correlated.

In practice, investors can reduce non-systematic risk (the company related risk) by diversifying their investment in shares of a large number of companies. Systematic risk (the market related risk) is not diversifiable. Therefore, investors do not pay any premium for diversifying total risk via reduction in non-systematic risk that they can do on their own, cheaply and quickly. For example, an investor who holds one per cent of shares of Company X and one per cent share of Company Y could achieve the same share of earnings and assets if Companies X and Y are merged and he holds one per cent of shares of the merged company. The risk from his point of view has been diversified by his acquiring shares of the two companies. Of course, the merger of two companies may reduce the viability of earnings, but it would not necessarily reduce the variability of earnings vis-à-vis the market-related variables. What advantage can result from conglomerate mergers for shareholders who can diversify their portfolios to reduce non-systematic risk? The reduction of total risk, however, is advantageous from the combined company's point of view, since the combination of management and other systems strengthen the capacity of the combined firm to withstand the severity of the unforeseen economic factors which could otherwise endanger the survival of individual companies. Conglomerate mergers can also prove to be beneficial in the case of shareholders of unquoted companies since they do not have opportunity for trading in their company's shares.

An example of diversification through mergers to reduce total risk improve profitability is that of RPG Enterprises (Goenka Group). The group started its takeover activity in 1979. It comprises a large number of companies, most of which have been takeover. The strategy has been to look out for any foreign disinvestment, or any cases of sick companies which could prove right target at low takeover prices. In 1988, RPG took over ICIM and Harrisons Malayalam Limited. In the case of ICIM, the parent company, ICL, continued to hold 40 per cent the equity stake with the Goenkas acquiring 10 per cent of the equity by private placement of shares. For the Goenkas, this has provided an easy access to the electronics industry.

Reduction in Tax Liability

In a number of countries, a company is allowed to carry forward its accumulated loss to set-off against its future earnings for calculating its tax liability. A loss-making or sick company may not be in a position to earn sufficient profits in future to take advantage of the carry forward provision. If the company is allowed to merge with a sick company to set-off against its profits the accumulated loss and unutilised depreciation of that company. A number of companies in India have merged to take advantage of this provision.

An example of a merger to reduce tax liability is the absorption of Ahmedabad Cotton Mills Limited (ACML) by Arvind Mills in 1979. AMCL was closed in August 1977 on account of labour problem. At the time of merger in April 1979, ACML had an accumulated loss of Rs. 3.34 crore. Arvind Mills saved about Rs. 2 crore in tax liability for the next two years because it could set-off ACML's accumulated loss against its profits. Yet another example of a merger induced by tax saving is the takeover of Sidhpur Mills by Reliance in 1979. The carry forward losses and unabsorbed depreciation of Sidhpur amounted to Rs. 2.47 crore. In addition to tax savings, the merger provided Reliance with an opportunity for vertical integration (Sidhpur would supply grey cloth to Reliance) and capacity expansion (Sidhpur had 490 looms and 50,000 spindles and 40 acres of land). ICICI taking new bank of

Madurai in another case in point where tax benefits have been gained.

When two companies merge through an exchange of shares, the shareholders of selling company can save tax. The profit arising from the exchange of shares are not taxable until the shares are actually sold. When the shares are sold, they are subject to capital gains tax which is much lower than the ordinary income tax rate. For example, in India capital gains tax rate is 20 per cent while for the corporate tax rate is 35 per cent.

A strong urge to reduce tax liability, particularly when the marginal tax rate is high (as has been the case in India), is a strong motivation for the combination of companies. For example, the high tax rate was the main reason for the post-war merger activity in the USA. Also, tax benefits are responsible for one-third of mergers in the USA.

Financial Benefits

There are many ways in which a merger can result into financial synergy and benefits. A merger may help in:

- Eliminating the financial constraint
- Deploying surplus cash
- Enhancing debt capacity
- Lowering the financing costs

Financing constraint

A company may be constrained to grow through internal development due to shortage of funds. The company can grow externally by acquiring another company by the exchange of shares and thus, release the financing constraint.

Surplus cash

A different situation may be faced by a cash-rich company. It may not have enough internal opportunities to invest its surplus cash. It may either distribute its surplus cash to its shareholders or use it to acquire some other company. The shareholders may not really benefit much if surplus cash is returned to them since they would have to pay tax at ordinary income tax rate. Their wealth may increase through an increase in the market value of their shares if surplus cash is used to acquire another company. If they sell their shares they would pay tax at a lower, capital gains tax rate. The company would also be enabled to keep surplus and grow through acquisition.

Debt capacity

A merger of two companies, with fluctuating, but negatively correlated, cash flows, can bring stability of cash flows of the combined company. The stability of cash flows reduces the risk of insolvency and enhances the capacity of the new entity to service a larger amount of debt. The increased borrowing allows a higher interest tax shield which adds to the shareholders' wealth.

Financing cost

The enhanced debt capacity of the merged firm reduces its cost of capital, Since the probability of insolvency is reduced due to financial stability and increased protection to lenders, the merged firm should be able to borrow at a lower rate of interest. This advantage may, however, be taken off partially or completely by increase in the shareholders' risk on account of providing better protection to lenders.

Increased Market Power

A merger can increase the market share of the merged firm. As discussed earlier, the increased concentration or market share improves the profitability of the firm due to economies of scale. The bargaining power of the firm vis-à-vis labour, suppliers and buyers is also enhanced. The merged firm can also exploit technological breakthroughs against obsolescence and price wars. Thus, by limiting competition, the merged firm can earn super-normal profit and strategically employ the surplus funds to further consolidate its position and improve its market power.

We can once again refer to the acquisitions of Universal Luggage by Blow Plast as an example of limiting competition to increase market power. Before the merger, the two companies were competing fiercely with each other leading to a severe price war and increased marketing costs. As a result of the merger, Blow

Plast has obtained a strong hold on the market and now operates under near monopoly situation.

Merger is not the only route to obtain market power. A firm can increase its market share through internal growth or joint ventures or strategic alliances. Also, it is not necessary that the increased market power of the merged firm will lead to efficiency and optimum allocation of resources. Market power means undue concentration which could limit the choice of buyers as well as exploit suppliers and labour.

To summarise the above, in a nutshell, the motives which add shareholders' value are:

- **Synergy:** This refers to the fact that the combined company can often reduce duplicate departments or operations, lowering the costs of the company relative to the same revenue stream, thus increasing profit.
- **Increased revenue/Increased Market Share:** This motive assumes that the company will be absorbing a major competitor and thus increase its power (by capturing increased market share) to set prices.
- **Cross selling:** For example, a bank buying a stock broker could then sell its banking products to the stock broker's customers, while the broker can sign up the bank's customers for brokerage accounts. Or, a manufacturer can acquire and sell complementary products.
- **Economies of Scale:** For example, managerial economies such as the increased opportunity of managerial specialisation. Another examples are purchasing economies due to increased order size and associated bulk-buying discounts.
- **Taxes:** A profitable company can buy a loss maker to use the target's loss as their advantage by reducing their tax liability. In the United States and many other countries, rules are in place to limit the ability of profitable companies to "shop" for loss making companies, limiting the tax motive of an acquiring company.

- **Geographical or other diversification:** This is designed to smooth the earning results of a company, which over the long term smoothen the stock price of a company, giving conservative investors more confidence in investing in the company. However, this does not always deliver value to shareholders.
- **Resource transfer:** Resources are unevenly distributed across firms (Barney, 1991) and the interaction of target and acquiring firm resources can create value through either overcoming information asymmetry or by combining scarce resources.

The motives those are considered not to add shareholder's value:

- **Empire building:** Managers have larger companies to manage and hence more power.
- **Manager's compensation:** In the past, certain executive management teams had their payout based on the total amount of profit of the company, instead of the profit per share, which would give the team a perverse incentive to buy companies to increase the total profit while decreasing the profit per share (which hurts the owners of the company, the shareholders); although some empirical studies show that compensation is linked to profitability rather than mere profits of the company.
- **Vertical integration:** Companies acquire part of a supply chain and benefit from the resources. However, this may not add any value since although one end of the supply chain may receive a product at a cheaper cost, the other end now has lower revenue. In addition, the supplier may find more difficulty in supplying to competitors of its acquirer because the competition would not want to support the new conglomerate.

M&A marketplace difficulties

At present, the process by which a company is bought or sold can prove difficult, slow and expensive. A transaction typically requires six to nine months and involves many steps. Locating parties with whom to conduct a transaction forms one step in the overall process and perhaps the most difficult one. Qualified and interested buyers of multimillion dollar corporations are hard to find. Even more difficulties attend bringing a number of potential buyers forward simultaneously during negotiations. Potential acquirers in an industry simply cannot effectively "monitor" the economy at large for acquisition opportunities even though some may fit well within their company's operations or plans. An industry of professional "middlemen" exists to facilitate M&A transactions.

These professionals do not provide their services cheaply and generally resort to previously-established personal contacts, direct-calling campaigns, and placing advertisements in various media. In servicing their clients they attempt to create a one-time market for a one-time transaction. Certain types of merger and acquisition transactions involve securities and may require that these "middlemen" be securities licensed in order to be compensated. Many, but not all, transactions use intermediaries on one or both sides. The role played by legendary Warren Buffet in the P&G and Gillette merger and the way of charging a fortune for the deal is worth mentioning here.

The market inefficiencies can prove detrimental for this important sector of the economy. Beyond the intermediary's high fees, the current process for mergers and acquisitions has the effect of causing private companies to initially sell their shares at a significant discount relative to what the same company might sell for had it been already publicly traded. An important and large sector of the entire economy is held back by the difficulty in conducting corporate M&A (and also in raising equity or debt capital).

Varieties of Merger

As mentioned earlier, a **merger,** simply put, is a combination of two companies into one larger company. Such actions are commonly voluntary and involve stock swap or cash payment to the target. Stock swap is often used as it allows the shareholders of the two companies to share the risk involved in the deal. A merger results in a new company name (often combining the names of the original companies) and in new branding. The outstanding organization absorbs the properties of the other companies. There are several **types of merger** that organizations can engage in:

- Vertical merger consists of the combination of two or more companies that are at different levels of the supply chain for one specific product or service. It also means companies that are in direct competition and share the same product lines and markets).
- Horizontal merger occurs when two or more businesses that produce the same or similar products or services combine under one name. Think of a cone supplier merging with an ice cream maker.
- Extensional merger occurs when similar businesses combine to enter a new product market separate from what they already specialize in.
- **Market-extension merger:** Two companies that sell the same products in different markets.
- **Product-extension merger:** Two companies selling different but related products in the same market.
- **Conglomeration:** Two companies that have no common business areas. There are two types of mergers that are distinguished by how the merger is financed. Each has certain implications for the companies involved and for investors:
  - **Purchase Mergers:** As the name suggests, this kind of merger occurs when one company purchases another. The purchase is made with cash or through the issue of some kind of debt instrument; the sale is taxable. Acquiring companies often prefer this type of merger because it can provide them with a tax benefit. Acquired assets can be written-up to the actual purchase price, and the difference between the book value and the purchase price of the assets can depreciate annually, reducing taxes payable by the acquiring company. We will discuss this later.
  - **Consolidation Mergers:** With this merger, a brand new company is formed and both companies are bought and combined under the new entity. The tax terms are the same as those of a purchase merger.

Like mergers, acquisitions are actions through which companies seek economies of scale, efficiencies and enhanced market visibility.

Unlike all mergers, all acquisitions involve one firm purchasing another. There is no exchange of stock or consolidation as a new company. Acquisitions are often congenial, and all parties feel satisfied with the deal. Acquisitions are more hostile. In an acquisition, as in some of the merger deals we discussed above, a company can buy another company with cash, stock or a combination of the two. Another possibility, which is common in smaller deals, is for one company to acquire all the assets of another company. Company X buys all of Company Y's assets for cash, which means that Company Y will have only cash (and debt, if they had debt before). Company Y becomes merely a shell and will eventually liquidate or enter another area of business. Another type of acquisition is a reverse merger, a deal that enables a private company to get publicly-listed in a relatively short time period. A reverse merger occurs when a private company that has strong prospects and is eager to raise financing buys a publicly-listed shell company, usually one with no business and limited assets. The private company reverse merges into the public company, and together they become an entirely new public corporation with tradable shares. Regardless of their category or structure, all mergers and acquisitions have one common goal: they are all meant to create synergy that makes the value of the combined companies greater than the sum of the two parts. The success of a merger or acquisition depends on whether this synergy is achieved.

As discussed above, an acquisition, also known as a takeover or a buyout, is the buying of one company (the 'target') by another. An acquisition may be **friendly or hostile**. In the former case, the companies cooperate in negotiations; in the latter case, the takeover target is unwilling to be bought or the target's board has no prior knowledge of the offer.

Acquisition usually refers to a purchase of a smaller firm by a larger one. Sometimes, however, a smaller firm will acquire management control of a larger or longer established company and keep its name for the combined entity. This is known as a **reverse takeover**. Another type of acquisition is reverse merger—a deal that enables a private company to get publicly listed in a short time period. A reverse merger occurs when a private company that has strong prospects and is eager to raise financing buys a publicly listed shell company, usually one with no business and limited assets.

- Friendly acquisition occurs when the target firm agrees to give up ownership due to certain circumstances, such as a looming bankruptcy.
- Hostile takeover occurs when the target firm is simply taken over and ownership is lost. The larger, more profitable company generally takes over the smaller, target company without its consent.

M&As involve buying, selling or combining company resources of two or more organizations to enter new markets, increase the overall company price tag or gain market share. With the current market in an economic slump, should mergers and acquisitions (M&A) be explored? Especially during times like this when the economy is struggling, many businesses strategically do decide to merge with or acquire less profitable or smaller companies to gain financial resources and market share With the help of organizational charting, M&A's are much more foreseeable because they visually display the current situations of each of the companies before the M&A begins.

As the economy slumps, it is strategic for companies with substantial resources to merge or acquire other companies which no longer can keep up with the difficult economy. By entering a merger or accepting an acquisition, companies can grow substantially without creating a whole new entity. In some cases, the companies merging together can altogether save what might have elsewhere become bankrupt. The use of organizational charting, especially in these circumstances, companies can quickly combine the multiple entities, map out the future company layout, and visualize the company logistics before the M&A is set in stone. This will help company leaders to make important decisions pre-merger, during the implementation stage, and in the management stages of adjustment that follow.

As companies increasingly look to mergers and acquisitions as a source of new growth and revenue in today's competitive environment, company leaders need reliable answers to questions like:

- Why do some mergers fail miserably and others prosper?
- Is there a common denominator for failures?
- Can businesses learn from merger mistakes?
- What potential buyers should look for when picking a target?
- Pitfalls to avoid during merger and acquisition process
- Analyze some of the successful mergers and reasons for the ones who have failed

Recent trends in M&As around the world reveal that this area is fraught with difficulties and there are lessons to be learnt for Indian companies which seek to enter the foray. For example, in a survey of *Fortune 1000* companies conducted by Braxton Associates, it was found that less that 30 per cent of acquisitions were successful. *The Economist* reports that in a survey of 300 major mergers conducted over a 10-year period, in 57 per cent of the merged companies, the returns lagged behind their industry average.

Till recent past, the incidence of Indian entrepreneurs acquiring foreign enterprises was not so common. The situation has undergone a sea change in the last couple of years. Acquisition of foreign companies by the Indian businesses has been the latest trend in India. There are different factors that played their role in facilitating the mergers and acquisitions in India. Favourable government policies, buoyancy in economy, additional liquidity in the corporate sector, and dynamic attitudes of the Indian entrepreneurs are the key factors behind the changing trends of mergers and acquisitions in India.

The Indian IT and ITES sectors have already proved their potential in the global market. The other Indian sectors are also following the same trend. The increased participation of the Indian companies in the global corporate sector has further facilitated the merger and acquisition activities in India.

SOME MORE INSIGHT INTO M&A

One plus one makes three (1+1=3) - this equation is of special importance in a **merger** or an **acquisition**. The key principle behind buying a company is to create shareholder value over and above that of the sum of the two companies. Two companies together are more valuable than two separate companies—at least, that's the reasoning behind M&A.

The phrase **mergers and acquisitions** (abbreviated **M&As**) refers to the aspect of corporate strategy, corporate finance and management dealing with the buying, selling and combining of different companies that can aid, finance, or help a growing company in a given industry grow rapidly without having to create another business entity.

This rationale is particularly alluring to companies when times are tough. Strong companies will act to buy other companies to create a more competitive, cost-efficient company. The companies will come together hoping to gain a greater market share or to achieve greater efficiency. Because of these potential benefits, target companies will often agree to be purchased when they know they cannot survive alone.

FRIENDLY TAKEOVERS

Before a bidder makes an offer for another company, it usually first informs that company's board of directors. If the board feels that accepting the offer serves shareholders better than rejecting it, it recommends the offer be accepted by the shareholders.

In a private company, because the shareholders and the board are usually the same people or closely connected with one another, private acquisitions are usually friendly: if the shareholders agree to sell the company then the board is usually of the same mind or sufficiently under the orders of the shareholders to cooperate with the bidder. This point is not relevant to the UK concept of takeovers, which always involves the acquisition of a public company.

OFFER

Tender offer is a corporate finance term denoting a type of takeover bid. The tender offer is a public, open offer (usually announced in a newspaper advertisement) by an acquirer to all stockholders of a publicly traded corporation to tender their stock for sale at a specified price during a specified time, subject to the tendering of a minimum and maximum number of shares. In tender offers, the bidder contacts shareholders directly, inviting them to sell their shares at an offer price. To induce the shareholders of the target company to sell, the **acquirer's offer price usually includes a premium** over the current market price of the target company's shares. For example, if a target corporation's stock were trading at a value of $1/share, an acquirer might offer $1.15/share to its shareholders on the condition that 51% of shareholders agree. Cash or other securities may be offered to the target company's shareholders as consideration, although a tender offer in which securities are offered as consideration is generally referred to as an "exchange offer."

TYPES OF ACQUISITION

The **buyer buys the shares**, and therefore control of the target company being purchased. Ownership control of the company in turn conveys effective control over the assets of the company, but since the company is acquired intact as a going business, this form of transaction carries with it all of the liabilities accrued by that business over its past and all of the risks that company faces in its commercial environment.

Demerger *is the converse of a merger or acquisition. It describes a form of restructure in which shareholders or* ***unit holders*** *in the parent company gain* ***direct ownership in a subsidiary (the 'demerged entity').***

The **buyer buys the assets** of the target company. The cash the target receives from the sell-off is paid back to its shareholders by dividend or through liquidation. This type of transaction leaves the target company as an empty shell, if the buyer buys out the entire assets. A buyer often structures the transaction as an asset purchase to "cherry-pick" the assets that it wants and leave out the assets and liabilities that it does not. This can be particularly important where foreseeable liabilities may include future, unquantifiable damage such as those that could arise from litigation over defective products, employee benefits or terminations, or environmental damage. A disadvantage of this structure is the tax that many jurisdictions, particularly outside the United States, impose on transfers of the individual assets. The terms **"demerger", "spin-off" and "spin-out"** are sometimes used to indicate a situation where one company splits into two, generating a second company separately listed on a stock exchange.

Demerger is the converse of a merger or acquisition. It describes a form of restructure in which **shareholders or unit holders** in the parent company gain direct ownership in a subsidiary (the 'demerged entity'). Underlying ownership of the companies and/or trusts that formed part of the group does not change. The company or trust that ceases to own the entity is known as the 'demerging entity'. If the parent company holds a majority stake in the demerged entity, the resulting company is referred to as the subsidiary. Demergers can also result from government intervention, usually by way of anti-trust/competition law, or through decartelization.

Spin out refers to a type of spin off **where a company "splits off"** sections of itself as a separate business. The common definition of spin out is when a division of a company or organization becomes an independent business. The "spin out" company takes assets, intellectual property, technology, and/or existing products from the parent organization.

Many times the management of the new company are from the same parent organization. Often, a spin-out offers the opportunity for a division to be backed by the company but not be affected by the parent company's image or history, giving potential to grow existing ideas that had been languishing in an old environment and help them grow in a new environment.

In most cases, the parent company or organization offers support doing one or more of the following:

- investing equity in the new firm,
- being the first customer of the spin-out (helps to create cash flow),

- providing incubation space (desk, chairs, phones, internet access, etc.) or
- providing services such as legal, finance, technology, etc.

All the support from the parent company is provided with the explicit purpose of helping the spin-out grow.

MERGERS: FURTHER CLASSIFICATION

In business or economics a **merger** is a combination of two companies into one larger company. Such actions are commonly voluntary and involve stock swap or cash payment to the target. Stock swap is often used as it allows the shareholders of the two companies to share the risk involved in the deal. A merger can resemble a takeover but result in a new company name (often combining the names of the original companies) and in new branding; in some cases, terming the combination a "merger" rather than an acquisition is done purely for political or marketing reasons.

A **stock swap**, also known as a **share swap**, is a business takeover or acquisition in which the acquiring company uses its own stock to pay for the acquired company. Each shareholder of the newly acquired company receives a certain number of shares of the acquiring company's stock for each share of stock they previously held in the acquired company. Sometimes some shareholders are required to wait for an agreed-upon period of time before they are allowed to sell their new shares of stock. A unique type of merger called a reverse merger is used as a way of going public without the expense and time required by an IPO.

The occurrence of a merger often raises concerns in **antitrust** circles. Devices such as the **Herfindahl index** can analyze the prevent it. Regulatory bodies such as the European Commission, the United States Department of Justice and the U.S. Federal Trade Commission may investigate anti-trust cases for monopolies dangers, and have the power to block mergers.

Competition law, known in the United States as **antitrust law**, has three main elements prohibiting agreements or practices that

Assretive mergers are those in which the acquiring company's earnings per share increase.

Dilutive mergers are those in which the acquiring companies earnings per share decrease.

restrict free trading and competition between business entities. This includes in particular the repression of cartels, banning abusive behaviour by a firm dominating a market, or anti-competitive practices that tend to lead to such a dominant position. Practices controlled in this way may include predatory pricing, tying, price gouging, refusal to deal, and many others.

CLASSIFICATION OF MERGERS

- **Horizontal mergers** take place where the two merging companies produce similar products in the same industry.
- **Vertical mergers** occur when two firms, each working at different stages in the production of the same good, combine
- **Congeneric merger/concentric mergers** occur where two merging firms are in the same general industry, but they have no mutual buyer/customer or supplier relationship, such as a merger between a bank and a leasing company. Example: Prudential's acquisition of Bache & Company.
- **Conglomerate mergers** take place when the two firms operate in different industries.

Transactions that are considered to threaten the competitive process can be prohibited altogether, or approved subject to "remedies" such as an obligation to divest part of the merged business or to offer licenses or access to facilities to enable other businesses to continue competing in the market.

In US and some European countries, merger or acquisition involves, from a competition law perspective, the concentration of economic power in the hands of fewer than before. This usually means that one firm buys out the shares of another. The reasons for oversight of economic concentrations by the state are the same as the reasons to restrict firms who **abuse a position of dominance**, only that regulation of mergers and acquisitions attempts to deal with the problem before it arises, *ex ante* prevention of creating dominant firms. Competition law requires that firms proposing to merge gain authorisation from the relevant government authority, or simply go ahead but face the prospect of demerger should the concentration later be found to lessen competition. The anti-trust law against Microsoft is a case for example.

Analysis of Mergers and Acquisitions

There are three important steps involved in the analysis of mergers and acquisitions:

- Planning
- Search and screening
- Financial evaluation

Planning

The acquiring firm should review its objective of acquisition in the context of its strengths and weaknesses, and corporate goals. This will help in indicating the product-market strategies that are appropriate for the company. It will also force the firm identify business units that should be dropped and those that should be added.

The planning of acquiring a firm will require the analysis of industry-specific and the firm-specific information. The acquiring firm will need industry data on market growth, nature of competition, ease of entry, capital and labour intensity, degree of regulation etc. About the target firm the information needed will include the quality of management, market size, capital structure, profitability, production and marketing capabilities etc.

Search and Screening

Search focuses on how and where to look for suitable candidates for acquisition. Screening process short-lists a few candidates from many available. Detailed information about these candidates is obtained.

Merger objectives may include attaining faster growth, improving profitability, improving managerial effectiveness, gaining market power and leadership, achieving cost reduction etc. These objectives can be achieved in various ways rather than through mergers alone. The alternatives to merger include joint ventures, strategic alliances, elimination of inefficient operations, cost reduction and productivity improvement, hiring capable managers etc. If the merger is considered the best alternative, the acquiring firm must satisfy itself that it is the best available option in terms of its own screening criteria and economically most attractive.

Financial Evaluation

Financial evaluation of a merger is needed to determine the earnings and cash flows, areas of risk, the maximum price payable to the target company and the best way to finance the merger. The acquiring firm must pay a fair consideration to the target firm for acquiring its business. In a competitive market situation with capital market efficiency, the current market value is the correct and fair value of the share of the target firm. The target firm will not accept any offer below the current market value of its share. The target firm may, in fact, expect the offer price to be more than the current market value of its share since it may expect that merger benefits will accrue to the acquiring firm. A merger is said to be at a premium when the offer price is higher than the target firm's pre-merger market value. The acquiring firm may pay the premium if it thinks that it can increase the target firm's profit after merger by improving its operations and due to synergy. It may have to pay premium as an incentive to the target firm's shareholders to induce them to sell their shares so that the acquiring firm is enabled to obtain the control of the target firm. What is the benefit of merger to the acquiring firm?

Value Created by Merger

A merger will make economic sense to the acquiring firm if its shareholders benefit. Merger will create an economic advantage (EA) when the combined present value of the merged firms is greater than the sum of their individual present values as separate entities. For example, if firm P and firm Q merge, and they are separately worth V_P and V_Q, respectively, and worth V_{PQ} in combination, then the economic advantage will occur if:

$$V_{PQ} > (V_P + V_Q)$$

and it will equal to:

$$EA = V_{PQ} - (V_P + V_Q)$$

Suppose that firm P acquires firm Q. After merger P will gain the present value of Q i.e., V_Q, but it will also have to pay a price (say in cash) to Q. Thus, the cost of merging to P is [Cash paid – V_Q]. For P, the net economic advantage of merger (NEA) is positive if the economic advantage exceeds the cost of merging. Thus

Net economic advantage = economic advantage – cost of merging

$$NEA = [V_{PQ} - (V_P + V_Q) - (\text{cash paid} - V_Q)$$

The economic advantage i.e., $[V_{PQ} - (V_P + V_Q)]$, represents the benefits resulting from operating efficiencies and synergy when two firms merge. If the acquiring firm pays cash equal to the value of the acquired firm, i.e. cash paid – V_Q = 0, then the entire advantage of merger will accrue to the shareholders of the acquiring firm. In practice, the acquiring and the acquired firm may share the economic advantage between themselves.

The acquiring firm should appraise merger as a capital budgeting decision, following the discounted cash flow (DCF) approach. The acquiring firm incurs a cost (in buying the business of the target firm) in the expectation of a stream of benefits (in the form of cash flows) in the future. The merger will be advantageous to the acquiring company if the present value of the target merger is greater than the cost of acquisition.

Mergers and acquisitions involve complex set of managerial problems than the purchase of an asset. Nevertheless, DCF approach is an important tool in analyzing mergers and acquisitions. In order to apply DCF technique, the following information is required:

- Estimation of cash flows
- Timing of cash flows
- Discount rate

Earnings are the basis for estimating cash flows. Cash flows include adjustments for depreciation, capital expenditure and working capital. In summary, the following steps are involved in the financial evaluation of a merger:

- Identify growth and profitability assumptions and scenarios
- Project cash flows magnitudes and their timing
- Estimate the cost of capital
- Compute NPV for each scenario
- Decide if the acquisition is attractive on the basis of NPV
- Decide if the acquisitions should be financed through cash or exchange of shares
- Evaluate the impact of the merger on EPS and price-earnings ratio.

Above the process, analysis and the different types of merger and acquisition has been discussed, but it was seen that many CEOs and other organizations believe in friendly mergers and takeovers rather than going for hostile takeovers. Also, many mergers and acquisitions fail because many times the people involved in the process are not the right people for instance Cypress, Cisco and the Mittals group have at their core a small group of people, a dedicated team which has worked together for years and has an excellent operational background. Having an inner circle of people who are familiar with each other facilitates coordination and communication. The reason why at this point I am discussing this is because the above stated process of valuation and everything will bear fruit only if the team which is behind the process is experienced, dedicated and focused. Many deals have failed because the people slacked once they think the deal is theirs.

Thus, people, due diligence and the process all play a very important role when it comes to mergers and acquisitions.

Regulation of Mergers and Takeover in India

Mergers and acquisitions may degenerate into the exploitation of shareholders, particularly minority shareholders. They may also stifle competition and encourage monopoly and monopolistic corporate behaviour. Therefore, most countries have legal framework to regulate the merger and acquisition activities. In India, mergers and acquisitions are regulated through the provision of the Companies Act, 1956, the Monopolies and Restrictive Trade Practice (MRTP) Act, 1969, the Foreign Exchange Regulation Act (FERA), 1973, the Income Tax Act, 1961, and the Securities and Controls (Regulations) Act, 1956. The Securities and Exchange Board in India (SEBI) has issued guidelines to regulate mergers, acquisitions and takeovers.

Legal Measures against Takeovers

The Companies Act restricts and individual or a company or a group of individuals from acquiring shares, together with the shares held earlier, in a public company to 25 per cent of the total paid-up capital. Also, the Central Government needs to be intimated whenever such holding exceeds 10 per cent of the subscribed capital. The Companies Act also provides for the approval of shareholders and the Central Government when a company, by itself or in association of an individual or individuals purchases shares of another company in excess of its specified limit. The approval of the Central Government is necessary if such investment exceeds 10 per cent of the subscribed capital of another company. These are precautionary measures against the takeover of pubic limited companies.

Refusal to Register the Transfer of Shares

In order to diffuse situation of hostile takeover attempts, companies have been given power to refuse to register the transfer of shares. If this is done, a company must inform the transferee and the transferor within 60 days. A refusal to register transfer is permitted if:

- A legal requirement relating to the transfer of shares have not be compiled with; or
- The transfer is in contravention of the law; or
- The transfer is prohibited by a court order; or
- The transfer is not in the interest of the company and the public.

Protection of Minority Shareholders' Interests

In a takeover bid, the interests of all shareholders should be protected without a prejudice to genuine takeovers. It would be unfair if the same high price is not offered to all the shareholders of prospective acquired company. The larger shareholders (including financial institutions, banks and individuals) may get most of the benefits because of their accessibility to the brokers and the takeover deal makers. Before the small shareholders know about the proposal, it may be too late for them. The Companies Act provides that a purchaser can force the minority shareholder to sell their shares if:

- The offer has been made to the shareholders of the company;
- The offer has been approved by at least 90 per cent of the shareholders of the company whose transfer is involved, within 4 months of making the offer, and
- The minority shareholders have been intimated within 2 months from the expiry of 4 months referred above.

If the purchaser is already in possession of more than 90 per cent of the aggregate value of all the shares of the company, the transfer of the shares of minority shareholders is possible if:

- The purchaser offers the same terms of all shareholders and
- The tenders who approve the transfer, besides holding at least 90 per cent of the value of shares should also form at least 75 per cent of the total holders of shares.

Guidelines for Takeovers

SEBI has provided guidelines for takeovers. The guidelines have been strengthened recently to protect the interests of the shareholders from takeovers. The salient features of the guidelines are:

- **Notification of takeover:** If an individual or a company acquires 5 per cent or more of the voting capital of a company, the target company and the stock exchange shall be notified immediately.
- **Limit to share acquisition:** An individual or a company can continue acquiring the shares of another company without making any offer to other shareholders until the individual or the company acquires 10 per cent of the voting capital.

- **Public Offer:** If the holding of the acquiring company exceeds 10 per cent, a public offer to purchase a minimum of 20 per cent of the shares shall be made to the remaining shareholders through a public announcement.
- **Offer price:** Once the offer is made to the remaining shareholders, the minimum offer price shall not be less than the average of the weekly high and low of the closing prices during the last six months preceding the date of announcement.
- **Disclosure:** The offer should disclose the detailed terms of the offer, identity of the offerer, details of the offerer's existing holdings in the offeree company etc. and the information should be make available to all the shareholders at the same time and in the same manner.
- **Offer document:** The offer document should contain, the offer's financial information, its intention to continue the offeree company's business and to make major change and long-term commercial justification for the offer.

The objectives of the Companies Act and the guidelines for takeover are to ensure full disclosure about the mergers and takeovers and to protect the interests of the shareholders, particularly the small shareholders. The main thrust is that public authorities should be notified within two days.

In a nutshell, an individual or company can continue to purchase the share without making and offer to other shareholders until the shareholding exceeds 10 per cent. Once the offer is made to other shareholders, the offer price should not be less than the weekly average price in the past 6 months or the negotiated price.

Legal Procedures

The following is the summary of legal procedures for merger or acquisition laid down in the Companies Act, 1956:

Permission for merger

Two or more companies can amalgamate only when amalgamation is permitted under their memorandum of association. Also, the acquiring company should have the permission in its object clause to carry on the business of the acquired company. In the absence of these provisions in the memorandum of association, it is necessary to seek the permission of the shareholders, board or directors and the Company Law Board before affecting the merger.

Information to the stock exchange

The acquiring and the acquired companies should inform the stock exchanges where they are listed about the merger.

Approval of board of directors

The boards of the directors of the individual companies should approve the draft proposal for amalgamation and authorize the management of companies to further pursue the proposal.

Application in the High Court

An application for approving the draft amalgamation proposal duly approved by the boards of directors of the individual companies should be made to the High Court. The High Court would convene a meeting of the shareholders and creditors to approve the amalgamation proposal. The notice of meeting should be sent to them at least 21 days in advance.

Shareholders' and creditors' meetings

The individual companies should hold separate meetings of their shareholders and creditors for approving the amalgamation scheme. At least, 75 per cent of shareholders and creditors in separate meeting, voting in person or by proxy, must accord their approval to the scheme.

Sanction by the High Court

After the approval of shareholders and creditors, on the petitions of the companies, the High Court will pass order sanctioning the amalgamation scheme after it is satisfied that the scheme is fair and reasonable. If it deems so, it can modify the scheme. The date of the court's hearing will be published in two newspapers and also, the Regional Director of the Company Law Board will be intimated.

Filling of the Court Order

After the Court order, its certified true copies will be filed with the Registrar of Companies.

Transfer of assets and liabilities
The assets and liabilities of the acquired company will be transferred to the acquiring company in accordance with the approved scheme, with effect from the specified date.

Payment by cash or securities
As per the proposal, the acquiring company will exchange shares and debentures and/or pay cash for the shares and debentures of the acquired company. These securities will be listed on the stock exchange.

Accounting for Mergers and Acquisitions

Mergers and acquisitions involve complex accounting treatment. A merger, defined as amalgamation in India, involves the absorption of the target company by the acquiring company, which results in the uniting of the interests of the two companies. The merger should be structured as pooling of interest. In the case of acquisition, where the acquiring company purchases the shares of the target company, the acquisition should be structured as a purchase.

Pooling of Interests Method

In the pooling of interests method of accounting, the balance sheet items and the profit and loss items of the merged firms are combined without recording the effects of merger. This implies that assets, liabilities and other items of the acquiring and the acquired firms are simply added at the book value without making any adjustments. Thus, there is no revaluation of assets or creation of goodwill.

Purchase Method

Under the purchase method, the assets and liabilities of the acquiring firm after the acquisition of the target firm are adjusted for the purchase price paid to the target company. Thus, the assets and liabilities after merger are re-valued. If the acquirer pays a price more than the fair market value of assets and liabilities, the excess amount is shown as goodwill in the acquiring company's books. On the contrary, if the fair value of assets and liabilities is less than the purchase price paid, then this difference is recorded as capital reserve.

Separate chapters are dedicated to legal issues and takeover codes that govern any M&A. It is noteworthy to point out that the entire world is converging on developing common guidelines for M&A that would increasingly enhance cross-border mergers and acquisitions and make it hassle free and synergetic.

3

Genesis of Mergers and Acquisitions

Although they are often uttered in the same breath and used as though they were synonymous, the terms **merger** and **acquisition** mean slightly different things.

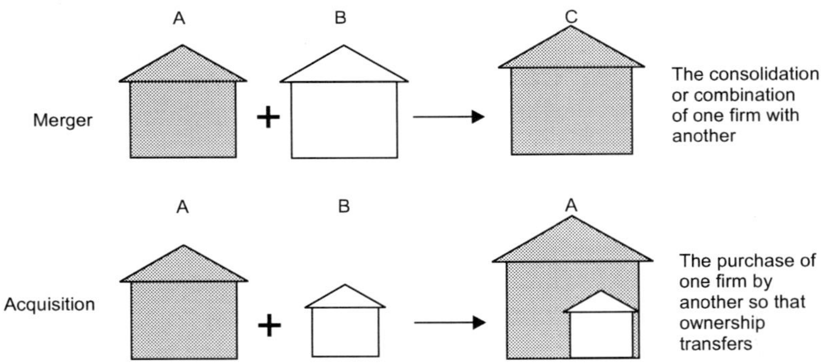

Figure 3.1: Merger vs. Acquisition

Source: Mergers and Acquisitions report, 2005

When one company takes over another and clearly established itself as the new owner, the purchase is called acquisition. From a legal point of view, the target company ceases to exist, the buyer "swallows" the business and the buyer's stock continues to be traded.

In the pure sense of the term, a merger happens when two firms, often of about the same size, agree to go forward as a single new company rather than remain separately owned and operated. This kind of action is more precisely referred to as "merger of equals". Both companies' stocks are surrendered and new company stock is issued in its place. For example, both Daimler-Benz and Chrysler ceased to exist when the two firms merged, and a new company, DaimlerChrysler, was created.

The real difference lies in how the purchase is communicated to and received by the target company's board of directors, employees and shareholders. *It is quite normal though for M&A deal communications to take place in a so called 'confidentiality bubble' whereby information flows are restricted due to confidentiality agreements.*

In practice, however, actual mergers of equals don't happen very often. Usually, one company will buy another and, as part of the deal's terms, simply allow the acquired firm to proclaim that the action is a merger of equals, even if it is technically an acquisition. Being bought out often carries negative connotations, therefore, by describing the deal euphemistically as a merger, deal makers and top managers try to make the takeover more palatable.

A purchase deal will also be called a merger when both CEOs agree that joining together is in the best interest of both of their companies. But when the deal is unfriendly—that is, when the target company does not want to be purchased—it is always regarded as an acquisition. This is challengeable. An acquisition can be either friendly or hostile. An example of a recent friendly takeover was when Microsoft bought Fast Search and Transfer (OSE Stock Exchange, Ticker FAST). CEO of the acquired company (FAST) revealed that they had been working with Microsoft for more than 6 months to get the deal which was announced in January, 2008.

Whether a purchase is considered a merger or an acquisition really depends on whether the purchase is friendly or hostile and how it is announced. In other words, the real difference lies in how the purchase is communicated to and received by the target company's board of directors, employees and shareholders. It is quite normal though for M&A deal communications to take place in a so called 'confidentiality bubble' whereby information flows are restricted due to confidentiality agreements.

The distinction between "merger" and "acquisition" is described this way by F. Ducoulombier, Candesic Analysis which slightly differs from the above: Corporate Restructuring is all activities involving expansion or contraction of a firm's operations or changes in its assets or financial structure. Merger: A transaction in which at least one firm ceases to exist and the assets of that firm are transferred to a surviving firm so that only one separate legal entity remains. Acquisition: A transaction in which both firms in the transaction survive but the acquirer increases its percentage ownership in the target.

THE FIVE MERGER WAVES

United States has witnessed five periods of merger activity, often referred to as merger waves, each wave having been dominated by a particular type of merger. These periods were characterized by high level of cyclic activity, that is, high levels of mergers followed by periods of relatively fewer mergers. All the merger movements occurred when the economy experienced sustained high growth rates and coincided with particular developments in business environments, because firms are motivated to make large investments outlay only when the business prospects are favourable.

When such favourable business prospects are joined with changes in competitive conditions directly motivating a new business strategy, M&A activity will be stimulated.

The First Wave—1897–1904

The mergers of the first wave consisted mainly of horizontal mergers, which resulted in a near monopolistic market structure. This merger period is known for its role in creating large monopolies. The first billion-dollar mega merger deal between **US steel** and **Carnegie** took place during this period. The resulting steel giant merged 785 separate firms.

Another feature of this wave is the formation of trusts, where the investors invested funds in a firm and entrusted their stock certificates with directors who ensured that they received the dividends for their trust certificates.

These trusts were formed by dominant business leaders, such as JP Morgan of the house of Morgan and John D. Rockefeller of Standard Oil and National City bank, as a response to the poor performance of many of the nations businesses as they struggled with the weak economic climate.

As firms expanded, they exploited economies of scale in production and distribution. In pursuit of economies of scale, an expansion process took place in many manufacturing industries in the US economy.

Financial factors led to the end of the first merger wave.

The Second Wave—1916–1929

Like the first wave, second merger movement also began with an upturn in business activity. Several industries were consolidated during the second merger wave. The result was an oligopolistic industry structure rather than monopolies. The consolidation pattern which was established in the first merger wave, continued in the second merger wave also. The combination in this period occurred

Table 3.1

Year	Number of mergers
1897	69
1898	303
1899	1208
1900	340
1901	423
1902	379
1903	142
1904	79

Source: *Mergers, Acquisitions and Corporate Restructuring* by Patrick A Gaughan

outside the previously consolidated heavy manufacturing industries. A large number of mergers occurred in industries like primary metals, petroleum products, chemicals and transportation equipment.

The second merger period witnessed the formation of many prominent corporations that still operate today. These include General Motors, IBM, Union Carbide Corporation and John Deere.

The second merger wave came to an end when the stock market crashed on October 29, 1929.

The Third Wave—1965–1969

The merger activity reached its then historically highest level during this period. This was due to the booming economy of this period. This period is also known as a conglomerate merger period, as small or medium sized firms adopted a diversification strategy into business activities outside their traditional areas of interest.

Around 6000 mergers took place in the US economy during this period and led to the disappearance of about 25,000 firms.

Investment bankers did not finance most of the mergers in this period. Many of the acquisitions that took place during this period were followed by poor financial performance.

Table 3.2

Year	Number of mergers
1963	1361
1964	1950
1965	2125
1966	2377
1967	2975
1968	4462
1969	6107
1970	5152

Source : *Mergers, Acquisitions and Corporate Restructuring* by Patrick A Gaughan

Table 3.3: Major mergers in the telecom sector

Acquirer	Target
Vodafone	Mannesman
MCI Worldcom	Spirit
Bell Atlantic	GTE
AT&T	MeCaw Cellular
SBC	Ameritech
Bell Atlantic	NYNEX

The Fourth Wave—1981–1989

Following the recession in the 1974–1975, the US economy entered a long period of expansion during which merger and acquisition trend went upward. Hostile mergers played a significant role in the fourth wave.

There was a great degree of concentration within the oil industry, as it experienced a high level of merger activity. Another important feature is the increased use of debt to finance acquisitions.

The yield on junk bonds was significantly higher than that of investment grade bonds. Hence, the ready availability of the finance helped even small firms to acquire large well established firms.

The Fifth Wave—1992–Till Date

The current merger activity can be described as the fifth wave. Mega mergers, as in the fourth wave, began to take place in fifth wave also. The number of hostile deals was less than strategic mergers.

ENTRY MODES

The choice between Greenfield and Acquisition modes of entry is explained by the degree of multinationality, product diversity and the size of the parent firm. There is also the industry effect on the pattern of mode selection. Nitsch *et al.* (1996) considered three ownership based entry modes: Greenfield, acquisition and joint ventures.

- The Greenfield venture is mostly deploying the existing resources in a new market. While acquisition is acquiring new

Table 3.4: Costs associated with entry modes

Mode	Resource costs	Control costs	Total costs
Greenfield	Low	Low	Low
Joint venture	Medium	High	Medium/high
Acquisition	High	High	High

resources, there is little uncertainty about efficiency of a firm to improve its performance through Greenfield ventures. On the other hand, acquisition will have many risks including risk of overpayment by the acquirer.

- Greenfield ventures perform better than acquisitions due to lower control costs. The acquisition involves additional control costs in integrating different corporate cultures.
- Joint ventures are modes for a firm to gain access to resources that are not available within the firm. The costs associated with joint ventures are search costs in finding a partner and risk of exposing ownership of core resources to a partner.
- There will be high control costs in a joint venture than the wholly owned mode. In Greenfield investments, the control cost is low due to sole management by the parent firm.
- Both acquisitions and joint ventures have higher costs than the Greenfield mode. However, risks are less in an acquisition than in joint ventures.
- Management control costs in acquisition involve integration costs of the different sets of organizational cultures, procedures etc. In case of joint ventures, there will be interdependencies among the partners.

The choice between acquisition and Greenfield depends on many factors. Some of them for acquisition mode are:

- The larger, the initial operating scale in the US market, the preference is for acquisition.
- MNE which are diversified among countries and product markets, preferred acquisition.
- Acquisition is favoured when the market entered is growing very rapidly or very slowly. In the former case, it is quicker to enter and latter case the price of assets are depressed and work out cheaper. (S. Shiva Ramu, *Cross Border Mergers and Acquisitions*)

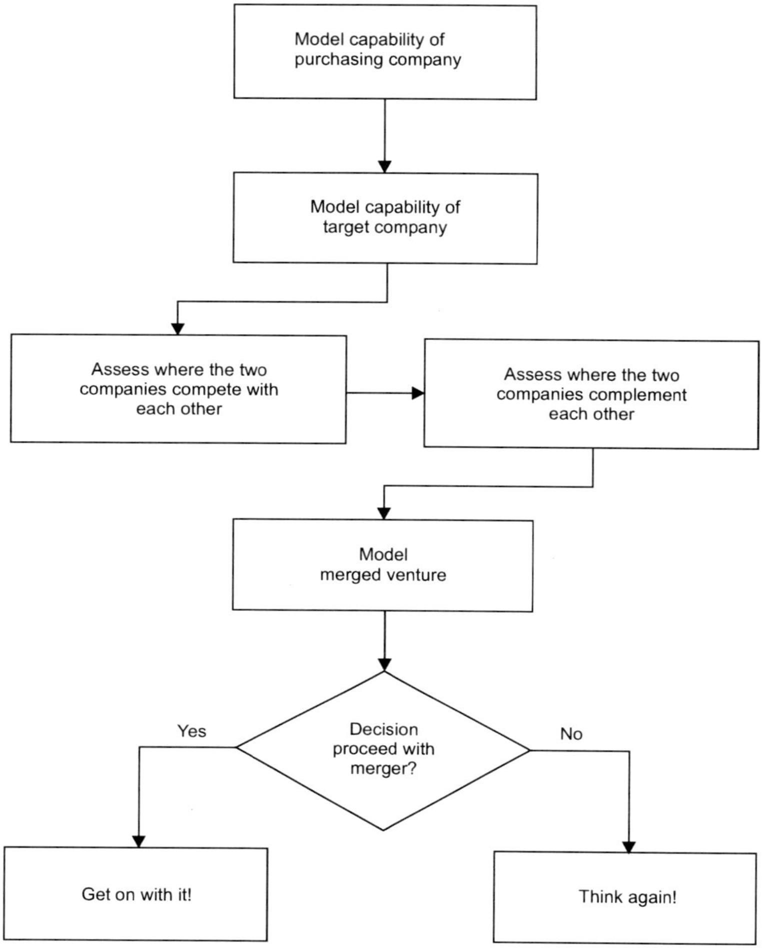

Figure 3.2: Mergers and acquisitions ... doing the deal

Source: Mergers and Acquisitions Report 2005, version 1.3

START WITH AN OFFER

When the CEO and top managers of a company decide that they want to do a merger or acquisition, they start with a tender offer. The process typically begins with the acquiring company carefully and discreetly buying up shares in the target company, or building a position. Once the acquiring company starts to purchase shares in the open market, it is restricted to buying 5% of the total outstanding shares before it must file with the SEBI (in the USA it is SEC). In the filing, the company must formally declare how many shares it owns and whether it intends to buy the company or keep the shares purely as an investment. Working with financial advisors and investment bankers, the acquiring company will arrive at an overall price that it's willing to pay for its target in cash, shares or both.

TARGET'S RESPONSE

Once the tender offer has been made, the target company can do one of several things:

- **Accept the Terms of the Offer:** If the target firm's top managers and shareholders are happy with the terms of the transaction, they will go ahead with the deal.
- **Attempt to Negotiate:** The tender offer price may not be high enough for the target company's shareholders to accept, or the specific terms of the deal may not be attractive. In a merger, there may be much at stake for the management of the target their jobs, in particular. If they're not satisfied with the terms laid out in the tender offer, the target's management may try to work out more agreeable terms that let them keep their jobs. Not surprisingly, highly sought-after target companies that are the objects of several bidders will have greater latitude for negotiation. Furthermore, managers have more negotiating power if they can show that they are crucial to the merger's future success.
- **Execute a Poison Pill or Some Other Hostile Takeover Defense:** A poison pill scheme can be triggered by a target company when a hostile suitor acquires a predetermined percentage of company stock. To execute its defense, the target company grants all shareholders – except the acquiring company – options to buy additional stock at a dramatic discount. This dilutes the acquiring company's share and intercepts its control of the company.
- **Find a White Knight:** As an alternative, the target company's management may seek out a friendlier potential acquiring

company, or white knight. If a white knight is found, it will offer an equal or higher price for the shares than the hostile bidder.

CLOSING THE DEAL

Finally, once the target company agrees to the tender offer and regulatory requirements are met, the merger deal will be executed by means of some transaction. In a merger in which one company buys another, the acquiring company will pay for the target company's shares with cash, stock or both. A cash-for-stock transaction is fairly straightforward: target company's shareholders receive a cash payment for each share purchased. If the transaction is **made with stock instead of cash, then it's not taxable**. There is simply an exchange of share certificates. The desire to steer clear of the tax man explains why so many M&A deals are carried out as stock-for-stock transactions. When a company is purchased with stock, new shares from the acquiring company's stock are issued directly to the target company's shareholders, or the new shares are sent to a broker who manages them for target company's shareholders. The shareholders of the target company are only taxed when they sell their new shares. When the deal is closed, investors usually receive a new stock in their portfolios—the acquiring company's expanded stock.

RATIONALE FOR M&A

The rationale for M&A for the acquiring company and the selling company is as follows:

Acquiring company:

- Diversification to achieve economic protection
- Adding new products faster
- Acquiring management or technical personnel
- Acquiring profitable operations

Selling company

- Major stockholders wishing to retire
- Need for further financing

- Means of survival
- Prospect of marketing or technology changes
- Attractive purchase or exchange offer

Successful M&A

- The committee approach is suitable for M&A deals
- Defining general objectives and policies
- Prospective acquirer information:
  - History and background
  - Organizational structure and personnel
  - Product lines
  - Marketing methods and areas served
  - Research and development
  - Financial position
- Prospective companies for acquisition
  - Horizontal, vertical or diversified
  - Method of deal: cash or stock
  - Size of companies: sale and profit range
  - Product lines
  - Research and development
  - Management

Unsuccessful M&A

- Major pitfalls
  - Insufficient investigation of acquired company
  - Corporate indigestion: too many companies acquired in too short time in diverse industries
  - Loss companies in unrelated fields present greater acquisition risks
- Failure of mergers:
  - No plan for fit of plant, personnel and facilities
  - Inadequate diligence by merger partners
  - Lack of strategic rationale
  - Unrealistic expectations of synergies
  - Paying too much
  - Conflicting corporate cultures
  - Failure to move quickly to meld the two companies

MERGER MOTIVES

To assess whether mergers work, it is necessary to examine the motives and reasons underlying the move before evaluating the results. The basic motive of a merger can be understood as an attempt to create value. Merger motives can be classified into the following categories:

- **Efficiency theory:** Efficiency theory states that the more efficient firms will acquire less efficient firms and realize gains through improved managerial efficiency.
- **Market power theory:** Market power theory suggests that merger gains result from increased concentration, leading to collusion and monopoly benefits. Increased market power may be in terms of higher market share or operating in monopoly conditions.
- **Operating synergies theory:** This theory holds that mergers achieve levels of activity at which economies of scale can be achieved due to synergies in technical, marketing, commercial or research activities between the merging and merged firms.
- **Financial synergies theory:** Financial theories assume complementarities between the merging firms in the availability of investment opportunities and internal cash flows. For instance, a firm in a declining industry might have large cash flows with few investment opportunities. A growth industry, on the other hand, has more investment opportunities but less cash to finance it. If two such firms merge, the merged firm will have lower cost of capital due to lower cost of internal funds as also due to higher leveraging capacity, leading to tax efficient funding.
- **Tax motives merger:** These occur due to tax savings achieved by merging a high tax bracket company with loss making or lower tax bracket company. Financial engineering through

To assess whether mergers work, it is necessary to examine the motives and reasons underlying the move before evaluating the results. Post merger economic gain will be generated only if the two units are worth more together than apart. The basic motive of a merger can be understood as an attempt to create value.

Table 3.5

Acquirer/Intent	Target / Intent	Year of Acquisition
STAR/increasing content production in India	Balaji Telefilms/ Achieving a higher level of growth	2004
Grasim/ consolidating cement business	L&T Cement/ spin off non-core business	2004
eBay/ entry into Indian market	Bazee.com/ get rid of accumulated loss of Rs. 518.9 million	2004
Tata Motors/ entry to East Asian market	Daewoo Commercial Motors/ spin off commercial vehicle unit	2003
Tata Steel/ entry to East Asian market	NatSteel/ Access to significant resources and to overcome volatility in steel industry	2004
AFK Sistema/ entry to Indian market	Aircel/ book profit and exit business	2005
Hutch/ consolidating its mobile interests under a single entity	Essar/ become a part of second largest cellular company	2005
Reliance Infocomm/ entry to international market and getting 50000 km submarine cable	FLAG Telecom/ To get rid of loss and achieve higher growth	2003
IBM/ Access to Indian call centre	Daksh eServices/ Access to higher resources to achieve faster growth	2004
VSNL/ To strengthen worldwide fibre optics cable	Tyco Global Network/ to get rid of loss making unit	2004
Oriental Bank/ Acquire nearly 8,00,000 depositors in the South	Global Trust Bank/ get rid of the bad debt and liabilities	2004
DHL/ strengthening logistic services in India	Blue Dart/ entry to world market	2004
Mahindra & Mahindra/ entry into international market and tractor business	Jiangling Tractor/ Strategic partnership will help in faster growth	2005
Avaya Mauritius/ consolidating presence in Indian market	Tata Telecom/ to import and distribute telecom solutions	2004

(Contd.)

(Table 3.5 Contd.)

Parkville Holdings/ investment in growing business; book profit and exit business at appropriate time later	Max India/ to meet long term funding needs	2004
Sajjan Jindal/ increasing wire rod capacity from 5 lakh ton to 3 MT	SISCOL/to get rid of accumulated loss of Rs 4.3 billion	2004
Reliance Petroleum/ becomes world's largest producer of polyester fibre and yarn	Trevira GmbH/ benefit from the resources of world's largest integrated polyester producer	2004

mergers can be attained by offering file creditors of a sick company equity stakes in the healthy company in view of their dues.

TRADING AND MARKET CAPITALISATION

The shares of a public company are often traded on a stock exchange. The value or "size" of a public company is called its market capitalization, a term which is often shortened to "market cap". This is calculated as the number of shares outstanding (as opposed to authorized but not necessarily issued) times the price per share. For example, a company with two million shares outstanding and a price

For example: If all the shareholders were to simultaneously try to sell their shares in the open market, this would immediately create downward pressure on the price for which the share is traded unless there were an equal number of buyers willing to purchase the security at the price the sellers demand. Thus, the number of trades in a given period of time, commonly referred to as the "volume" is important when determining how well a company's **market capitalization** reflects true fair market value of the company as a whole. The higher the volume, the more the fair market value of the company is likely to be reflected by its market capitalization.

per share of Rs. 40 would have a market capitalization of Rs. 80 million. However, a company's market capitalization should not be confused with the fair market value of the company as a whole since the price per share is influenced by other factors such as the volume of shares traded.

Another example of the impact of volume on the accuracy of market capitalization is when a company has little or no trading activity and the market price is simply the price at which the most recent trade took place, which could be days or weeks ago. This occurs when there are no buyers willing to purchase the securities at the price being offered by the sellers and there are no sellers willing to sell at the price the buyers are willing to pay. While this is rare when the company is traded on a major stock exchange, it is not uncommon when shares are traded over-the-counter (OTC). Since individual buyers and sellers need to incorporate news about the company into their purchasing decisions, a security with an imbalance of buyers or sellers may not feel the full effects of recent news.

4

Business Valuation

Valuation is a critical part of the merger process. A deal that may be sound from a business standpoint may be unsound from a financial standpoint if the bidder firm pays too much. The purpose of valuation analysis is to provide a disciplined procedure for arriving at a price. If the buyer offers too little, the target may resist and, since it is in play, seek to interest other bidders. If the price is too high, the premium may never be recovered from post-merger synergies. These general principles are illustrated by the following simple model.

ANALYSIS

Mergers increase value when the value of the combined firm is greater than the sum of the pre-merger values of the independent entities.

$$\text{NVI} = VBT - (VB + VT)$$

where NVI = net value increase
VB = value of bidder alone
VT = value of target alone
VBT = value of firms combined

A simple example will illustrate. Company B (the bidder) has a current market value of Rs. 40 (it is understood that all the numbers are in millions). Company T (the target) has a current market value of Rs. 40. The sum of the values as independent firms is therefore

Rs. 80. Assume that as a combined company (CC) synergies will increase the value to Rs. 100. The amount of value created is Rs. 20.

How will the increase in value be divided? Targets always (usually) receive a premium. What about the bidders? If the bidder pays a premium of less than Rs. 20, it will share in the value increase. If B pays a premium larger than Rs. 20, the value of the bidder will decline. If the bidder pays Rs. 50 for the target, a premium of 25 per cent has been paid to T. The value increases are shared equally.

USE OF STOCK IN ACQUISITIONS

A high percentage of the large transactions beginning in 1992 has been stock-for-stock transactions. Some hold the view that this does not represent real money. But this is not valid.

Suppose B exchanges 1.0 of its shares for 1.0 share of T. Since the combined firm is valued at Rs. 100, T will receive 5 × Rs. 100, which equals Rs. 50. The premium paid is 25 per cent. Based on their previous Rs. 40 values, B and T each owned 50 per cent of the premerger combined values. Post-merger, the percentages of ownership will remain 50-50. If B exchanges 1.5 of its own shares per share of T, this is equivalent to paying Rs. 60 in value for the target. Company T shareholders will own 60 per cent of the combined company. None of the synergy gains will be received by the bidder shareholders.

Also note that the target shareholders will have 1.5 shares in the new company for every 1.0 share held by the bidder shareholders.

The situation is even worse if B pays more than Rs. 60 for the target. Assume B pays Rs. 70 for the target (1.75 to 1 shares). Since the combined company has a value of Rs. 100, the value of the bidder shares must decline to Rs. 36.36. The consequences are terrible. The shares of the bidder will decline in value by Rs. 3.64, or 9.1 per cent. Furthermore, the B shareholders will own only 36.36 per cent of the combined company; for every 1.0 share that they own, the target shareholders will own 1.75 shares.

Investors in a company that is aiming to take over another one must determine whether the purchase will be beneficial to them. In order to do so, they must ask themselves how much the company being acquired is really worth.

Naturally, both sides of an M&A deal will have different ideas about the worth of a target company: its seller will tend to value the company at as high a price as possible, while the buyer will try to get the lowest price that he can.

There are, however, many legitimate ways to value companies. The most common method is to look at comparable companies in an industry, but deal makers employ a variety of other methods and tools when assessing a target company.

The five most common ways to valuate a business are:

- asset valuation,
- historical earnings valuation,
- future maintainable earnings valuation,
- relative valuation (comparable company & comparable transactions),
- discounted cash flow (DCF) valuation.

Professionals who valuate businesses generally do not use just one of these methods but a combination of some of them, as well as possibly others that are not mentioned above, in order to obtain a more accurate value. These values are determined for the most part by looking at a company's balance sheet and/or income statement and withdrawing the appropriate information. The information in the balance sheet or income statement is obtained by one of three accounting measures: a Notice to Reader, a Review Engagement or an Audit. Accurate business valuation is one of the most important aspects of M&A as valuations like these will have a major impact on the price that a business will be sold for. Most often

Investors in a company that are aiming to take over another one must determine whether the purchase will be beneficial to them. In order to do so, they must ask themselves how much the company being acquired is really worth.

this information is expressed in a Letter of Opinion of Value (LOV) when the business is being valuated for interest's sake. There are other, more detailed ways of expressing the value of a business. These reports generally get more detailed and expensive as the size of a company increases, however, this is not always the case as there are many complicated industries which require more attention to detail, regardless of size.

In finance, **valuation** is the process of estimating the potential **market value** of a financial asset or liability. Valuations can be done on assets (for example, investments in marketable securities such as stocks, options, business enterprises, or intangible assets such as patents and trademarks) or on liabilities (e.g., bonds issued by a company). Valuations are required in many contexts including investment analysis, capital budgeting, merger and acquisition transactions, financial reporting, taxable events to determine the proper tax liability, and in litigation.

OVERVIEW OF VALUATION

Valuation of financial assets is done using one or more of these types of model:

1. Relative value models determine the value based on the market prices of similar assets.
2. Absolute value models determine the value by estimating the expected future earnings from owning the asset discounted to their present value.
3. Option pricing models are used for certain types of financial assets (e.g., warrants, put options, call options, employee stock options, investments with embedded options such as a callable bond) and are a complex present value model. The most common option pricing models are the Black-Scholes-Merton models and lattice models.

Common terms for the value of an asset or liability are fair market value, fair value and intrinsic value. The meanings of these terms differ. The most common term in use is probably *fair market value* defined as the cash price an item would sell for between a willing buyer and willing seller assuming they both have knowledge of the relevant facts and they have no compulsion to buy or sell. *Fair value* is used in different contexts and has multiple meanings. Some people use the term to mean the same thing as fair market value. Furthermore, fair value is also used in accounting and law. In accounting, the term is used as part of generally accepted accounting principles (GAAP) in financial reporting. In law, fair value is often used in state statutes for shareholder rights. In both cases, fair value is defined in the accounting literature or the law, respectively. Fair value in the accounting and legal contexts may be different from each other and may also be different from fair market value. Another term—*intrinsic value*—is the "true" value of an asset regardless of the asset's market price. For instance, when an analyst believes a stock's intrinsic value is greater than its market price, the analyst makes a "buy" recommendation and vice versa. Moreover, an asset's intrinsic value may be subject to personal opinion and vary among analysts.

Accurate business valuation is one of the most important aspects of M&A as valuations like these will have a major impact on the price that a business will be sold for. Most often this information is expressed in a Letter of Opinion of Value (LOV) when the business is being valuated for interest's sake. There are other, more detailed ways of expressing the value of a business. These reports generally get more detailed and expensive as the size of a company increases; however, this is not always the case as there are many complicated industries which require more attention to detail, regardless of size.

Investors in a company that is aiming to take over another one must determine whether the purchase will be beneficial to them. In order to do so, they must ask themselves how much the company being acquired is really worth.

Naturally, both sides of an M&A deal will have different ideas about the worth of a target company: its seller will tend to value the company at as high of a price as possible, while the buyer will try to get the lowest price that he can. There are, however, many legitimate ways to value companies. The most common method is to look at comparable companies in an industry, but deal makers employ a variety of other methods and tools when assessing a target company. Some of them are:

- **Comparative Ratios -** The following are two examples of the many comparative metrics on which acquiring companies may base their offers:
  - Price-Earnings Ratio (P/E Ratio) - With the use of this ratio, an acquiring company makes an offer that is a multiple of the earnings of the target company. Looking at the P/E for all the stocks within the same industry group will give the acquiring company good guidance for what the target's P/E multiple should be.
  - Enterprise-Value-to-Sales Ratio (EV/Sales) - With this ratio, the acquiring company makes an offer as a multiple of the revenues, again, while being aware of the price-to-sales ratio of other companies in the industry.

Replacement Cost - In a few cases, acquisitions are based on the cost of replacing the target company. For simplicity's sake, suppose the value of a company is simply the sum of all its equipment and staffing costs. The acquiring company can literally order the target to sell at that price, or it will create a competitor for the same cost. Naturally, it takes a long time to assemble good management, acquire property and get the right equipment. This method of establishing a price certainly wouldn't make much sense in a service industry where the key assets—people and ideas—are hard to value and develop.

MAIN BUSINESS VALUATION METHOD

Discounted Cash Flows Method

This method estimates the value of an asset based on its expected future cash flows, which are discounted to the present (i.e., the present value). This concept of discounting future cash flows is commonly known as the time value of money. For instance, an asset that matures and pays Re. 1 in one year is worth less than Re. 1 today. The size of the discount is based on an opportunity cost of

*This method estimates the value of an asset based on its expected future cash flows, which are discounted to the present (i.e., the present value). This concept of discounting future monies is commonly known as the **time value of money***

Table 4.1: Valuation of NTPC

Initial Growth Period (in Rs. Crores)	1	2	3	4	5	6	7	8	9	10	11
Years	2007	2008	2009	2010	2011	2012	2013	2014	2015	2016	2017
1 Revenues	35385	40011	43634	48283	56052	65204	75845	88156	102438	119202	139315
2 Operating Expenses	22538	25545	28866	32618	36859	41650	47065	53183	60097	67910	76738
3 Depreciation	2075	2138	2202	2268	2336	2406	2479	2553	2629	2708	2790
4 EBIT = NOI	10772	12328	12566	13397	16857	21147	26302	32420	39711	48584	59787
5 Less: Interest Expense	1859	1798	1744	1692	1641	1592	1544	1498	1453	1409	1367
6 EBT = (4) – (5)	8913	10530	10822	11705	15216	19555	24758	30922	38258	47174	58420
7 Less: Tax @ 33%	2941	3475	3571	3863	5021	6453	8170	10204	12625	15568	19279
8 Net Income = (6) – (7)	5972	7055	7251	7842	10195	13102	16588	20718	25633	31607	39142
9 Add: Interest Expense (1-T) = 5(1-T)	1246	1205	1169	1133	1099	1066	1034	1003	973	944	916
10 NOPAT = 4(1-T) = (8) – (9)	7217	8260	8419	8976	11294	14169	17622	21721	26606	32551	40057
10a Add: depreciation	2075	2138	2202	2268	2336	2406	2479	2553	2629	2708	2790
10b Less: capital expenditures	1262	1611	2062	2639	3379	4324	5535	7085	9069	11608	14859
10c Less changes in working capital	5770	2459	2459	2459	2459	2459	2459	2459	2459	2459	2459
11 Free cash flow = (10) + (10a) – (10b) – (10c)	2260	6328	6100	6146	7793	9791	12106	14730	17708	21192	25529
12 Discount factor @ WACC	0.929	0.862	0.801	0.744	0.691	0.641	0.596	0.553	0.514	0.477	0.443
13 Present values of free cash flow	2099	5457	4886	4571	5383	6281	7212	8149	9097	10111	11311
14 Sum of initial period present values	74556										

Table 4.2: Terminal period (in crore)

1.	EBITDA of 2017	62,577
2.	Free cash flow, 2017	25,529
3.	Terminal period discount rate	10.00%
4.	Terminal value in 2017	255,292
5.	Present value factor: 1 / (1 + WACC) × n	0.443
6.	Present value of terminal period	113,111

Table 4.3: Calculation of equity value (in crore)

1.	Sum of initial period present values	74556
2.	Present value of terminal period	113111
3.	DCF enterprise value	187667
4.	Add: excess cash	–1118
5.	Less: debt	21726
6.	Equity value	164823
7.	Number of shares outstanding	825
8.	Value per share	200

Table 4.4: WACC calculation

WACC= Wequity * Kequity + Wdebt * Kdebt (1- T_c)

Wequity and Wdebt are the weights of the Equity and debt portion respectively

Kequity is the Cost of Raising Equity and Kdebt the Cost of Debt

T_c is the Corporate Tax Rate, which is equal to 33%

Now, Kdebt = 6%

Cost of Equity, Kequity, can be found out by the Capital Asset Pricing Model(CAPM)

Required Rate of Return on Equity = Rf + ß (Rm – Rf)

Where, ß = Market Sensitivity of the NTPC Stock = 0.75

Rf is the Risk free Rate = 7%

Rm is the Return on the Market Portfolio = 10%

Thus, Cost of Equity = 0.07 + 0.75 (0.10 – 0.07) = 0.1 = 9.25%

Now Wequity = 0.7 and Wdebt = 0.3. This is based on the Capital Structure of NTPC

Thus inserting all the values in the WACC formula,

WACC= 0.7 * 9.25% + 0.3 * 6% *(1 – 0.33) = 6.475 + 1.206 = 7.681%

capital and it is expressed as a percentage. Some people call this percentage a discount rate.

The idea of opportunity cost can be illustrated in an example. A person with only Rs. 100 to invest can make just one Rs. 100 investment even when presented with two or more investment choices. If this person is later offered an alternative investment choice, the investor has lost the opportunity to make that second investment since Rs. 100 is spent to buy the first opportunity. This example illustrates that money is limited and people make choices in how to spend it. By making a choice, they give up other opportunities.

In finance theory, the amount of the **opportunity cost** is based on a relation between the risk and return of some sort of investment. Classic economic theory maintains that people are rational and adverse to risk. They, therefore, need an incentive to accept risk. The incentive in finance comes in the form of higher expected returns after buying a risky asset. In other words, the more risky the investment, the more return investors want from that investment. Using the same example as above, assume the first investment opportunity is a government bond that will pay interest of 5% per year and the principle and interest payments are guaranteed by the government. Alternatively, the second investment opportunity is a bond issued by small company and that bond also pays annual interest of 5%. If given a choice between the two bonds, virtually all investors would buy the government bond rather than the small-firm bond because the first is less risky while paying the same interest rate as the riskier second bond. In this case, an investor has no incentive to buy the riskier second bond. Furthermore, in order to attract capital from investors, the small firm issuing the second bond must pay an interest rate higher than 5% that the government bond pays. Otherwise, no investor is likely to buy that bond and, therefore, the firm will be unable to raise capital. But by offering to pay an interest rate more than 5%. The firm gives investors an incentive to buy a riskier bond.

For a valuation using the discounted cash flow method, one first estimates the future cash flows from the investment and then estimates a reasonable discount rate after considering the riskiness of those cash flows and interest rates in the capital markets. Next, one makes a calculation to compute the present value of the future cash flows.

VALUATION PROCEDURES

The procedure for valuing an acquisition candidate depends on the source of the estimated gains. Different sources of *synergy* have different risks. Tax gains can be estimated fairly accurately and should be discounted at the cost of debt. Cost reductions through operating efficiencies can also be determined with some confidence. Such savings should be discounted at a normal weighted average cost of capital. Gains from strategic benefits are difficult to estimate and are often highly uncertain. A discount rate greater than the overall cost of capital would thus be appropriate for creation of value.

The net present value (NPV) of the acquisition is equal to the gains less the cost of the acquisition. The cost depends on whether cash or stock is used as payment. The cost of an acquisition when cash is used is just the amount paid. The cost of the merger when common stock is used as the consideration (the payment) is equal to the percentage of the new firm that is owned by the previous shareholders in the acquired firm *multiplied* by the value of the new firm. In a cash merger the benefits go entirely to the acquiring firm, whereas in a stock-for-stock exchange the benefits are shared by the acquiring and acquired firms.

Whether to use cash or stock depends on three considerations. First, if the acquiring firm's management believes that its stock is *overvalued*, then a stock acquisition may be cheaper. Second, a cash acquisition is usually taxable, which may result in a higher price. Third, the use of stock means that the acquired firm will share in any gains from merger; if the merger has a negative NPV, however, then the acquired firm will share in the loss.

In valuing acquisitions, the following factors should be kept in mind. First, market values must not be ignored. Thus, there is no need to estimate the value of a publicly traded firm as a separate entity. Second, only those cash flows that are incremental are relevant to the analysis. Third, the discount rate used should reflect the risk associated with the incremental cash flows. Therefore, the acquiring firm should not use its own cost of capital to value the cash flows of another firm. Finally, acquisition may involve significant investment banking fees and costs.

SYNERGY: THE PREMIUM FOR POTENTIAL SUCCESS

For the most part, acquiring companies nearly always pay a substantial premium on the stock market value of the companies they buy. The justification for doing so nearly always boils down to the notion of synergy; a merger benefits shareholders when a company's post-merger share price increases by the value of potential synergy. It would be highly unlikely for rational owners to sell if they would benefit more by not selling. That means buyers will need to pay a premium if they hope to acquire the company, regardless of what pre-merger valuation tells them. For sellers, that premium represents their company's future prospects. For buyers, the premium represents part of the post-merger synergy they expect can be achieved. The following equation offers a good way to think about synergy and how to determine whether a deal makes sense.

A Simple Example to Explain Merger and Acquisition

Scenario: Two Companies A and B is planning to Merge then the worth of deal can be calculated as follows:

- **Gains From Merger is the Value Created and is calculated as follows**
  1. Company A + Company B = Company AB
  2. Value of Company (A) + Value of Company (B) < Value of Merged Company (AB)
  3. GAIN = Value of Merged Company (AB) - [Value of Company (A) + Value of Company (B) = WEALTH CREATION
  4. Estimate Gain which is = Present Value of Merged Company AB - (Present Value of Company A + Present Value of Company B)
  5. If Gain is Positive There is an Economic Justification for the Merger

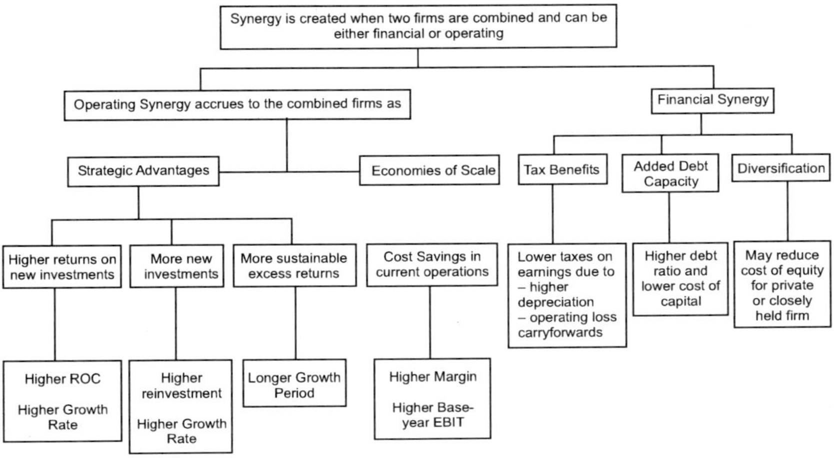

Figure 4.1: Source of Synergy

Source: Mergers and Acquisition Report 2005.

- **Cost of Acquiring Firm B**
  1. Cost of Buying Firm B - The Value of B as Separate Entity
  2. Cost = Cash Paid Out to Buy Company B – Current Value of Company B
- **NPV of Merger is given as follows :**
  1. NPV = Gains From Merger — Cost of Acquiring Firm
  2. Present Value of Merged Company AB = (Present Value of Company A + Present Value of Company B)-(Cash paid to Acquire B –Present Value of B)
  3. Present Value of Merged Company AB =PVAB — PVA – Cash
  4. One Should Go Ahead with Merger if NPV is Positive

EXAMPLE OF COST AND GAINS

1. Assume Present Value of Company A = Rs. 100 million
2. Assume Present Value of Company B = Rs. 50 million
3. Gain from the merger is + Rs. 25 million
4. Value of Merged Company AB is Rs. 175 million
5. Assume B is bought for Rs. 65 million Then
   - Cost = Cash paid to acquire B - Value of Merged Company AB

- 65 – 50 = Rs. 15 mill
- Hence NPV = 25 – 15 = Rs. 10 mill

Thus Shareholders of the target Firm B have Captured Rs. 15 million of the Total gain of Rs. 25 million. Bidding Firm Shareholders Gain is Rs. 10 mill. They start with a Firm worth Rs. 100 mill, Pay Rs. 65 mill in Cash to Acquire Firm B, and End with Combined Firm Value of Rs. 175 million

ADDITIONAL CONDITION

Case 1: Suppose the merger was unanticipated. The announcement will cause the value of firm B to rise from Rs. 50 million to Rs. 65 million (30 % increase).

- If the market is able to correctly assess the merger gain (= Rs. 25 mill), market value of firm A will rise from Rs. 100 million to Rs. 110 million (10%)
- Estimating Gains

	Firm A	Firm B
Market Price / Share	Rs. 75	Rs. 15
No. of Shares	1,000,000	600,000
Market Value of Firm	Rs. 75 m	Rs. 9 m
A intends to acquire B for Rs. 12 million		

If due to rumours, price of B share rises by Rs. 2 prior to A's announcement

Cost = (cash- MVB) + (MVB - PVB) = (12 - 9) + (9 - 9) = Rs. 3 m

If rumours raise price of B, true vale of B is only Rs. 7.8 m

Cost == (12 - 9) + (9 - 7.8) = Rs. 4.2 m

If true value of B is more than Rs. 9 million (market undervalues B), cost would be negative

Case 2: Suppose A plans to offer 160,000 shares instead of Rs. 12 m.

- Apparent Cost = 160,000 x 75 - 9 million = Rs. 3 million

- The shares were worth Rs. 75 before the merger was announced. Suppose the merger provides cost savings worth Rs. 4.75 m i.e.

Present Value of Merged Company AB = 75+9+4.75 = 88.75

Gain = PV of AB - (PV of A + PV of B) = 88.75 - (75 + 9) = 4.75

- Hence after the announcement, we can now expect the market price of A's share to be = 88750,000/1160,000 = Rs. 76.50
- Hence Cost = (160,000 × 76.5) - 9 m = Rs. 3,240,000 = Rs. 3.24 m

WHAT TO LOOK FOR

It's hard for investors to know when a deal is worthwhile. The burden of proof should fall on the acquiring company. To find mergers that have a chance of success, investors should start by looking for some of these simple criteria:

- **A reasonable purchase price -** A premium of, say, 10% above the market price seems within the bounds of level-headedness. A premium of 50%, on the other hand, requires synergy of stellar proportions for the deal to make sense. Stay away from companies that participate in such contests.
- **Cash transactions -** Companies that pay in cash tend to be more careful when calculating bids and valuations come closer to target. When stock is used as the currency for acquisition, discipline can go by the wayside.
- **Sensible appetite –** An acquiring company should be targeting a company that is smaller and in businesses that the acquiring company knows intimately. Synergy is hard to create from companies in disparate business areas. Sadly, companies have a bad habit of biting off more than they can chew in mergers.

Mergers are awfully hard to get right, so investors should look for acquiring companies with a healthy grasp of reality.

Taxable versus Tax-Free Transactions

Mergers and acquisitions can be either tax-free or taxable events. The tax status of a transaction may affect its value from both the buyer's and the seller's viewpoints. In a taxable acquisition, the assets of the selling firm are revalued or "written up."

Certain exchanges of stock are considered tax-free reorganizations, which permit the owners of one company to exchange their shares for the stock of the acquirer without Therefore, the depreciation deduction will rise (assets are not revalued in a tax-free acquisition). But the selling shareholders will have to pay capital gains taxes and thus will want more for their shares to compensate. This is known as the capital gains effect. The capital gains and write-up effects tend to cancel each other out. paying taxes. There are three basic types of tax-free reorganizations. In order for a transaction to qualify as a type A tax-free reorganization, it must be structured in certain ways. In contrast to a type B reorganization, the type A transaction allows the buyer to use either voting or nonvoting stock. It also permits the buyer to use more cash in the total consideration since the law does not stipulate a maximum amount of cash that can be used. At least 50 per cent of the consideration, however, must be stock in the acquiring corporation. In addition, in a type A reorganization, the acquiring corporation may choose not to purchase all the target's assets.

In instances where at least 50 per cent of the bidder's stock is used as the consideration—but other considerations such as cash, debt, or no equity securities are also used—the transaction may be partially taxable. Capital gains taxes must be paid on those shares that were exchanged for no equity consideration.

A type B reorganization requires that the acquiring corporation use mainly its own voting common stock as the consideration for purchase of the target corporation's common stock. Cash must comprise no more than 20 per cent of the total consideration, and at least 80 per cent of the target's stock must be paid for by voting stock by the bidder.

Target stockholders who receive the stock of the acquiring corporation in exchange for their common stock are not immediately taxed on the consideration they receive. Taxes will have to be paid only if the stock is eventually sold. If cash is included in the transaction, this cash may be taxed to the extent that it represents a gain on the sale of stock.

In a type C reorganization, the acquiring corporation must purchase 80 per cent of the fair market value of the target's assets. In this type of reorganization, a tax liability results when the acquiring corporation purchases the assets of the target using consideration other than stock in the acquiring corporation. The tax liability is measured by comparing the purchase price of the assets with the adjusted basis of these assets.

Financial Accounting for Mergers and Acquisitions

The two principal accounting methods used in mergers and acquisitions are:

- Pooling of interests method
- The purchase method.

The main difference between them is the value that the combined firm's balance sheet places on the assets of the acquired firm, as well as the depreciation allowances and charges against income following the merger.

The pooling of interests method assumes that the transaction is simply an exchange of equity securities. Therefore, the capital stock account of the target firm is eliminated, and the acquirer issues new stock to replace it. The two firms' assets and liabilities are combined at their historical book values as of the acquisition date. The end result of a pooling of interests transaction is that the total assets of the combined firm are equal to the sum of the assets of the individual firms. No goodwill is generated, and there are no charges against earnings. A tax-free acquisition would normally be reported as a pooling of interests.

Under the purchase method, assets and liabilities are shown on the merged firm's books at their market (not book) values as of the acquisition date. This method is based on the idea that the resulting values should reflect the market values established during the *bargaining* process. The total liabilities of the combined firm equal the sum of the two firms' individual liabilities. The equity of the acquiring firm is increased by the amount of the purchase price.

Accounting for the excess of cost over the *aggregate* of the fair market values of the identifiable net assets acquired applies only in purchase accounting. The excess is called *goodwill*, an asset which is charged against income and amortized over a period that cannot exceed 40 years. Although the *amortization* "expense" is deducted from reported income, it cannot be deducted for tax purposes.

Purchase accounting usually results in increased depreciation charges because the book value of most assets is usually less than fair value because of inflation. For tax purposes, however, depreciation does not increase because the tax basis of the assets remains the same. Since depreciation under pooling accounting is based on the old book values of the assets, accounting income is usually higher under the pooling method. The accounting treatment has no cash flow consequences. Thus, value should be *unaffected* by accounting procedure. However, some firms may dislike the purchase method because of the goodwill created. The reason for this is that goodwill is amortized over a period of years.

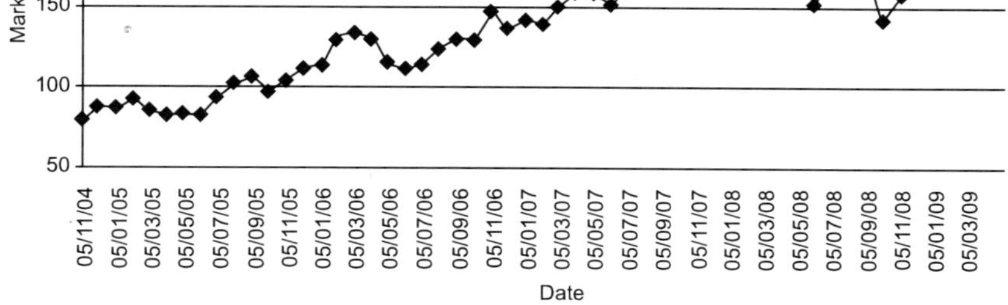

Figure 4.2: NTPC

Guideline Companies Method

This method determines the value of a firm by observing the prices of similar companies (guideline companies) that sold in the market. Those sales could be shares of stock or sales of entire firms. The observed prices serve as valuation benchmarks. From the prices, one calculates price multiples such as the price-to-earnings or price-to-book value ratios. Next, one or more price multiples are used to value the firm. For example, the average price-to-earnings multiple of the guideline companies is applied to the subject firm's earnings to estimate its value.

Many price multiples can be calculated. Most are based on a financial statement element such as a firm's earnings (price-to-earnings) or book value (price-to-book value) but multiples can be based on other factors such as price-per-subscriber.

USAGE OF VALUATION

In finance, valuation analysis is required for many reasons including tax assessment, wills and estates, divorce settlements, business analysis, and basic book-keeping and accounting. Since the value of things fluctuates over time, valuations are as of a specific date e.g., the end of the accounting quarter or year. They may alternatively be mark-to-market estimates of the current value of assets or liabilities as of this minute or this day for the purposes of managing portfolios and associated financial risk (for example, within large financial firms including investment banks and stockbrokers).

Some balance sheet items are much easier to value than others. Publicly traded stocks and bonds have prices that are quoted frequently and readily available. Other assets are harder to value. For instance, private firms that have no frequently quoted price. Additionally, financial instruments that have prices that are partly dependent on theoretical models of one kind or another are difficult to value. For example, options are generally valued using the Black-Scholes model while the liabilities of life assurance firms are valued using the theory of present value. Intangible business assets, like goodwill and intellectual property, are open to a wide range of value interpretations.

It is possible and conventional for financial professionals to make their own estimates of the valuations of assets or liabilities.

FINANCING MERGERS AND ACQUISITIONS

Mergers are generally differentiated from acquisitions partly by the way in which they are financed and partly by the relative size of the companies. Various methods of financing an M&A deal exist.

Cash

Payment by cash: Such transactions are usually termed acquisitions rather than mergers because the shareholders of the target company are removed from the picture and the target comes under the (indirect) control of the bidder's shareholders alone.

A cash deal would make more sense during a downward trend in the interest rates. Another advantage of using cash for an acquisition is that there tends to lesser chances of EPS dilution for the acquiring company. But a caveat in using cash is that it places constraints on the cash flow of the company.

> *A* ***leveraged buyout*** *(or* ***LBO****, or highly-leveraged transaction (HLT), or "bootstrap" transaction) occurs when a financial sponsor acquires a controlling interest in a company's equity and where a significant percentage of the purchase price is financed through leverage (borrowing).*

Financing

Financing capital may be borrowed from a bank, or raised by an issue of bonds. Alternatively, the acquirer's stock may be offered as consideration. Acquisitions financed through debt are known as leveraged buyouts if they take the target private, and the debt will often be moved down onto the balance sheet of the acquired company.

A **leveraged buyout** (or LBO, or highly-leveraged transaction (HLT), or "bootstrap" transaction) occurs when a financial sponsor acquires a controlling interest in a company's equity and where a significant percentage of the purchase price is financed through leverage (borrowing). The assets of the acquired company are used as collateral for the borrowed capital, sometimes with assets of the acquiring company. The bonds or other papers issued for leveraged buyouts are commonly considered not to be investment grade because of the significant risks involved.

Companies of all sizes and industries have been the target of leveraged buyout transactions, although because of the importance of debt and the ability of the acquired firm to make regular loan payments after the completion of a leveraged buyout, some features of potential target firms make for more attractive leverage buyout candidates, including:

- Low existing debt loads;
- A multi-year history of stable and recurring cash flows;
- Hard assets (property, plant and equipment, inventory, receivables) that may be used as collateral for lower cost secured debt;
- The potential for new management to make operational or other improvements to the firm to boost cash flows;
- Market conditions and perceptions that depress the valuation or stock price.

Management buyouts: A special case of such acquisition is a management buyout (MBO), which occurs when a company's managers buy or acquire a large part of the company. The goal of an MBO may be to strengthen the managers' interest in the success of the company. In most cases, the management will then make the company private. MBOs have assumed an important role in corporate restructuring beside mergers and acquisitions. Key considerations in an MBO are fairness to shareholders, price, the future business plan, and legal and tax issues. One recent criticism of MBOs is that they create a conflict of interest—an incentive is created for managers to mismanage (or not manage as efficiently) a company, thereby depressing its stock price, and profiting handsomely by implementing effective management after the successful MBO.

Hybrids

An acquisition can involve a combination of cash and debt or of cash and stock of the purchasing entity.

Factoring

Factoring can provide the extra impetus to make a merger or sale work. **Factoring** is a financial transaction whereby a business **sells its accounts receivable** (i.e., invoices) at a discount. Factoring differs from a bank loan in three main ways. First, the emphasis is on the value of the receivables (essentially a financial asset), not the firm's creditworthiness. Secondly, factoring is not a loan – it is the purchase of a financial asset (the receivable). Finally, a bank loan involves two parties whereas factoring involves three.

Factoring is a method used by a firm to obtain cash when the available cash balance held by the firm is insufficient to meet current obligations and accommodate its other cash needs, such as new orders or contracts. The use of factoring to obtain the cash needed to accommodate the firm's immediate cash needs will allow the firm to maintain a smaller ongoing cash balance. By reducing the size of its cash balance, more money is made available for investment in the firm's growth. A company sells its invoices at a discount to their face value when it calculates that it will be better off using the proceeds to bolster its own growth than it would be by effectively functioning as its "customer's bank." Accordingly, factoring occurs when the rate of return on the proceeds invested in production exceed the costs associated with Factoring the Receivables. Therefore, the trade off between the return the firm earns on investment in production and the cost of utilizing a factor is crucial in determining both the extent factoring is used and the quantity of cash the firm holds on hand.

Financing of Corus Deal by Tata

On January 31, 2007, **Tata Steel Limited (Tata Steel**), one of the leading steel producers in India, acquired the Anglo Dutch steel producer **Corus Group Plc** (Corus) for US$ 12.9 billion. The process of acquisition concluded only after nine rounds of bidding against the **other bidder** for Corus – the Brazil based **Companhia Siderurgica Nacional (CSN).**

Total Amount Required to Finance the Acquisition : **$12.9 billion**

Tata Steel's committed equity contribution : $ **4.1 billion**

Out of its share of $4.1 billion Tata Steel invested : $ **1.8 billion**

Rs. 7900 crore, which was made through **internal generation** of **$700 million (Rs. 3000 crore), external commercial borrowings** of **$500 million (Rs. 2170 crore)** and funds from **preferential issue of equity shares** to Tata Sons at an average price of Rs. 499.7 per share that fetched **$640 million (Rs. 2770 crore).**

Tata Steel approved two rights issues and one foreign issue to raise remaining **$ 2.3 billion** of its committed contribution. The remaining **$8.8 billion** was financed through a non- recourse **debt** arranged by a consortium of banks for **$ 6.14 billion** at **Tata Steel UK** and the balance **$2.66 billion** raised in the form of bridge finance by its subsidiary **Tata Steel Asia Singapore.**

MERGERS AND ACQUISITIONS – BREAK UPS

As mergers capture the imagination of many investors and companies, the idea of getting smaller might seem counter-intuitive. But **corporate break-ups, or demergers, can be very attractive options for companies and their shareholders.**

Advantages

The rationale behind a spinoff, tracking stock or carve-out is that "**the parts are greater than the whole**." These corporate restructuring techniques, which involve the separation of a business unit or subsidiary from the parent, can help a company raise additional equity funds. A break-up can also boost a company's valuation by providing powerful incentives to the people who work in the separating unit, and help the parent's management to **focus on core operations.**

Most importantly, shareholders get better information about the business unit because it issues separate financial statements. This is particularly useful when a company's traditional line of business differs from the separated business unit. With separate financial disclosure, investors are better equipped to gauge the value of the parent corporation. The parent company might attract more investors and, ultimately, more capital. Also, separating a subsidiary from its parent can reduce internal competition for corporate funds. For investors, that's great news: it curbs the kind of negative internal wrangling that can compromise the unity and productivity of a company.

For employees of the new separate entity, there is a publicly traded stock to motivate and reward them. Stock options in the parent often provide little incentive to subsidiary managers, especially because their efforts are buried in the firm's overall performance.

Disadvantages

That said, demerged firms are likely to be **substantially smaller** than their parents, possibly making it harder to tap credit markets and costlier finance that may be affordable only for larger companies. And the smaller size of the firm may mean it has less representation on major indexes, making it more difficult to attract interest from institutional investors. Meanwhile, there are the extra **costs that the parts of the business face if separated**. When a firm divides itself into smaller units, it may be losing the synergy that it had as a larger entity. For instance, the division of expenses such as marketing, administration and research and development (R&D) into different business units may cause redundant costs without increasing overall revenues.

5

Companies Act and SEBI Takeover Code

As far as India is concerned, every M&A activity is regulated by the following legal and regulatory issues.

- Companies Act
- Competition Act
- Income Tax Act
- Indian Stamp Act
- SEBI Takeover Code
- FEMA

COMPANIES ACT

Mergers and acquisitions in India are governed by the Indian Companies Act, 1956, more particularly Sections 391 to 394. This Act consolidates provisions pertaining to mergers and acquisitions and other related issues of compromise, arrangements and reconstruction. Though mergers and acquisitions may be initiated through agreements between the parties, the process remains largely court driven as the sanction of the concerned High Court is required for bringing such a merger/acquisition into effect.

Under the existing law in India, the scheme for merger and/ or acquisition or any such arrangement should be approved by a majority in number representing not less than 3/4th in value of shareholders/creditors present and voting during the General Body Meetings of the companies concerned. However, different courts in

India follow different procedures of holding meetings of the creditors and shareholders or dispensing with the requirement of such meetings.

The Government has a role to play in this process and it acts through an Official Liquidator (OL) or the Regional Director of the Ministry of Company Affairs. After hearing all the concerned parties including shareholders, the concerned High Court approves acquisition and merger proposals.

Compared to mergers and acquisitions, joint venture arrangements are easier to set up under Indian law. Joint venture companies can be formed by entering into a joint venture agreement for incorporating a new company with equity participation of the joint venture parties or by picking up equity stakes in an existing company.

The Act lays down the legal procedures for mergers or acquisitions:

- **Permission for merger:** Two or more companies can amalgamate only when the amalgamation is permitted under their memorandum of association. Also, the acquiring company should have the permission in its object clause to carry on the business of the acquired company. In the absence of these provisions in the memorandum of association, it is necessary to seek the permission of the shareholders, board of directors and the Company Law Board before affecting the merger.
- **Information to the stock exchange:** The acquiring and the acquired companies should inform the stock exchanges (where they are listed) about the merger.
- **Approval of board of directors:** The board of directors of the individual companies should approve the draft proposal for amalgamation and authorise the managements of the companies to further pursue the proposal.
- **Application in the High Court:** An application for approving the draft amalgamation proposal duly approved by the board of directors of the individual companies should be made to the High Court.
- **Shareholders' and creditors' meetings:** The individual companies should hold separate meetings of their

shareholders and creditors for approving the amalgamation scheme. At least, 75 per cent of shareholders and creditors in separate meetings, voting in person or by proxy, must accord their approval to the scheme.

- **Sanction by the High Court:** After the approval of the shareholders and creditors, on the petitions of the companies, the High Court will pass an order, sanctioning the amalgamation scheme after it is satisfied that the scheme is fair and reasonable. The date of the Court's hearing will be published in two newspapers, and also, the regional director of the Company Law Board will be intimated.
- **Filing of the Court order:** After the Court order, its certified true copies will be filed with the Registrar of Companies.
- **Transfer of assets and liabilities:** The assets and liabilities of the acquired company will be transferred to the acquiring company in accordance with the approved scheme, with effect from the specified date.
- **Payment by cash or securities:** As per the proposal, the acquiring company will exchange shares and debentures and/or cash for the shares and debentures of the acquired company. These securities will be listed on the stock exchange.

COMPETITION ACT

The Act regulates the various forms of business combinations through Competition Commission of India. Under the Act, no person or enterprise shall enter into a combination, in the form of an acquisition, merger or amalgamation, which causes or is likely to cause an appreciable adverse effect on competition in the relevant market and such a combination shall be void. Enterprises intending to enter into a combination may give notice to the Commission, but this notification is voluntary. But, all combinations do not call for scrutiny unless the resulting combination exceeds the threshold limits in terms of assets or turnover as specified by the Competition Commission of India. The Commission while regulating a 'combination' shall consider the following factors:

- Actual and potential competition through imports;
- Extent of entry barriers into the market;
- Level of combination in the market;
- Degree of countervailing power in the market;

- Possibility of the combination to significantly and substantially increase prices or profits;
- Extent of effective competition likely to sustain in a market;
- Availability of substitutes before and after the combination;
- Market share of the parties to the combination individually and as a combination;
- Possibility of the combination to remove the vigorous and effective competitor or competition in the market;
- Nature and extent of vertical integration in the market;
- Nature and extent of innovation;
- Whether the benefits of the combinations outweigh the adverse impact of the combination.

The Competition Act does not seek to eliminate combinations and only aims to eliminate their harmful effects.

SECURITIES AND EXCHANGE BOARD OF INDIA (SEBI)

M&A and takeovers are powerful ways to achieve corporate growth, but because of their complex nature, to protect the interest of all the parties, curb the malpractices and to facilitate orderly development these activities are regulated by a takeover code in most part of the world. In India after liberalization Govt. started to regulate these activities by introducing a takeover code. This code has gone through various major and minor changes since then to respond the challenges it faced during implementation and also to overcome its shortcomings.

NEED FOR TAKEOVER CODE

In India activities of the companies from the point of view of M&A and takeover can be seen in terms of three waves.

First Wave: The first wave of takeover was witnessed in India during 80s and in the beginning of 90s. It was altogether different from current scenario. There were hardly any regulation and making a tender offer was not compulsory. Takeover was considered a willing buyer-seller negotiation. Mostly two types of cases were there. First, it was a case of foreign owner, who had diluted his stake to less than 50% and therefore lost interest in Indian company and sold it out to Indians (e.g. Shaw Wallace). Secondly, due to the pressure of financial crisis. During this period some cases were where acquirer was a strong person and loser were generally small investors e.g. Tata's acquisition of Special Steel and HLL's acquisition of Stepan Chemicals. During this period Swaraj Paul, RP Goenka, Manu Chabbria, Ambanis and Murrugappa group were the pioneers.

Second Wave: Second wave in the Indian context however started after 1994. This was the era of expansion, consolidation and restructuring and a marked shift from friendly to hostile takeover was witnessed during this period. In fact liberalization of Indian economy, dismantling of MRTP and licensing regime, relaxation under FERA, availability of foreign funds etc had led to a rise in the number of mergers and takeovers during this period.

Third Wave: The wave gaining momentum now is the third wave. It is significantly different from earlier two because role of banks and FIS becomes important now. Because of the complexity of the nature of takeover, to protect the interest of small investors as well as the target company a need was felt to develop a code to regulate the whole process of acquisition and takeovers based on the principle of transparency, fairness and equal opportunity to all. The impact of the SEBI's initiative on the takeover code in the interest of investors seems to be visible. According to a presentation made by SEBI in 2001, introduction of takeover code has been resulted in a benefit of Rs. 4250 crore to the shareholders of various companies.

EVOLUTION OF TAKEOVER CODE

PRIOR TO 1990

The first attempts at regulating takeovers were made in a limited way by incorporating a clause, viz. Clause 40, in the listing agreement, which provided for making a public offer to the shareholders of a company by any person who sought to acquire 25% or more of the voting rights of the company. Before 1990s M&A and takeovers were regulated by Companies Act, 1956, IDRA 1951, MRTP Act, 1969, FERA, 1973, and SCRA, 1956 (with respect to transfer of shares of listed companies vide clauses 40A and 40B). It was frustrating to the person who wanted to achieve corporate growth through this route. For example, in case of MNC related acquisitions, provisions of the FERA applied which imposed a general limit on foreign ownership at 40%. In addition, MRTP gave powers to the union government to prevent an acquisition if it was considered to lead to 'concentration of economic power to the common detriment'. Moreover, in the event of a hostile bid for the company, the board of a company had the power to refuse transfer to a particular buyer, thereby making it almost impossible for a takeover to occur without the acquiescence of the management of the target company. In the due course Govt. found that the companies circumvented the threshold limit of 25% for making a public offer, simply by acquiring voting rights a little below the threshold limit of 25%. Besides it noted that it was possible to acquire control over a company in the Indian context with even holding 10% directly. Existing provisions were also not sufficient to consider issues like pricing and change in the management and control.

RELEVANT CASES

Swaraj Paul- Escorts/ DCM

In 1980s London-based NRI Swaraj Paul sought to control the management of two Indian companies, Escorts Limited and DCM (Delhi Cloth Mills) Limited by picking up their shares from the stock market. Paul apparently used the tacit support of the then Prime Minister Indira Gandhi. But had to face major obstacle from government-run financial institutions like the Life Insurance Corporation opposed him and the two companies refused to register the transfer of shares in his name. Promoters of the two companies—the Nanda and Shri Ram families—also used their political links to defeat Paul.

Though Swaraj Paul failed to fulfill his dream of controlling Escorts and DCM, but was successful in highlighting how particular families were able to exercise managerial control over large corporate entities despite holding a minuscule proportion of the concerned company's shares

IN 1990

Govt. in consultation with SEBI made following amendments in the Clause 40:

- Lowering the threshold acquisition level for making a public offer by the acquirer, from 25% to 10%.
- Bringing within its fold the aspect of change in management and control (even without acquisition of shares beyond the threshold limit), as a sufficient ground for making a public offer;
- Introducing the requirement of acquiring a minimum of 20% from the shareholders;
- Stipulating a minimum price at which an offer should be made;
- Providing for disclosure requirements through a mandatory public announcement
- Requiring a shareholder to disclose his shareholding at level of 5% or above to serve as an advance notice to the target company about the possible takeover threat.

Problems

These changes helped in making the process of acquisition of shares and takeovers transparent, provided for protection of investors' interests in greater measure and introduced an element of equity between the various parties concerned by increasing the disclosure requirement. But the clause suffered from several deficiencies, particularly in its limited applicability and weak enforceability. Being a part of the listing agreement, it could be made binding only on listed companies and could not be effectively enforced against an acquirer unless the acquirer itself was a listed company.

The penalty for non-compliance was one common to all violations of a listing agreement, namely, delisting of the company's shares, which ran contrary to the interest of investors. The amended clause was unable to provide a comprehensive regulatory framework governing takeovers.

IN 1994

In 1992, SEBI was given statutory power to regulate the substantial acquisition of shares and takeovers. In November 1994 SEBI issued 'Substantial Acquisition of Shares and Takeovers Regulation, 1994' The Regulations preserved the basic framework of Clause 40 (A & B) by retaining the requirements of initial disclosure at the level of 5%, threshold limit of 10% for public offer to acquire minimum percentage of shares at a minimum offer price and making of a public announcement by the acquirer followed by a letter of offer.

Several new provisions were introduced enabling both negotiated and open market acquisitions, competitive bids, revision of offer, withdrawal of offer under certain circumstances and restraining a second offer in relation to the same company within 6 months by the same acquirer, post-offer public holding, etc. The takeover code covers three types of takeovers—negotiated takeovers, open market takeovers and bailout takeovers (to help financially weak companies which do not fall under the purview of BIFR).

Features:

- Requiring a shareholder to disclose his holding at 5%
- Threshold limit at 10% for making public offer
- Changes in management and control dropped as a requirement for making open offer
- If holding crosses to15% than open offer compulsory (no creeping facility for promoters).
- Min. price offered to shareholders through open offer will be average of 26 weeks high and low
- Price can be paid either in cash or through exchange of shares
- If a person were to cross the threshold of 10%, he must make a public offer to acquire a minimum of 20% of the share capital of the company, and consequent upon such offer, the public share holding must not fall below 20%. In addition, if a person holding more than 10% shares in a company, and who has not made any public offer before, were to acquire any further shares, the public offer will have to be made to the extent of the difference between his present holding and 30%.
- Acquisition of shares in companies pursuant to a scheme of arrangement or reconstruction including amalgamation or

merger or demerger under any law or regulation, whether Indian or foreign has been exempted from the public offer provisions. However, prima facie it does not exempt international acquisitions or mergers carried out under normal course of business as a result of which there is a change in control of an Indian listed company. For that matter, the Code defines control very broadly to include both direct and indirect control.

Problems

The above provisions raised some issues. First, in companies where public holding was less than 20%, or might fall below that level to comply with the minimum public offer requirement, it was not possible to comply with the requirement of maintaining a minimum level of post-offer public holding. The two provisions were thus conflicting with each other. Further, a harmonious construction of all the three provisions implied that if a person was holding more than 30%, no public offer was required to be made by him, for further acquisition of shares in the company, even though he has not made any public offer earlier to reach his present holding. Thirdly, it was not clear from the three provisions whether full offer for a company could be made, i.e. a bid for 100% shares of the company could be made.

It does not clearly specify obligations on the part of the acquirer, the board of directors of the target company and the merchant banker. Again it lends to an interpretation that further acquisitions outside of public offer, from the market or otherwise, may be permitted, once the public announcement of offer has been made.

Regulations do not specify the circumstances and the time limit within which a revised offer can be made; nor do the regulations specify whether revision of all the terms of offer, upward or downward, is permissible, and circumstances under which withdrawal of offer can be made. Existing Regulation on the competitive bids was not very clear. First, there was the question of definition of a competitive bid. Secondly, was the position of the first bid if the acquirer did not want to compete in the offer?

These provisions were used later by some acquirers to launch hostile and competitive bids.

RELEVANT CASES

Sesa Goa-Mitsui

In 1996, Mitsui of Japan acquired the parent company of Sesa-Goa India Limited, a publicly traded listed company in India. As a result of this acquisition, Mitsui indirectly became the single largest shareholder of Sesa-Goa. The question then raised was whether Mitsui should make an open offer to other shareholders of Sesa-Goa under the Takeover Code. Mitsui applied to SEBI stating that the Takeover Code should not be triggered as the change in control of Sesa-Goa was a result of its acquisition of Sesa-Goa's parent. Luckily for Mitsui, the case was evaluated under the 1994 takeover code and the Ministry of Finance ruled that under the 1994 takeover code, SEBI had no jurisdiction over the developments abroad and therefore could not pass sentence on something that happened outside its jurisdiction and thereby no open offer was required.

Schenectady International Inc.

Schenectady International Inc. of USA filed an application with SEBI seeking exemption from the application of public offer provisions of the Takeover Code for its acquisition of 51% of the equity capital of Dr. Beck & Co. (India) Limited .The acquirer proposed to acquire 32.67% and 18.33% of the target from Beck and BASF AG of Germany respectively. The acquirer in its application stated that this acquisition of 51% of the target company was a part of the global acquisition of the Beck division from BASF which includes BASF and Beck's equity holding in the target company. The takeover panel rejected above application and accordingly SEBI ordered the acquirer to make open offer for 20% to the public.

Herbertsons Case

In 1993 Kishore Chabbaria acquired 27% stake in Vijay Mallaya's Herbertsons Ltd at Mallaya's invitation. Later on Chabbaria tried to takeover the Herbertsons. This is a very controversial case, which took around a decade for SEBI to solve it. During this period SEBI changed its verdict several times, which made it more controversial. In this case both Chabbaria and Mallya are alleged to violate the code. Chhabbria used loopholes of the 1994 code to avoid an open offer. A drafting flaw in the 1994 regulations created a loophole allowing him to use a two-step route to raising his stake without attracting the open offer provision Chabbaria acquired 10.9% stake in 1993. Later on he acquired another 9% in February 97, before the notification of New takeover code. In May 1996, SEBI reacted in the case and ordered Chabbaria to make an open offer, which was against the interest of Mallaya because open offer was to give Chabbaria enough power to takeover Herbertsons. So Mallaya strongly opposed the SEBI verdict.

In this case a new turn came when Herbertsons file and earlier letters lost from SEBI office. Later on even the secret documents were even found in the hands of both the parties.

This case came at a conclusion recently in August this year, when SAT ordered Kishore Chhabria to make an open offer to acquire an additional 20 per cent of Herbertsons' equity within three months at a price worked out with October 27, 1994, as the reference date. It has also ordered him to pay interest at the rate of 15 per cent to those investors who have been holding the shares as on January 25, 1995, and continue to be shareholders. Which worked out around Rs. 210.74 per share.

A committee was therefore set up by SEBI in November 1995, under the Chairmanship of Justice P.N. Bhagwati, former Chief Justice of India, to review the SEBI (Substantial Acquisition of Shares and Takeovers) Regulations, 1994.Committee discussed all the issues, which came up before SEBI in the course of administration of the Regulations over the past two years or so, keeping in view the imminent scenario in the corporate sector following the economic reforms.

The committee examined the principles and practices and the regulatory framework governing takeovers in as many as 14 countries. The committee noted that the regulatory framework in these countries had evolved over a period of time drawing extensively upon the corporate culture and practice in these countries. Without an appreciation of these factors, a mere comparison of the procedures, regulatory requirements and various quantitative limits in these countries would be meaningless.

The committee submitted its report in January, 1997 based on the recommendations of this committee SEBI enacted " substantial Acquisition of Shares and Takeover Code 1997."

SUBSTANTIAL ACQUISITION OF SHARES AND TAKEOVER CODE 1997

Main Features

• **Compulsory disclosure:** New regulation made it compulsory to disclose holdings at the levels of 5%. So any person whose total holding in the company (inclusive of shares and voting right already held) reaches to this limit has to compulsorily disclose his level of holding to the concerned company and stock exchange.

• **Continual disclosures:** If a person held more than 10% shares or voting right in a company, he has to disclose his holding within 21 days from the financial year ending on 31 march. (Note: This limit was revised to 15% in Oct. 98)

Trigger of takeover code: If a person wants to increase his holding beyond 10% (this 10% would be inclusive of the rights or shares already held by the acquirer or by the persons acting in concert with him), he has to do make an open offer.

Consolidation of holdings/Creeping acquisition: If a person holds more than 10% but less than 51% shares or voting right in a company and wants to acquire more than 2% in a financial year can do only through public offer. (Note: In Oct. 98, 10%, 51 % and 2% limits were revised as 15%, 75 % and 5% respectively.)

Acquisition of any additional shares or voting rights when the acquirer already has 51 % of the shares or voting rights of the company can be done through open offer only. (Note: in Oct. 98, this limit was revised to 75%.)

Minimum number of shares to be acquired: The public offer made by the acquirer to the shareholders of the target company shall be for a minimum 10% of the voting capital of the company.) (Revised in Feb 98 as 20%) Minimum Price: Minimum price to be offered to shareholders will be average of highest and lowest in the preceding 26 weeks.

If the public offer results in the public shareholding being reduced to 10% or less of the voting capital of the company, or if the public offer is in respect of a company which has public shareholding of less than 10% of the voting capital of the company, the acquirer shall either, make an offer to buy the outstanding shares remaining with the shareholders or undertake to disinvest through an offer for sale or by a fresh issue of capital to the public, which shall open within a period of 6 months from the date of closure of the public offer, such number of shares so as to satisfy the listing requirements offer conditional upon level of acceptance. An acquirer may make an offer conditional as to the level of acceptance which may be less than 20%. Conditional offer will be for minimum 20%, although acceptance level may be less than 20%.

Competitive bid: Any person other than the acquirer can made a competitive offer within 21 days of the public announcement of the offer. Competitive offer shall be at least for the number of shares for which first public announcement has been made. In case of a competitive bid, the acquirer who made the first announcement shall have the option to revise his original offer within 14 days of such competitive offer, if no such announcement is made by acquirer within 14 days than original offer will continue to be valid. The acquirers who have made the public announcement of offer(s) including the public announcement of competitive bid(s) shall have the option to make upward revisions in his offer(s), in respect to the price and the number of shares to be acquired, at any time up to seven working days prior to the date of closure of the offer.

Withdrawal of offer: Withdrawal of offer can be made consequent to competitive offer or under following circumstances: (1) the statutory approval(s) required have been refused; (2) the sole acquirer, being a natural person, has died; (3) such circumstances as in the opinion of the Board merits withdrawal.

Bail out takeovers: Separate provisions are given for substantial acquisition of shares in a financially weak company not being a sick industrial company, in pursuance to a scheme of rehabilitation approved by a public financial institution or a scheduled bank. The financial institution shall be responsible for ensuring compliance with the provisions of this chapter.

Exemptions from open offer: The public offer provisions of the Takeover Code will not be apply in the following cases.

i) Allotment in pursuance of an application made to a public issue.
ii) Allotment pursuant to an application made by the shareholder for rights issue. (Subject to such rights issue not resulting in change in control and management of the company).
iii) Preferential allotment of shares, subject to the condition that at least 75% of the shareholders of the company shall have approved the preferential allotment and that sufficient disclosures relating to the post-allotment shareholding pattern, offer price etc., have been made to the shareholders.
iv) Allotment to the underwriters pursuant to any underwriting agreement;
v) Issue of American Depository Receipts and Global Depository Receipts or Foreign Currency Convertible Bonds, till such time, as they are not converted into equity shares.
vi) Shares held by banks and financial institutions by way of security against loans.
vii) in addition to the above cases, even when there is a change in control and management of the company, the Takeover Code would still not apply if at least 51% of the shareholders of the company have approved the acquisition by the acquirer after being made aware that such acquisition would result in change in control and management.

• **Preferential offers:** Companies adopt the preferential offer route in varied situations for the purpose of consolidation of stake by the existing Indian or foreign promoters, induction of foreign collaborators with foreign technology, gaining management control of the company, injection of fresh funds for turning around sick companies. Regulations provide that the Board resolution is to be sent to the stock exchanges, SEBI will grant exemption on case to case basis under the powers granted to it under section 4 of the regulation.

• **Acquisitions during offer period:** Except where an offer is made conditional as to minimum level of acceptances, the acquirer may be allowed to make acquisitions during offer period subject to the condition that highest price paid for such acquisition be paid to the shareholders under the public offer, unless it is less than the minimum offer price.

SOME IMPORTANT CHANGES IN TAKEOVER CODE AFTER 1997

i) **February 1998** SEBI proposes to revise the takeover code and make it mandatory for acquirers to make a minimum open offer for 20% (and not 10% as earlier) of the target company's equity, even if the holding goes beyond 51% as a result of the offer.

ii) **June 1998** SEBI proposes to raise the creeping acquisition limit under the Takeover Code from 2% to 5%. It also proposes to increase the share acquisition limit for triggering the takeover code from minimum 10% to 15% and maximum from 51% to 75%.

iii) **November 1998** takeover panel amends the takeover code to incorporate buy-back offers by companies. The committee decides to allow takeover offers to be made when a buy-back offer is open and vice versa. .

iv) **January 2000** SEBI again proposes that all open offers made by promoters for consolidating their holding in a company will have to be for a minimum of 20% of equity. Exemption to the minimum 20% requirement should be given only in the case of such companies in which promoters hold over

75%. The SEBI takeover committee also recommends that a special resolution approved by 75% of the shareholders should be made mandatory for effecting a change in the management of professionally managed companies. The step aims to avoid misuse of the earlier provision, under which certain groups with 51% stake could effect the changes through a simple resolution. Another recommendation that follows was that venture capital funds should be treated on par with state financial institutions. And like financial institutions, they should be exempted from making a public offer, in the event of acquiring a 15% stake in a company.

v) **November 2000** SEBI made it mandatory for an 'acquirer' to disclose his holdings in the target company, to the company as well exchanges at three levels - 5%, 10% and 14% – instead of the existing stipulation of only 5%.

vi) **August 2001** SEBI relaxes the creeping acquisition limit for shareholders (holding between 15-75%) to 10% till March 2002 without the compulsion to obtain shareholder approval.

vii) **September 2002** The Takeover Committee, headed by former chief justice of India P. N. Bhagwati, comes out with recommendations to amend the Code. SEBI approves the recommendations of the Takeover Committee with minor modifications and notifies the new Takeover Code. The new regulations are a finer version of the earlier code and largely aim at benefiting the investing community. It aimed at increasing the ambit of open offer.

SUBSTANTIAL ACQUISITION OF SHARES AND TAKEOVER CODE 2002

Main Features: (Where changes were made)

Creeping acquisition: Reducing the creeping acquisition limit from 10 per cent to 5 per cent with effect from October 1, 2002. Also, that to calculate this limit financial year ending on 31st march will be considered instead of existing 12 month period.

Preferential allotments: SEBI has done well to remove the exemption altogether. Hereafter, all preferential allotment of shares aggregating to an equity stake of 15 per cent or more will be automatically referred to the Takeover Panel for applicability of open offers.

Offer price: Offer price should be the average of past 26 weeks prices or average of past 2 weeks preceding the date of the public announcement, whichever is higher. Thus it dropped the concept of average of high and low for last 26 weeks.

Consolidation of holdings: Acquirers who already hold 75% in a company and wish to increase their stake further will have to make a minimum offer of 20%, as against the earlier provision allowing them to make an offer of less than 20%.

Interse transfer: A share transfer among different promoters or groups will not attract the provisions of the code if it is made at a price above less than 25% of that arrived at by the SEBI formula. However, if the price exceeds 25%, it will attract the provisions of the code. Interse transfers are transfers between shareholders who have been promoters for at least three years and hold over 5% in the target company. So far, transfer of stakes between promoters were fully exempt from the Takeover Code.

Indirect acquisition: Indirect acquisitions were brought under the purview of takeover code. Any indirect acquisition of over 5% will trigger an open offer. Earlier this was applicable (with a limit of 15%) only for listed companies.

Conditional offer: An acquirer or any person acting in concert with him may make an offer conditional as to the level of acceptance which may be less than 20% only in case the acquirer.

i. Has deposited in escrow account in cash a sum of 50% of the consideration payable under the public offer; Only if he binds himself to rescind the acquisition under the Memorandum of understanding, in case the desired level of acceptance is not received."

Competitive bid: Here a change made in the manner that competitive bid shall be for such number of shares which will make the total holding of the bidder at least equals to the holding of the original acquirer together with the shares or voting power already held.

Withdrawal of offer: No public offer, once made, shall be withdrawn except under the following circumstances:

i) The statutory approval(s) required have been refused
ii) The sole acquirer, being a natural person, has died
iii) Such circumstances as in the opinion of the Board merits withdrawal. Earlier provision of withdrawal consequent to competitive bid was removed also if acquirer withdraws the offer, he cannot make another offer for the same company for 6 months.

Exemptions from code (new added): If shares are transferred from state level financial corporations or its subsidiaries to the co-promoters or their successors or assignee(s) or acquirer who has substituted erstwhile promoter.

Investors have been given the freedom to withdraw shares already tendered in an open offer. On the other hand, if competitive bids exist, the code has removed the facility of the first acquirer withdrawing from the offer. The code has done away with the need for acquirers to inform SEBI and the stock exchanges two days prior to a public announcement. A newspaper advertisement would suffice.

The capital markets regulator has also amended the takeover code to stipulate that an "acquirer" who has made a public offer and seeking to acquire further shares under the creeping acquisition route cannot acquire shares at a price higher than the offer price during the period of six months from the date of closure of public offer. This stipulation, however, will not be applicable in cases where the acquisition is made through the stock exchanges.

(Where status quo maintained)

Disclosure of holdings: Three-stage disclosure – at 5%, 10% and 14% of equity to the target company and the stock exchanges.

Minimum offer: Minimum size of the offer kept at existing 20%.

Mode of payment: Acquirer can pay either in cash or in terms of exchange of shares.

Changes in control: Change in control" is possible only when a special resolution (as against a general resolution applicable currently) is passed by shareholders in a general meeting. In addition, postal ballots are to be allowed at such meetings.

Indirect acquisitions/global level arrangement: In the case of indirect acquisition or change in control, a public announcement has to be made by the acquirer within three months of the consummation of such acquisition or change in control or restructuring of the parent or the company holding shares of or control over the target company in India.

viii) November 2002 A SEBI committee suggests closed book-building (where the book will not be made public) so that applicants have to take a call on the price at which they make the bid without having access to information regarding the bids made by other applicants. Further, companies may be allowed to disclose the minimum floor price just prior to the bid opening date.

The SEBI has decided to make promoters of companies more accountable for the information disclosed in offer documents and has made it mandatory for the board of directors to approve and sign the draft offer document. The committee recommended that companies should not be allowed to come out with a public or rights issue unless 75% of the stated means of finance are tied up.

COMPARISON WITH OTHER COUNTRIES

Although before preparing the takeover code, Bhagwati Committee made an attempt to analyse different takeover codes prevalent in different countries. The Committee observed that the selection of a particular type of code depends upon the fundamental character of that market, for example, takeover code in the UK is not imposed by any regulatory body but has evolved as a self-regulatory framework. Similarly, if we compare Indian takeover with that of prevalent in US (Williams Act, 1968) we can notice that it is on the same route. In US also there is a compulsory initial disclosure provision at 5% and also a creeping facility for 2% in 12 months period.

6

Legal Procedures for Mergers and Acquisitions

The control exercised by the government over mergers is articulated in an elaborate legal framework embodied in the Companies Act and the MRTP Act. The general law relating to mergers, amalgamations and reconstruction is embodied in sections 391 to 396 of the Companies Act, 1956 which jointly deal with the compromise and arrangement with creditors and members of a company needed for a merger. Section 391 gives the High Court the power to sanction a compromise or arrangement with creditors and members, subject to certain conditions. Section 392 gives the power to the High Court to enforce and supervise the carrying out of such compromises or arrangements with creditors and members. Section 393 provides for the availability of the information required by the creditors and members of the concerned company when acceding to such an arrangement. Section 394 makes provisions for facilitating reconstruction and amalgamation of companies. And Section 396 deals with the power of the central government to provide for an amalgamation of companies in the national interest.

In any scheme of amalgamation, both the amalgamating company or companies and the amalgamated company should comply with the requirements specified in sections 391 to 394 and submit details of all the formalities for consideration to the High Court. It is not enough if one of the companies alone fulfils the necessary formalities. Sections 394, 394A of the Companies Act deal with the procedures and the requirements to be followed in order to effect amalgamation of companies coupled with the provisions relating to the powers of the court and the central government in the matter of bringing about amalgamation of companies.

PROVISIONS IN THE MRTP ACT

The law relating to mergers also explicitly prescribed that any merger or amalgamation, which increased concentration of asset ownership, should not be approved by the High Court. Thus wherever such a possibility existed the role of the High Court as the agency which ensured that a merger was not prejudicial to the interests of its members or the public was superseded by the role of the central government as an agency that safeguards the national interest. This was done under Section 23 of the MRTP Act. According to sub-section (2) of this section, Government approval for amalgamations was necessary in the following circumstances: (i) if one MRTP undertaking amalgamated with another undertaking; and (ii) if, on amalgamation of two or more undertakings, an undertaking came into existence which became registrable under the MRTP Act.

As per the law, the power of the central government under section 23 of the MRTP Act overrode the power of the Court to sanction a scheme of merger or amalgamation under sections 391 to 396 of the Companies Act. According to this section, no scheme for the merger or amalgamation of an undertaking could be sanctioned by any Court or would be recognised for any purpose or would be given effect to unless the scheme for such merger or amalgamation had been approved by the central government under the specific provisions of this section. The owner of the undertaking had to make an application to the central government for the approval. The scheme of approval could not be modified without the previous approval of the central government. The approval of the central government was not necessary for the merger or amalgamation of interconnected undertakings (which were not dominant undertakings) if they produced the same goods or provided the same services. If one of the transacting parties is a non-resident Indian, then transfer of shares could be made only with the permission of the RBI.

Finally, the provisions under the Sections 23 and 24 of Chapter 3 of MRTP Act were abolished in 1991. As a result, the MRTP commission does not play a role in mergers and acquisitions in the same manner in which it used to. But, it does play a role in cases where it believes that a merger or a takeover would lead to restrictive trade practices regarding takeovers there were no comprehensive regulations to govern these activities until the new clauses 40A and 40B were incorporated in May 1990 although both the companies Act (section 395) and the MRTP Act (section 24) had provisions for corporate takeovers. According to this clause, any person who acquires 5% or more of the shares in a company must notify the stock exchange and when the holdings cross 10%, a public offer to purchase shares must be made. However, this agreement was restricted to only listed companies and was effective only when either of the parties in an acquisition was a listed company. In November 1994, the Securities and Exchange Board of India came out with SEBI (Substantial acquisition of shares and take-overs) Regulation, 1994 to regulate the take-over of the companies. But this code was inadequate to address all the complexities and therefore a new committee was set up to review the present code. The committee under the chairmanship of P. N. Bhagwati suggested substantial modifications in the existing code.

The important changes are:

- Consolidation of holdings by an existing shareholder holding not less than 10 per cent of voting rights will be allowed;
- Conditional bid will be allowed;
- Acquirer will be required to deposit upfront 10 per cent of the total consideration in an Escrow account;
- Time limit for competitive bidding has been extended to 21 days;
- The consideration shall be payable even by exchange and/ or transfer of secured instruments with a minimum of 'A' grade rating from a credit rating agency. The valuation of the instrument will be duly certified by an independent category 1 merchant banker or a chartered accountant of 10 years standing;
- Acquisition of shares by the acquirer during offer period is permitted, except in case of conditional offer;

- Time schedule for each event in the takeover process has been specified;
- Waiting for offer letter by SEBI has been dispensed with.

Thus the revised code is applicable to the takeovers through acquisition of control over a company irrespective of whether or not there has been any acquisition of shares or voting rights in the company whereas, the present code restricts its applicability to takeovers through acquisition of shares or voting rights. However, mergers and amalgamations constitute a subject matter of Companies Act, 1956 and are outside the purview of SEBI.

PROCEDURES TO BE FOLLOWED FOR MERGERS

Examination of Object Clauses

The MOA of both the companies should be examined to check the power to amalgamate is available. Further, the object clause of the merging company should permit it to carry on the business of the merged company. If such clauses do not exist, necessary approvals of the shareholders, board of directors, and company law board are required.

Intimation to Stock Exchanges

The stock exchanges where merging and merged companies are listed should be informed about the merger proposal. From time to time, copies of all notices, resolutions, and orders should be mailed to the concerned stock exchanges.

Approval of the Draft Merger Proposal by the Respective Boards

- The draft merger proposal should be approved by the respective BOD's.
- The board of each company should pass a resolution authorizing
- Its directors/executives to pursue the matter further.

Application to High Courts

Once the drafts of merger proposal is approved by the respective boards, each company should make an application to the High Court of the state where its registered office is situated so that it can convene the meetings of shareholders and creditors for passing the merger proposal.

Dispatch of notice to shareholders and creditors

In order to convene the meetings of shareholders and creditors, a notice and an explanatory statement of the meeting, as approved by the High Court, should be dispatched by each company to its shareholders and creditors so that they get 21 days advance intimation. The notice of the meetings should also be published in two newspapers.

Holding of meetings of shareholders and creditors

A meeting of shareholders should be held by each company for passing the scheme of mergers at least 75% of shareholders who vote either in person or by proxy must approve the scheme of merger. Same applies to creditors also.

Petition to High Court for confirmation and passing of High Court Orders

Once the merger scheme is passed by the shareholders and creditors, the companies involved in the merger should present a petition to the High Court for confirming the scheme of merger. A notice about the same has to be published in two newspapers.

Filing the Order with the Registrar

Certified true copies of the High Court order must be filed with the registrar of companies within the time limit specified by the Court.

Transfer of Assets and Liabilities

After the final orders have been passed by both the High Courts, all the assets and liabilities of the merged company will have to be transferred to the merging company.

Issue of Shares and Debentures

The merging company, after fulfilling the provisions of the law, should issue shares and debentures of the merging company. The new shares and debentures so issued will then be listed on the stock exchange. With the increase in the number of cross-border mergers and acquisitions, it would be worth while to study the competition laws of some major nations.

EUROPEAN UNION

Merger Regulations

EC Merger Control Regulation lays down a mandatory system of notification of concentrations which have a strong relation to the European community. In mergers, a notification must be made jointly by parties and in other cases responsibility is with acquiring companies.

- First three weeks—the mergers are not to be put into effect after the notification
- The Commission carries a preliminary examination within a month. Most are cleared on this stage. Some may enter second stage.
- Second stage takes three/four months to carry out an in-depth examination. If concentration is proved, it may prohibit.

There are some features such as:

- Reciprocal exclusivity between the Community and the Member State level. If a concentration is vetted by EC Commission, national competition authority cannot prohibit.
- In case a national competition authority clears, and it is not vetted by the Commission, then another Member State can prohibit.
- There is a timetable. Case under MCR takes one month.
- MCR expects the notifying company to provide information.

USA

There are two legislations which have a direct impact on mergers and acquisitions in USA. They are Securities Act of 1933 and Securities and Exchange Act of 1934. Under the Securities Act of 1933, any offering by an issuer of its own securities for the business is unlawful except in acquisitions where there is no offering of stock or securities by an issuer to public. The Act lists the requirements for filling the registration statements of securities. Securities and

Exchange Act of 1934 provides the requirements for proxy material which must be submitted to stockholders in connection with stockholders' meetings for the purpose of approving statutory mergers.

There are three anti-trust federal acts:

- The Sherman Act declares any combination which may result in restraint of trade of commerce. It prohibits price fixing, boycotts allocation of territories through concert of action by competitors
- The Federal Trade Commission Act deals with unfair methods of competition in commerce. The Commission requires a 60-day notice prior to the consummation of an acquisition by a buyer
- The Robinson-Patman Act is an amendment to the Clayton Act. This act prohibits discrimination in prices.

ANTI-TRUST HISTORY

The **Sherman Act of 1890** outlawed monopoly and monopolization. It was supplemented in **1914** by the **Clayton Act**, which made it illegal to have tying agreements, stock acquisitions, and interlocking directorates that would tend to reduce competition. Both acts assumed that high concentration (dominance of an industry by a few firms) would weaken competition and damage the public by reducing output, increasing prices, and slowing technological advance.

This legislation responded to public anger and fears over the ongoing concentration of business, which at the time the Sherman Act was passed assumed the form of "trusts," which brought separate firms under common control. Most notorious were Rockefeller's Standard Oil Trust and James Duke's American Tobacco Company, both of which employed ruthless tactics (local price cutting, denial of pipeline or other distribution access) to acquire large market shares and the power to charge high prices.

But the federal government only minimally enforced the Sherman Act until the election of Theodore Roosevelt in 1900. The Act did not interfere with the great merger movement of 1897-1903, although the Roosevelt administration's successful prosecution of a great railroad merger in the 1904 Northern Securities case may have helped to quiet merger activity. The government successfully prosecuted the Standard Oil and American Tobacco trusts, as the Supreme Court decided in 1911 that both companies were "bad trusts" because of their predatory tactics, and ordered their dismantling. Later, the Court refused in 1920 to condemn the U.S. Steel consolidation, because it was a "good trust" that didn't attack its smaller rivals. This set the stage for a long period when the Antitrust Division and the courts approved mergers that produced industries with a few dominant firms (oligopolies), but which were "well-behaved."

From 1897 onward, moreover, the courts took a harsher stand against price-fixing and market-sharing agreements among rival companies ("loose-knit combinations") than they did against the actual merger of rivals ("close-knit combinations"). This perverse double standard, based heavily on the assumption that mergers advance efficiency, has arguably encouraged mergers.

GOLDEN AGE OF ANTI-TRUST

The Roosevelt administration revived anti-trust during 1938 to 1941, and anti-trust law had its golden age from 1945 to 1974, fueled by a liberal Supreme Court, anti-merger legislation passed in 1950, and mildly progressive enforcement (though less so in the Republican years). During this period Alcoa (aluminum) was condemned under the Sherman Act and its monopoly was broken (1945), and the Court found the tobacco oligopoly guilty of "group monopoly" (1946), although no effective remedies were put in place (the companies were only assessed a modest fine).

Another danger to consumers is **"vertical" monopoly power"** which occurs when one company owns two or more stages of the production process (such as raw materials, manufacturing, and distribution). Rival firms may become dependent on buying or selling through the vertically integrated firm, as in the Paramount case (1948), where the linkage between motion picture production and distribution was severed. Tougher standards were imposed on both "horizontal" (within the same industry) and vertical mergers in decisions on Von's Grocery (1966), Brown Shoe (1962), and the Philadelphia National Bank (PNB, 1963). In the PNB case, a merger of banks which together held a 30% market share was condemned by the court as "inherently likely **to lessen competition substantially**."

Even conglomerate mergers involving unrelated firms were brought under the anti-trust orbit in the Procter and Gamble case (1967). P&G was prevented from acquiring Clorox on the grounds that P&G was a potential competitor that could enter the liquid bleach industry by routes other than buying up the leading producer—and thereby eliminating its potential competition. .

THREAT FROM MERGERS: CAN ANTI-TRUST MAKE A DIFFERENCE?

Anti-trust action by government assumes that **consumer interests** are served best when many companies compete to sell each product or service. Monopolies, or tight oligopolies (when a few firms are dominant, and face little threat of entry by new companies), are harmful in several ways. First, lacking the discipline of **competition,** they have less pressure to minimize costs, and may operate wastefully. Second, they restrict output in order to **keep prices and profits high**. Third, they may stifle technical progress, because their market power reduces the incentive for both themselves and outsiders to innovate. Finally, huge corporations can **exert great political power**, thereby undermining democracy.

An important example was the U.S. Steel merger of 1901, which the Supreme Court eventually sanctioned in a 1920 decision. The Court's decision allowed an inefficient and technologically backward firm to dominate a great industry for many decades, entailing heavy social costs. U.S. Steel only became vulnerable when superior, and much smaller, foreign firms were allowed a limited penetration of U.S. markets beginning in the 1960s. Subsequently, the industry's political power allowed it to obtain legislation protecting it from imports. This resulted in high steel prices, burdening numerous steel-using industries and reducing their competitiveness. Ultimately, hundreds of thousands of steel workers were laid off and local steel-making communities were devastated by the industry's backwardness.

Many other giants of U.S. industry, including American Can, United Shoe Machinery, International Harvester, General Motors, Eastman Kodak, and IBM have demonstrated poor long-term performance. A good argument can be made that their failures were a result of having comfortable monopolistic positions – which more aggressive anti-trust action by the government could have challenged.

HERFHINDAHL INDEX IN DETAIL

The **Herfindahl index**, also known as **Herfindahl-Hirschman Index** or **HHI**, is a measure of the size of firms in relation to the industry and an indicator of the amount of competition among them. Named after economists Orris C. Herfindahl and Albert O. Hirschman, it is an economic concept but widely applied in **competition law** and **anti-trust**. It is defined as the sum of the squares of the market shares of the 50 largest firms (or summed over all the firms if there are fewer than 50) within the industry, where the market shares are expressed as percentages. The result is proportional to the average market share, weighted by market share. As such, it can range from 0 to 10,000, moving from a huge number of very small firms to a single monopolistic producer. **Increases in the Herfindahl index generally indicate a decrease in competition and an increase of market power, whereas decreases indicate the opposite.**

The major benefit of the Herfindahl index in relationship to such measures as the concentration ratio is that it gives more weight to larger firms.

For instance, two cases in which the six largest firms produce 90 per cnt of the output:

- Case 1: All six firms produce 15 per cent each, and
- Case 2: One firm produces 80 per cent while the five others produce 2 per cent each.

Assuming that the remaining 10 per cent of output is divided among 10 equally sized producers.

The six-firm concentration ratio would equal 90 per cent for both case 1 and case 2, but in the first case competition would be fierce where the second case approaches monopoly. The Herfindahl index for these two situations makes the lack of competition in the second case strikingly clear:

- Case 1: Herfindahl index = $6 * 15^2 + 10 * 1^2 = 1360$
- Case 2: Herfindahl index = $80^2 + 5 * 2^2 + 10 * 1^2 = 6430$

This behavior rests in the fact that the market shares are squared prior to being summed, giving additional weight to firms with larger size.

The index involves taking the market share of the respective market competitors, squaring it, and adding them together (e.g. in the market for X, company A has 30 per cent, B, C, D, E and F have 10 per cent each and G through to Z have 1 per cent each). If the resulting figure is above a **certain threshold** then economists consider the market to have a high concentration (e.g. market X's concentration is "0.142" or "1420" if you multiply percentages in whole figures). This threshold is considered to be "0.18" in the US while the EU prefers to focus on the level of change, for instance that concern is raised if there's a "0.025" change when the index already shows a concentration of "0.1". So to take the example, if in market X company B (with 10% market share) suddenly bought out the shares of company C (with 10% also) then this new market concentration would make the index jump to "0.172". Here it can be seen that it would not be relevant for merger law in the U.S. (being under 0.18) but would in the EU (because there's a change of over 0.025). Put simply; now two firms control half the market, so serious competition questions are raised.

FORMULA

$$H = \Sigma S_i^{\ 2}$$

where s_i is the market share of firm i in the market, and N is the number of firms (i takes values from 1 to N). The Herfindahl Index (H) ranges from $1/N$ to one, where N is the number of firms in the market. Equivalently, the index can range up to 10,000, if percents

Table 6.1: Critical concentration levels

Post-merger HHI	Anti-trust challenge to a merger?
Less than 1000	No challenge—industry is unconcentrated
Between 100 and 1800	If HHI increased by 100, investigate
More than 1800	If HHI increased by 50, challenge

are used as whole numbers, as in 75 instead of 0.75. The maximum in this case is $100^2 = 10{,}000$.

A small index indicates a competitive industry with no dominant players. If all firms have an equal share the reciprocal of the index shows the number of firms in the industry. When firms have unequal shares, the reciprocal of the index indicates the "equivalent" number of firms in the industry. Using case 2, we find that the market structure is equivalent to having 1.55521 firms of the same size.

The completion of a merger does not ensure the success of the resulting organization; indeed, many mergers (in some industries, the majority) result in a net loss of value due to problems. Correcting problems caused by incompatibility—whether of technology, equipment, or corporate culture— diverts resources away from new investment, and these problems may be exacerbated by inadequate research or by concealment of losses or liabilities by one of the partners. Overlapping subsidiaries or redundant staff may be allowed to continue, creating inefficiency, and conversely the new management may cut too many operations or personnel, losing expertise and disrupting employee culture. These problems are similar to those encountered in takeovers. For the merger not to be considered a failure, it must increase shareholder value faster than if the companies were separate, or prevent the deterioration of shareholder value more than if the companies were separate.

7

Due Diligence

DUE DILIGENCE: LEARN FROM THE PAST, BUT LOOK TOWARD THE FUTURE

Due diligence is used to investigate and evaluate a business opportunity. The term due diligence describes a general duty to exercise care in any transaction. As such, it spans investigation into all relevant aspects of the past, present, and predictable future of the business of a target company. Due diligence sounds impressive but ultimately it translates into basic commonsense success factors such as "thinking things through" and "doing your homework". There are many reasons for conducting due diligence, including the following:

- Confirmation that the business is what it appears to be
- Identify potential "deal killer" defects in the target and avoid a bad business transaction
- Gain information that will be useful for valuing assets, defining representations and warranties, and/or negotiating price concessions
- Verification that the transaction complies with investment or acquisition criteria.

Lead and co-investors, corporate development staff, attorneys, accountants, investment bankers, loan officers and other professionals involved in a transaction may have a need or an obligation to conduct independent due diligence. Target management typically assists these parties in obtaining due diligence information but because it is unwise to totally rely on management third party consultants such as Astute Diligence are often brought in to conduct due diligence.

Initial data collection and evaluation commences when a business opportunity first arises and continues throughout the talks. Thorough detailed due dligence is typically conducted after the parties involved in a proposed transaction have agreed in principle that a deal should be pursued and after a preliminary understanding has been reached, but prior to the signing of a binding contract.

The parties conducting due diligence generally create a checklist of needed information. Management of the target company prepares some of the information. Financial statements, business plans and other documents are reviewed. In addition, interviews and site visits are conducted. Finally, thorough research is conducted with external sources—including customers, suppliers, industry experts, trade organizations, market research firms, and others.

Time allocated for completion can vary widely with each situation. Many preliminary agreements define the timeframes in which due diligence will be conducted. Time schedules through the closing of a transaction are typically tight—parties should ensure that adequate time is allocated to due diligence.

Due diligence costs are based on the scope and duration of the effort, which in turn are dependent on the complexity of the target business and other factors. Costs are typically viewed as an essential expense far outweighed by the anticipated benefits and the downside risks of failing to conduct adequate due diligence. The involved parties determine who will bear due diligence expense.

Although due diligence is routinely performed when acquiring or selling a business, it's often conducted too quickly or too narrowly, focusing on how a company has historically performed financially. In other words, businesses focus on the past rather than the future of the combined companies.

Traditional financial, legal, and environmental due diligence is crucial to the success of any acquisition; however, it has been found insufficient in predicting the long-term success of a transaction hence multidisciplinary approach plays an important role. In addition to financial due diligence, businesses should focus on four other, sometimes neglected, areas of due diligence: strategy, information technology (IT), operations, and human capital, including the organization's culture.

- **Strategic Due Diligence:** Strategic due diligence considers an acquisition in the context of its industry and asks a simple question: Does it make sense — will the acquisition benefit the organization? For example, for a manufacturing company, how is the organization positioned within their customers' supply chain? What does it currently manufacture? Who does it sell to? What do you know about the customers? This is key — it's possible that a seemingly flourishing company could be 12 months away from going out of business because their customers are shifting their supply base from North America to a low cost region. No matter how well a company performs, if the products a company manufactures are at risk, there's no reason to continue with the acquisition. Optimally, this is the first step in the due diligence process. Strategic due diligence will provide the acquiring organizations the information to drive change and improve profitability or help the buyer determine that the deal is not worth pursuing.
- **Financial Due Diligence:** Financial due diligence analyzes, qualitatively and quantitatively, how an organization has performed financially to get a sense of earnings on a normalized basis. It's crucial to look at the anticipated performance of a business as represented by the seller, look at the underlying assumptions they've used in preparing their projections, and ensure they're reasonable and objective. Often times, companies can understand the future by understanding the past — it's important to assure a plausible bridge can be built to meet the metrics the seller claims may be achieved going forward. In addition, financial due diligence analyzes the assets and liabilities to be acquired. For example, is the pricing for raw materials on par with market value? Are there finished goods in stock that are unlikely to be sold within the next three to six months? Regarding liabilities, it's important to acquire only the

liabilities that have been incurred by the seller for purchases of inventory or services that occurred prior to the closing date. Finally, financial due diligence will look at whether federal and state taxes have been filed appropriately by the seller. Does the seller have nexus in other states? Do they file in those states? It's important to ensure the seller has complied with all tax requirements.

- **Operational Due Diligence**: Operational due diligence looks at a transaction to determine what the buyer can do to realize improvements in productivity and profitability. This includes examining work centers, material flow, scrap generation, and inventory levels — in short, employing Lean manufacturing principles to achieve maximum profitability. A purchase price based on a multiple of earnings may include certain operational inefficiencies. Operational due diligence will define this potential along with the cost of implementing the efficiency improvements for the buyer. Likewise the seller can benefit from operational due diligence by identifying and implementing the changes necessary to increase EBITDA and increasing the multiples due to lower risk.
- **IT Due Diligence:** IT due diligence considers questions such as: What's the current level of technology? Is it up to date? How well does the company use the existing technology? Is it sufficient to allow the organization to continue to grow? How much money will the buyer need to invest to provide the company with the tools it needs to operate effectively? Technology in a key component of merger and acquisition activities; it's imperative to look at IT considerations early in the acquisition process. Careful planning early in the transaction greatly simplifies the post-merger integration of information systems.
- **Human Capital Due Diligence:** When an acquisition fails, it's frequently due to people or related issues. Key managers and scarce talent leave unexpectedly. Valuable operating synergies evaporate because cultural differences between companies aren't understood or are simply ignored. Cuts in pay or benefits programs create ill will, which reduces productivity. Management doesn't communicate its business rationale or its goals for the new company, and staffs flounders in the ensuring confusion.

75 per cent of all mergers and acquisitions fail to live up to expectations; this is often due to lack of an effective integration plan. It's crucial to consider staffing issues up front; otherwise, organizations often find themselves dealing with a quagmire of issues that could have been avoided.

Due diligence is the process by which buyers **investigate** and **evaluate** a potential acquisition. Thourough due diligence answers the question of whether a **deal is being done at the right time at the right place for the right reasons.** It involves an investigation into the affairs of an entity (which may be a division, a company, a group of companies or some other form of business entity). It results in the production of a report detailing relevant data and points. The investigation is performed prior to the business's acquisition, floatation, restructuring or other transaction. Due diligence is performed by many advisors on the team. For example, there may be separate legal due diligence, tax due diligence, environmental due diligence, commercial due diligence and information technology due diligence.

*Due diligence is the process by which buyers **investigate** and **evaluate** a potential acquisition.*

The broad term is used to describe activities in a variety of disciplines including law, accounting, environmental, human resources, and others. Of these different due diligence activities, the three that generally receive the greatest attention are **accounting, legal and environmental assessment** (usually for manufacturing businesses).These three activities are extremely important in helping to ensure the completion of successful acquisitions. Typically, companies will rely on professional service firms with specialized expertise to perform an objective appraisal of these due diligence areas.

Due diligence is the process by which buyers **investigate** and **evaluate** a potential acquisition.

The findings from the legal, accounting, and environmental reviews can result in renegotiating the transaction price or in some cases, abandoning a transaction. The information garnered from these assessments represents just the tip of the iceberg as to whether a potential acquisition will be successful. Legal, accounting, and environmental audits are fundamentally backward looking reviews. Their principal focus is to **evaluate a company's historical actions** or to uncover past problems that the buyer does not want to inherit or wants to receive compensation for in return. The key driver of the merit of a transaction is the expected value of the **future cash flows** attributable to the acquired company. Typically, the future value of items such as revenue growth, gross margin improvement, cost synergies, and balance sheet efficiencies dwarfs the cost of settling an outstanding legal claim or resolving an environmental problem. Additionally, the information disclosure requirements in the nonstrategic due diligence areas are much better defined. For example, public companies must have independently audited financial statements. This can make major accounting problems easier to identify. Similarly, regulations require the disclosure of known environmental issues when properties are exchanged.

In summary, rigorous accounting, legal, and environmental due diligence are key reviews for any acquisition. However, the expectation should be that the results will confirm what was previously disclosed by the sellers. Strategic due diligence, on the other hand, reveals the most important insights regarding a company's future value. Broadly defined, it represents the set of activities involved in evaluating a target company's markets, customer relationships, competitive position, and strategic direction. The knowledge gained from this evaluation becomes the critical input into determining the target's value to the acquirer. This information can then be leveraged to drive the bid and negotiation strategy to ensure that the largest portion of the value created from the transaction is captured by the buyer's shareholders.

BUYER'S DUE DILIGENCE

The main objective of undertaking due diligence by the buyer is to identify and to confirm the source of value and lessen the potential liability by trying to eliminate the flaws that reduce value.

The due diligence exercise is carried out by a team of executives from acquirer, their Investment Bankers, Solicitors and Chartered Accountants. The team should have members with experience of all dimensions of the business like finance, marketing, human resources, operations, legal, etc. the members should have in-depth knowledge of the industry and operations to be reviewed. The exercise should cover all material factors which are likely to affect the future of the business.

Due diligence exercise covers careful study of information in public domain like financial statements, corporate records like minutes of meetings, past prospectuses, share price movements, etc. all contracts entered into by the firm with lenders, suppliers, customers, franchisee, lease agreements, asset purchases agreements etc., need to be studied carefully. Special attention should be given to litigations, contingent liabilities, environmental disputes, liens and encumbrances, product warranties, inter- company transactions, tax disputes, etc.

Due diligence should always be conducted in the shortest possible period in the interest of maintaining a cooperative relationship at the time of negotiations. A long and detailed due diligence is likely to uncover all the items that the buyer will use as an excuse to lower the purchase price. Hence, there is possibility that the seller may seek to stop the process before the appropriate time. The best possible solution is to agree to a shortened period.

SELLER'S DUE DILIGENCE

Though the major part of the due diligence procedure is carried out by the buyer, the seller also has to perform certain aspects of due diligence on the buyer. In such a process, the seller determines whether the buyer has the financial resources to finance the agreed purchase price.

What due diligence involves?[1]

Each transaction is different, and the extent and scope of financial

---

1 Jonathan Reuvid, Mergers and Acquisitions: A Practical Guide for Private Companies and Their Advisors.

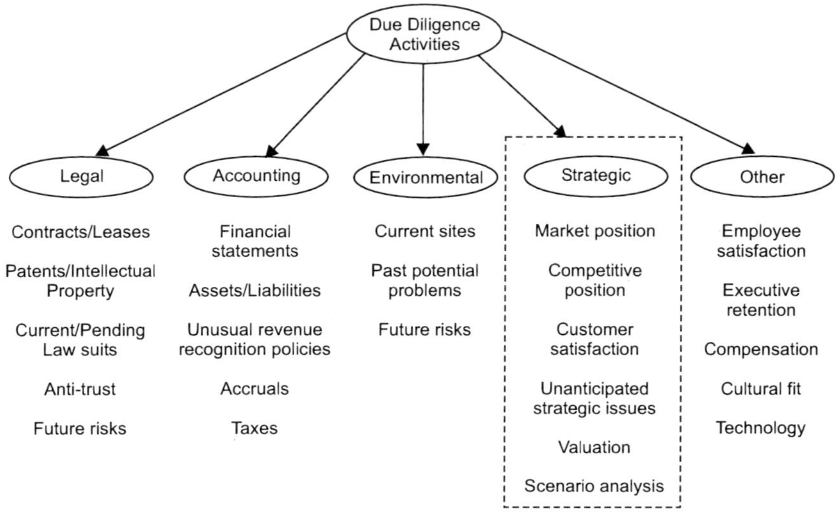

Figure 7.1: Due deligence process involves detailed evaluations across several areas.

due diligence has to be tailored to fit the needs of the buyer. For example, a MBO may entail less due diligence in certain areas as the management may have a full knowledge of the financial area concerned. By contrast, a venture capital investment may entail very thourough due diligence as the investing team will require full information on the target's financial affairs.

DUE DILIGENCE INVOLVES INVESTIGATING

- the history and commercial activities of the business
- its organization structure and employees
- its accounting policies
- the information systems
- a detailed review of financial systems
- a review of financial projections

History and Commercial Activities

The history and commercial activities review covers such things as historic milestones of the business, details of its shareholders and trading characteristics, and the influence of particular features of the industry sector. Such features may include legislative restrictions or freedoms, details of key competitors, the presence of any competitive technologies that may affect the business, and the need for any licences and the like. It also covers a review of the customer and supplier base, including identifying the key customers and suppliers, discovering pricing influences, trading seasonality, strength of the contract terms and credit worthiness.

When they are on the site reviewing these areas, the due diligence team will reveal the key customers and suppliers who do not have good contracts, or have pricing peculiarities, or have significant seasonality. Such features may not have been previously identified by the buyer. Problems with retention of title clauses on stocks, or extended credit afforded to certain customers, can all be uncovered. In some industry sectors customers may have retrospective discount clauses whereby the turnover threshold is exceeded post-deal with no provision having been made for the cost pre-deal.

The commercial activities review will also identify such things as key production processes, quality control issues, stock control issues and production planning issues. The review should highlight whether there are capacity problems, and whether efficiencies can be achieved post-deal.

Organization Structure and Employees

The organization structure and employees aspect of the review can identify management 'holes' where either pre- or post-deal a hole staff may become apparent, any problems in recruitment or training may be picked up, and unexpected trends in staff turnover may be uncovered. These days, pensions are a crucial aspect of any acquisition, and valuable financial information on pension commitments and other employee reward structures can be found and confirmed. Overall, the report will highlight the corporate culture and working environment, so the buyer can see whether there is a good fit between the parties, or get advance notice of a major culture clash.

Accounting Policies

A thorough review of the application of accounting policies is vital. A trend of reducing gross margins could be masked by a change in the application of stock provisioning policies. A rising gross margin could be the result of a reallocation of costs to distribution or administration cost centres instead of cost of sales. Even a simple change in the level at which a fixed asset becomes capitalized instead of written off to repairs and renewals can have an impact on the trend shown by the accounts. For some service industries there is a major impact of new generally accepted accounting policies for turnover recognition. A rise in turnover between this year and last year for a professional services company could be entirely caused by a change in turnover recognition policy or milestone billing policy rather than a true increase in the underling trade.

A buyer diversifying into a different industry sector may be unaware of the risks presented by such legitimate accounting policy factors. It's the job of the financial due diligence team to tailor their report to suit the buyer and cover the areas it needs to know about, as well as just the areas it thinks it needs to know about!

Overall the report should identify the consistency of application of the accounting policies, compare these with industry practice, and highlight unusual items and recent changes. Crucially, it should also identify those areas where the policies of each party to the deal differs; otherwise what one party understands to be a measure of financial performance may in fact be a very different measure when its own accounting policies are applied to the item.

For example, one party to the deal may make a general provision for warranty claims and returns, whereas the other may only recognize these as and when they arise. Each party would therefore have a different turnover and gross margin figure in mind even when looking at the same basic sales data. If there is an earn-out linked to turnover margins, such misunderstandings over accounting policies may prove expensive. Earn- outs are a key area where the input from the financial due diligence team into the wording of the sale and purchase agreement contract is vital.

Information Systems

Good information systems are vital to any business. The due diligence review may find that there is a need to budget for the replacement or major improvement of a business's systems.

There may have been **historic underinvestment** that the buyer will need to make good.

There may be **major shortfalls** in the systems, which means that the key information such as order book or stock record are found to be unexpectedly unreliable, which may impact on the whole rationale of the deal.

A classic information system problem is stock control. The information system might tell the user that the stock is current and saleable, but an inspection of the depot shelves then reveals that some stock is damaged or passed its 'best before' date. In manufacturing businesses, some goods recorded as valuable 'stock' may be found by the team to be in fact overruns of production with no current marketplace. A review of the sales information system may reveal that although sales are being recorded for a customer, there might not be any new orders in the pipeline to provide sales for the next year. A poor information system may mask this valuable information.

Detailed Review of the Financial Statements

The detailed review of financial statements has the aims of identifying hitherto unnoticed financial trends, of fleshing out the trend in numbers into an analysis of how the business is actually performing, and identifying whether the facts and figures as presented by management tally back to what the financial statements are actually saying.

The review should include cash flow analysis, adjusted for any changes caused by the inconsistent application of accounting policies. Such cash flow analysis may then feed into assumptions behind the projections that the buyer has prepared.

The review will analyze each key area of the accounts to glean useful information for the buyer. For example, a review of fixed assets may reveal a trend of underinvestment in the plant and equipment that the buyer will need to reverse. A review of debtors and creditors may reveal certain 'sundry' debtors or creditors which are in fact really bad debts or hidden liabilities. The review would also include comparison with budgets and industry trends. Related party transactions would also be identified, and in some situations post-deal changes to the pricing or occurrence of related party transactions could be crucial.

Review of Financial Projections

The due diligence team is placed in a key position to assess the reliability of any financial projections prepared by either of the parties to the deal. The detail they will have uncovered by being on

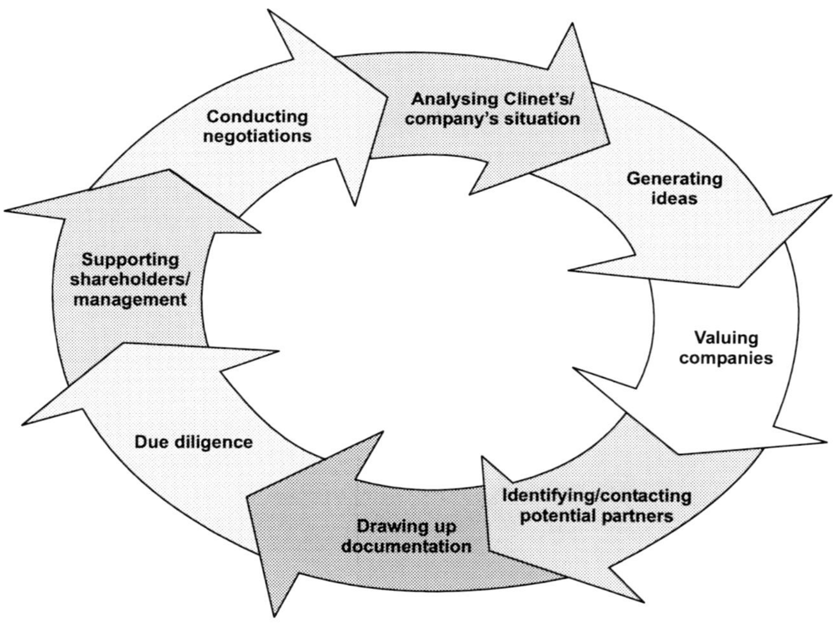

Figure 7.2: Due diligence process

site during the assignment allows them to both perform a high level credibility review of the projections, and pinpoint areas of the projection that do not tally with actual recorded performance. At present the financial assistance regulations of the Companies Act 1985 affect many bank-backed buyouts.

Due diligence is not just a process, it is also a **reality test**—a test of whether the factors driving the deal and making it look attractive to the parties are real or illusory. Due diligence is not a quest to find the deal breakers but a test of the value proposition underlying the transaction to make sure that the inside of the house is as attractive as the outside. Once the foundation has been dissected, it can either be rebuilt around a deal that makes sense or allow the buyer to walk away and prevent the consummation of a deal that doesn't make sense. It is also important to understand that due diligence is typically wider and deeper in its scope than ever before, especially if the prospective buyer is a public company or a company with plans to go public within the next 18 months. The seller's team must organize the documents, and the buyer's team must be prepared to ask all of the right questions, thereby conducting a detailed analysis of the documents provided. To the extent that the deal is structured as a merger, or where the seller will be taking the buyer's stock as all or part of its compensation, the process of due diligence is likely to be two-way, as the parties gather background information on each other. The due diligence work is usually divided between two working teams:

Due diligence is not a quest to find the deal breakers but a test of the value proposition underlying the transaction to make sure that the inside of the house is as attractive as the outside.

- financial and strategic, which is typically managed by the buyer's accountants and management team; and
- legal, to be conducted by the buyer's counsel.

Throughout the process, both teams compare notes on open issues and potential risks and problems. The **legal due diligence** focuses on the potential legal issues and problems that may serve as impediments to the transaction, as well as sheds light on how the transaction documents should be structured. The **business due diligence** focuses on the strategic and financial issues in the transaction, such as confirmation of the past financial performance of the seller; integration of the human and financial resources of the two companies; confirmation of the operating, production, and distribution synergies and economies of scale to be achieved by the acquisition; and the gathering of information necessary for financing the transaction. Overall, the due diligence process, when done properly, can be tedious, frustrating, time consuming, and expensive. Yet it is a **necessary prerequisite** to a well-planned acquisition, and it can be quite informative and revealing in its analysis of the target company and its measures of the costs and risks associated with the transaction.

Buyers should expect sellers to become defensive, evasive, and impatient during the due diligence phase of the transaction. Most business managers really don't enjoy having their business policies and decisions under the microscope, especially for an extended period of time and by a party searching for skeletons in the closet. Eventually, the seller is likely to give an ultimatum to the prospective buyer: "Finish the due diligence soon or the deal is off." When negotiations have reached this point, it is best to end the examination process soon thereafter. Buyers should resist the temptation to conduct a hasty "once over," either to save costs or to appease the seller. Yet at the same time, they should avoid "due diligence overkill," keeping in mind that due diligence is *not* a perfect process and should not be a tedious fishing expedition. Like any audit, a diligence process is designed **to answer the important claims** about the business are fair and legitimate. Information will slip through the cracks, which is precisely why broad representations, warranties, liability holdbacks, and indemnification provisions should be structured into the final purchase agreement. The nature and scope of these provisions are likely to be hotly contested in the negotiations. Remember that the key objective of due diligence is not only to "confirm that the deal makes sense" (e.g., confirm the factual assumptions and preliminary valuations underlying the terms by which the buyer negotiates the transaction), but also to determine whether the **transaction should proceed** at all. The buyer must recognize at all times that there may be a need to "jump ship" if the risks or potential liabilities in the transaction greatly exceed what is anticipated.

Effective due diligence is both an **art** and a **science**. The *art* is the style and experience to know which questions to ask and how and when to ask them. It's the ability to create an atmosphere of both trust and fear in the seller, which encourages full and complete disclosure. In this sense, the due diligence team is on a **risk discovery and assessment mission**, looking for potential problems and liabilities (the search), and finding ways to resolve these problems prior to closing and/or to ensure that risks are allocated fairly and openly after the closing. The *science* of due diligence is in the preparation of comprehensive and **customized checklists** of the specific questions to be presented to the seller, in maintaining a methodical system for organizing and analyzing the documents and data provided by the seller, and in quantitatively assessing the risks raised by those problems discovered in the process. One of the key areas is detection of the seller's obligations, particularly those that the buyer will be expected or required to assume after closing (especially in a stock purchase transaction; in an asset purchase, purchased liabilities are specifically defined). The due diligence process is designed first to detect the *existence* of the obligation and second to identify any *defaults or problems* in connection with these obligations that will affect the buyer after closing. The best way for the buyer to ensure that virtually no stone remains unturned is with effective due diligence preparation and planning.

The **legal due diligence** checklist in the following section is intended to guide the company's management team while it works closely with counsel to gather and review all legal documents that may be relevant to the structure and pricing of the transaction; to assess the potential legal risks and liabilities to the buyer following the closing; and to identify all of the consents and approvals, such as an existing contract that can't be assigned without consent, which must be obtained from third parties and government agencies. The checklist should be a guideline, not a crutch. The buyer's management team must take the lead in developing questions that pertain to the nature of the seller's business. These questions will set the pace for the level of detail and adequacy of the review.

The key point is that every type of business has its own issues and problems, and a standard set of questions will rarely be sufficient. When done properly, due diligence is performed in multiple stages. First, all the basic data are gathered and specific topics are identified. Follow-up questions and additional data gathering can be performed in subsequent rounds of due diligence; they must be custom-tailored to the target's core business industry trends and unique challenges.

Common wisdom suggests that post-deal one-half of the transactions succeed and one-half fail.

A cynical view would suggest that infact one third succeed, one third fail and, because of a lack of information, the management of one third are unsure whether they succeeded or not.

LOOK TOWARD THE FUTURE

Approximately one-third of due diligence investigations uncover serious problems—potential deal breakers. Of those, approximately half fail to complete the merger/acquisition process. It's crucial that, when conducting due diligence, organizations consider all aspects—strategic, financial, operational, IT, and human capital—to assure a successful transaction. Those who ignore the past are doomed to repeat it. Those who fail to look toward the future may fare similarly.

Where mergers go wrong: Most companies routinely overestimate the value of synergies they can capture from acquisitions. Lessons from the front lines can help.It's known as the winner's curse. In mergers, it is typically not the buyer but the seller who captures most of the shareholder value created. On average, in fact, acquirers pay sellers all of the value created by the merger in the form of a premium that typically ranges from 10 to 35 percent of the target company's preannouncement market value. But while the fact is well established, the reasons for it have been less clear. Our exploration of post merger integrations points to an explanation: the origins of the curse lie in the average acquirer materially overestimating the synergies that can be captured in a merger. Even a good faith acquisition effort can stumble over what appears to be a remarkably small margin for error in estimating synergy values.

No question, acquirers face an obvious challenge in coping with an acute lack of reliable information. They typically have little actual data about the target company, limited access to its managers, suppliers, channel partners, and customers, and insufficient experience to guide synergy estimation and benchmarks. Even highly experienced acquirers rarely capture their data systematically enough to improve their estimates for their next deal. And external transaction advisers—usually investment banks—are seldom involved in the kind of detailed, bottom-up estimation of synergies before the deal that are necessary for developing meaningful benchmarks. Fewer still get involved in the post merger work, when premerger estimates come face to face with reality.

Lessons learned: To address this challenge, we have begun developing a detailed database of estimated and realized merger synergies, grounded in our experience in post merger integration efforts across a range of industries, geographies, and deal types. We have accumulated data from 160 mergers so far, and combining it with industry and company knowledge we believe that there are practical steps executives can take to improve their odds of successfully capturing acquisition synergies. For starters, they should probably cast a gimlet eye on estimates of top-line synergies, which we found to be rife with inflated estimates. They ought to also look hard at raising estimates of one-time costs and better anticipate common setbacks or dissynergies likely to befall them. They might also vet pricing and market share assumptions, make better use of benchmarks to deliver cost savings, and get a better fix on how long it will take to capture synergies. When applied together, especially by savvy acquisition teams chosen for maximum expertise and ability to counter gaps in information, we believe acquirers can do more than merely avoid falling victim to the winner's curse—they can improve the quality of most of their deals.

- **Reduce top-line synergy estimates:** The area of greatest estimation error is on the revenue side—a particularly unfortunate state of affairs, since the strategic rationale of entire classes of deals, such as those pursued to gain access to the target's customers, channels, and geographies, is founded on these very synergies. Nearly 70 percent of the mergers in our database failed to achieve the revenue

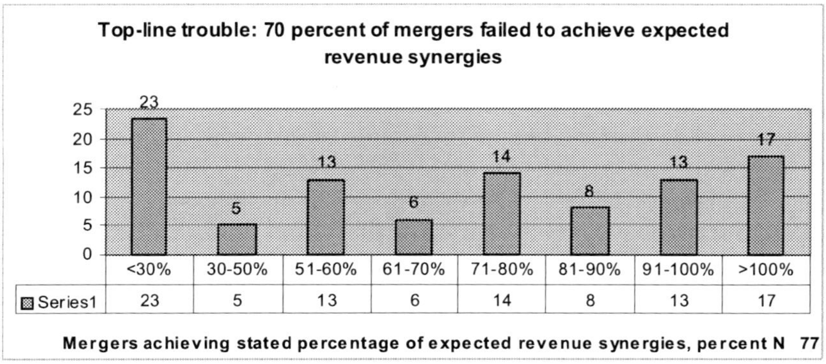

Typical sources of estimation error
• Ignoring or underestimating customer losses (typically 2% to 5%) that result from the integration
• Assuming growth or share targets out of line with overall market growth and competitive dynamics (no "outside view" calibration)
Source: McKinsey (2002) Postmerger Management Practice client survey; client case studies

synergies estimated by the acquirer's management as depicted in figure above.

- **Acknowledge synergy setbacks:** Another regular—and large—contributor to revenue estimation error is that few acquirers explicitly account for the common revenue dis-synergies that befall merging companies. Sometimes these stem from simple disruption of business as usual, but often they are the direct result of cost reduction efforts. For example, in retail banking, one of the most important cost savings comes from consolidating branches. Some customers may leave, but the cost savings are expected to more than make up for the losses. When one large US bank acquired a competitor with substantial geographic overlap, however, it suffered unusually high losses among the target company's customers, rendering the deal unprofitable and making the entire company vulnerable to takeover. Due diligence on the target's customer base would have revealed that they were heavy branch users and thus especially likely to defect during an integration that closed more than 75 percent of the acquired company's branches. This company's customer loss experience may be at the high end, but according to our research, the average merging company will see 2 to 5 percent of their combined customers disappear. Most acquiring companies can do better, especially in industries that have undergone considerable consolidation. Data on the severity of customer loss experienced by merging parties in retail banking, for example, can be gleaned from a variety of sources: industry associations, regulatory filings, and press articles. Examples are numerous enough not only to identify helpful benchmarks (e.g., 8 percent of retail deposits at closing branches will be lost to) but also underlying competitors drivers of whether a deal will see losses above or below the benchmark (e.g., the number of customers who also bank with a competitor, the distance to the next- closest remaining branch, or the presence of competitors to take over closing branches). In other industries, a search may yield only two or three good precedents and only limited data on those even this can greatly improve management's revenue estimates.

- Increase estimates of one-time costs many deal teams neglect or underestimate the impact of one-time costs. For example, one chemicals manufacturer publicly committed itself to reducing annual costs by $210 million at a one-time cost of $250 million. Had it put as much due diligence into that one-time figure as the annual synergy target, it would have found a few relevant precedent transactions suggesting that it was unlikely to spend less than $450 million . In trying to fulfil their original commitment, the company ended up running over budget, under- delivering on promised synergies, and falling well short of revenue growth targets. Compare pro forma projections with market and competitive realities. Many acquirers rely too heavily on assumptions about pricing and market share that are simply not consistent with overall market growth and competitive reality. Instead, acquirers must calibrate the assumptions in their pro-forma analysis with the realities of the market place. For example, one global financial concern estimated that a recent acquisition would net i1 billion in mostly top-line synergies within 5 years and 13 per cent profit growth in the first year. With limited overall

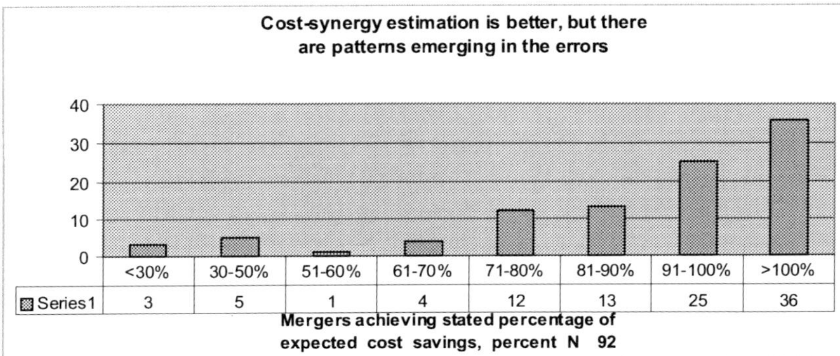

Typical sources of estimation error

- Underestimating one-time costs
- Using benchmarks from no comparable situations
- Not sanity-checking management estimates against precedent transactions
- Failing to ground estimates in bottom-up analysis (e.g., location by- location review of overlaps

Source: McKinsey (2002) Postmerger Management Practice client survey; client case studies

market growth, these goals could be achieved only by using cross-selling to increase market share without triggering a competitive response. Actual profit growth was a mere 2 per cent.

APPLY OUTSIDE-IN BENCHMARKS TO COST SYNERGIES

While managers in about 60 per cent of mergers can be commended for delivering nearly all of their planned cost synergies, we find that about a quarter overestimate cost synergies by at least 25 per cent. That can easily translate into a 5 to 10 per cent valuation error.6 one route to overestimating cost synergies starts by failing to use the benchmarks that are available as outside-in sanity-checks. One European industrial company, for example, planned a cost savings of 110 million from selling, general, and administrative (SG&A), even though precedent transactions suggested that a range of 25 million to 90 million was more realistic, and the company neglected to conduct bottom-up analysis to justify the higher figure. Worse, this was an especially risky area in which to aim high, because cutting sales and marketing expense puts revenue growth at risk, and the net present value of pre-synergy revenue growth was roughly four times more valuable than all synergies combined.

Important deal metrics such as near-term earnings and cash flow accretion can end up looking better than they deserve as a result, leading to a substantial overestimates of synergy net present value. One company we worked with had budgeted headcount cost savings (including severance) as if they were spread out evenly over each quarter. In practice, however, managers tended to wait until the last month of the quarter before making reductions. As it happens, this example did not have a material impact on the net present value of the transaction, but it did cause the post-merger integration leaders to miss their projections for first-year synergies, thereby undermining the credibility of their process. Neglecting to "phase out" certain synergies can be equally problematic. Companies often plan to reduce operating costs by squeezing production capacity and logistics across the merged organization. But if the merging companies are growing quickly on a standalone basis, sloppy incremental analysis will attribute benefits to the merger that would have been realized by the standalone companies.

Indeed, one medical products company, growing at 10 to 15 per cent a year, estimated that it would be using the full capacity of existing plants within three to four years without a merger. So many of the savings from closing or streamlining plants could not rightly be expected to last long, as the affected facilities would be quickly reopened. Many savings, while real, are not perpetual, and must be phased out. In general, we believe that it is overly optimistic to include the full amount of targeted annual synergies in the "continuing value" calculation of a net present value model. Moreover, the problem isn't just one of properly translating synergy timing into present values: bad timing can even affect whether synergies are captured at all. Persistent management attention matters in capturing synergies. We have found some evidence to suggest that synergies that are not captured within, say, the first full budget year after consolidation may never be captured, overtaken as they are by subsequent events. We have also observed that synergies are captured more quickly and efficiently when the transaction closes at the start of the two companies' annual operational planning and budgeting process. One financial institution even learned that its plans to migrate IT systems had to be radically altered (i.e., move onto the acquirer's platform rather than the target's) to accommodate the relatively narrow window of opportunity between peaks in the lending season.

Forming Effective Deal Teams

Estimating synergies is difficult, but the practice is critical and needs more investment than it usually receives. Companies have used a variety of ways to improve their synergy estimates.

Involve key line managers: Involving line managers in problem solving and due diligence not only improves the quality of estimates but also builds support for Postmerger integration initiatives.

Synergy analysis also illuminates issues that will shape due diligence, deal structure, and negotiations. For example, one client had its head of operations take the lead in estimating the savings from rationalizing manufacturing capacity, distribution networks, and suppliers. His knowledge of the unusual manufacturing requirements of a key product line and looming investment needs at the acquirer's main plant helped improve the estimates. He also used a due diligence interview with the target's head of operations to learn that they had recently renegotiated their supply contracts and had not yet implemented an enterprise resource planning (ERP) system; both of these facts refined synergy estimates even more. All of this helped during negotiations and deal structuring (e.g., knowing that it was all right to promise that the target's main European location would be retained, but to make no promises about their main US facility). Moreover, his involvement ensured that he was prepared to act quickly and decisively to capture savings once the deal closed. Another company with substantial acquisition experience left synergy estimation up to the mergers and acquisitions department, and paid the price. Based on accurate but high-level financial analysis (total cost per customer served), they concluded that there was no value in integrating customer service operations. Line managers would probably have discovered during due diligence that the target's smaller centers had much lower labour productivity but compensated for this with an innovative Web servicing program. Consolidating operations could have both improved labour productivity and brought the Web servicing program to the acquirer's larger service centre. But they missed the "unfreezing" time immediately following the merger announcement, and the acquirer lost the opportunity.

Codify experiences: Internal M&A teams should do more to codify and improve their synergy estimation techniques. Every deal represents a valuable lesson. Some specific actions we have seen make a difference include: holding a formal post-integration debrief session with both the integration and M&A teams (which ideally should overlap); requiring future M&A and integration leaders to review the results of past deals; tracking synergies relative to plan for two years; and calculating after the fact what the net present value of the transaction turned out to be. On the other hand, one must not overstate what can legitimately be learned from experience, since not all deals are alike. One bank balanced what it learned from one acquisition quite skilfully against the idiosyncrasies of its second major acquisition. The first had gone badly; the bank underestimated integration costs by a factor of three. The second went well because executives leading the deal understood that they needed to get the cost (and deposit loss) estimates right. Instead of simply applying the loss data from the first merger, which did not involve nearly as much geographic overlap as the second, they involved a line manager who had been part of a recent branch closure program. By applying benchmarks carefully and involving line management, the bank avoided making the same estimation error twice.

WHAT'S NEXT?

Companies with access to reliable data can develop sound benchmarks for estimating realizable synergies, insights into the sources and patterns of error in estimating synergies, and tools to estimate deal synergies. Obviously, these efforts can be thorny, but in our experience they are well worth the effort. Once companies have a database in place, they can explore other strategic issues, such as whether some synergies are consistently embedded in the acquisition premium paid while others are captured by the acquirer, or whether the stimulating effect of a transaction is even necessary to improve the standalone performance of an acquirer. The former will obviously inform price setting and negotiation strategies for acquiring companies, while the latter will lead companies to consider tactics other than an acquisition to accomplish the same ends. It's important to recognize, however, that a well-designed post-merger integration. Companies with access to reliable data can develop sound benchmarks for estimating realistic synergies. They can also find insight into the sources and patterns of error when estimating them.

THE OBSTACLES TO MAKING IT WORK

Coping with a merger can make top managers spread their time too thinly and neglect their core business, spelling doom. Too often, potential difficulties seem trivial to managers caught up in the thrill of the big deal. The chances for success are further hampered if the corporate cultures of the companies are very different. When a company is acquired, the decision is typically based on product or market synergies, but cultural differences are often ignored. It's a mistake to assume that personnel issues are easily overcome. For example, employees at a target company might be accustomed to easy access to top management, flexible work schedules or even a relaxed dress code. These aspects of a working environment may not seem significant, but if new management removes them, the result can be resentment and shrinking productivity. More insight into the failure of mergers is found in the highly acclaimed study from McKinsey, a global consultancy. The study concludes that companies often focus too intently on cutting costs following mergers, while revenues, and ultimately, profits, suffer. Merging companies can focus on integration and cost-cutting so much that they neglect day-to-day business, thereby prompting nervous customers to flee. This loss of revenue momentum is one reason so many mergers fail to create value for shareholders. But remember, not all mergers fail. Size and global reach can be advantageous, and strong managers can often squeeze greater efficiency out of badly run rivals. Nevertheless, the promises made by deal makers demand the careful scrutiny of investors. The success of mergers depends on how realistic the deal makers are and how well they can integrate two companies while maintaining day-to-day operations.

8
Merger Management

In the previous chapters, various aspects of M&As, such as motivation, evaluation, bidding, getting legal approvals have been described. Once, these are cleared, the important issue is to integrate the two organizations with distinct management styles into a coherent unit. This is one of the most difficult aspects of M&As when compared with Greenfield investments. The latter involve just transferring the management culture to the new establishment. While in M&As, there is an already existing management culture which has to be integrated. This is considered here in detail.

CULTURAL ASPECTS

Cultural Systems

The global corporations face difficult issues of reconfiguration and redeployment of resources. "Culture is a distinctly human capacity of adapting to circumstances and transmitting this coping skill and knowledge to subsequent generation."

There are perceptible cultural differences in managerial work styles in different countries. One of the distinctions based on communication is between high and low context cultures. A high context communication is mostly internalized or has a physical context. Compared to this, a low context culture uses mostly explicit codes. This can be noticed in the differences in perception between the US and other countries in their respective performance appraisal systems as explained below.

- *American:* The priorities accorded to equality, freedom, openness, self-reliance and co-operation are higher than authority, formality, group consensus, or seniority.
- *Japanese:* The priorities accorded to relationships, group harmony and family security are higher than openness, reputation and risk-taking.
- *Malaysian:* They value family security, co-operation and spirituality more than group consensus, privacy and risk-taking.
- *French:* They emphasize self-reliance, freedom and openness more than privacy, formality and reputation.

From the outside, a tree grown in California would probably look just like a tree grown in Japan. However, the growth of each tree is largely dependent on the soil that the roots of the trees have to 'interact' with in order to grow. The strength of the roots is also dependent on the environment the tree is exposed to, from sunshine to thunderstorms.

Imagine the values of a particular culture are represented by the roots of a tree. These roots are the source of strength needed to by the tree to survive in the surrounding environment (society). Of course, we don't really see the roots, but we are constantly exposed to the tree, nevertheless. The type of fertilizer and water fed to the tree contributes significantly to its growth (reward). In addition, you cannot transplant a tree unless you prepare the roots for the new soil. The roots of each tree may have different forms, much like the cultures they represent.

Cultural Dimensions

The word 'culture' is derived from Latin, meaning the cultivation of soil. The current usage of the term means collectivities within societies which distinguishes them from other human societies. The major issue is societal norms which is the value systems or 'mental programmes', shared by major groups of the population.

Another way of looking at culture is through the following four dimensions. They are:

- *Power Distance:* The acceptance of unequal power distribution in organizations.
- *Uncertainty Avoidance:* Whether a society feels threatened by uncertain situations.
- *Individualism/Collectivism:* Individualism represents a loosely knit society and the opposite is collectivism.
- *Masculinity/Femininity:* Masculinity places dominant values on assertiveness, money and material 'things'.

Different cultures exhibit differences based on these dimensions. International business management has to take cognizance of these differences in various management functions. This would enable the generation of synergies from the interface of different cultures.

Also, different societies have found different solutions to human inequality. This is normally formalized in hierarchical relationships in an organization. However, this depends on societally determined power distance. Inequality may be in different areas such as physical and mental characteristics, social status, wealth, power and laws. Inequality can also be found within an organization accounted for by members' abilities and power.

Power Distance: This is one of the dimensions of national culture. Societal inequality may be a result of prestige, wealth and power. In an organization, it is formalized in one hierarchical system. The equilibrium in an organization is determined by societal determined power distance. The Power Distance Index (PDI) was derived from country mean scores on three questions surveyed. The questions dealt with perceptions of the superior's style of decision-making and colleagues' fear to disagree with superiors and the type of decision-making preferred by the subordinates.

The PDI is a measure of values found in social systems and not in individuals. The PDI was classified into high and low for analytical purposes, though it is a continuum. For instance, in high PDI countries, subordinates tend towards dependence and counter-dependence versus their boss compared with low PDI countries, where they centre on interdependence. The attitudes toward power distance are different in low or high PDI countries. In high PDI countries all classes share the high PDI norm while in low PDI countries middle and upper classes hold low PDI values compared with lower classes.

Uncertainty Avoidance: Uncertainty is a fact of life. Humans try to cope with uncertainty through law, religion and technology. There are differences in uncertainty tolerance in different societies. With respect to the organization, three indicators are used to determine uncertainty: Rule orientation, employment stability and stress.

Rules try to render the behaviour of people predictable. For instance, Germans refer to *Befthl ist Befthl* (an order is an order). This is the authority of the rule. While French use *bon plaisir* (Good pleasure), this refers to the arbitrary will of the ruler. The former is high uncertainty avoidance and the later is high power distance. The rituals in an organization are manifested in their planning and control systems. These three indicators provide an Uncertainty Avoidance Index (UAI). A high level of UAI indicates rule orientation, employment stability and stress.

Individualism: The third dimension of culture is individualism. Relationships between the individual and the collectivity in society deal with not only living together but also the links with societal norms. These norms have influence on the nature of relationship between a person and the organization. The calculation of Individualism Index is based on the factors such as personal time, freedom, challenge, use of skills, physical conditions and training.

Masculinity: Different societies cope differently with the duality of the sexes. However, some of the important differences are in that men lay emphasis on advancement, earnings, training and 'up-to-dateness', while women tend towards friendly atmosphere, position security, physical conditions and co-operation. A masculinity index is based on factors such as manager co-operation, desirable area, employment security, challenge, advancement, recognition and earnings. This index lists Japan on top and followed by the German-speaking countries. Asian countries are in the middle. At the lower side end are the Latin countries and the lowest are the Scandinavian countries.

All these dimensions of culture have an impact on the structure and functioning of organizations. For instance, power distance and uncertainty avoidance indicate the following: In high PDI countries, power is the leading principle and in low PDI countries there may be two possibilities – either people have inner need for living up to the rules, i.e., is a high UAI and the leading principle is formal rules. In case of low UAI, the organization is based on *ad hoc* negotiation and high tolerance for uncertainty.

SYNERGY

It requires a multicultural management approach to achieve cultural synergy between (and among) the systems involved. Cultural synergy tries to increase effectiveness by sharing perceptions and co-operation is required in several situations such as:

- Acquisition
- Relocation
- Structural/environmental change
- Personnel change
- Role change
- Consortium
- Global consulting

Here, the context is mergers and acquisitions. In such situations, there is a need for a synthesis of two different cultures. Imposition of organizational culture of dominant company may not work. The merger of two organizational worlds can be facilitated through understanding policy, procedures and processes. Besides, there is necessity to understand corporate goals, attitudes and strategies. High synergy is achieved when employees of two organizations co-operate for mutual advantage. One has to work on the *values* in each of the existing organizations and build upon that. This needs a degree of sensitivity to cultural differences and opportunities for mutual growth and development.

In cases of mergers and acquisitions, the parties not only bring with them unique organizational history, management, and expertise, but also a distinct culture. Sometimes, the executives involved ignore these factors and concentrate on the task at hand. Managers who are sensitive to cultural differences take time to analyze the cultural dimensions of each participating organization and then develop strategies.

Response to Cultural Shocks

There are three possible responses to cultural shocks:

- **Resistance:** The rejection of the new culture and tendency towards defence of one's own traditional values.
- **Assimilation:** The wholesale rejection of one's own values in order to embrace another culture.
- **Acculturation:** Learning to talk the language of another culture, while remaining rooted in the values and language of one's own.

Those who resist, may become inflexible and either drop out of the mainstream and become marginal or try to impose their values on others. Those who assimilate forfeit their own culture. Those who resort to acculturation live in two worlds simultaneously. Out of these three responses, acculturation is the most practical choice in the present-day world.

This is similar to, '20 per cent of customers account for 80 per cent sales' or '20 per cent of employees account for 80 per cent of absenteeism'. In the 80-20 rule, the reverse holds true. One can assume that at least 80 per cent of a breakdown has cultural roots, while 20 per cent is personal. This will help resolve the issue instead of blaming individuals or groups. In addition, the **EXEC** formula is suggested for a leader to help build a powerful vision. It involves the following:

- Enter into the needs and aspirations of the people in the organization.
- EXpress how these needs will be fulfilled through the success of the enterprise.
- Enrol personally in this vision.
- Commit the vision into the hands of others.

Another concept is **empowerment.** This is an effort to renew organizational culture for productivity and service in response to the challenges of diversity and the global economy. This means changing the mindset and the rules to develop a new framework and acculturation in workplace. Normally, fear and empowerment are opposites. Diversity tends towards fear. This may lead to an adversarial stance instead of collaboration. The transcultural leaders have to create an empowered organization. This means that instead of planning and control on employee performance, empowerment leads to letting go, creating a learning organization and setting high standards for performance.

Each organization finds its own way to empowerment. The present corporate culture has to shift from a monocentric, linear mindset to a polycentric and circular and culturally diverse one. There are five C's which are critical for success. They are:

- *Continuous* Learning
- *Consistent* Leadership
- *Centredness* in one's own culture
- *Commitment* to a Vision

Acculturation

Most of the areas of concern *vis-a-vis* acquisitions are attributed to human resources problems. This is due to cultural clashes between the two organizations. One way of overcoming such problems is to choose a complementary culture and adopt a supportive integration management. However, in international cross-border acquisitions, neither cultural similarity nor complementarity are found to be significant. International acquisitions face additional societal barriers to acculturation.

Some cultural clashes are on account of differences in company philosophy, time attitude, disposition of profits, delegation of authority and function. However, another way of looking at the cultural conflicts is to adopt the four acculturation modes: Assimilation, integration, separation/rejection, and deculturation. These give the cross-cultural interactions:

- *Assimilation:* One culture replaces itself with the dominant one.
- *Deculturation:* One culture gives up without replacing it with the other culture.

- *Separation:* One's culture is maintained, withdrawing from the dominant one.
- *Integration:* One's culture is maintained while moving towards the dominant one.

Acculturation is defined "As the development of jointly shared meanings fostering co-operation between the joining firms".

The barriers of acculturation are:

- Initial *dilution* of the combined corporate culture. There will be more of an initial combination if there is strong shared meaning. The initial dilution occurs when the two organizations emphasize their common shared values. With this, the organizations can initiate socialization and maintenance mechanisms.
- Lack of joint *Socialisation Mechanisms:* This is another barrier in acquisitions, as both the acquirer and acquired view the other as newcomers. Both view the other as needing socialization of their own work.
- Separate *Maintenance Mechanisms:* Difference in organizational cultures leads to this barrier. Sometimes the intensified conversation protects its own culture against the imposed culture. There is a need for better mobilization of maintenance efforts.
- *Learned Helplessness:* This may reduce the motivation and can create fear over uncertain outcomes of the acquisition in the acquired firm.

There are four different types of cultural differences:

- *Complementary:* There are different shared meanings but provide the missing know-how to the other organization.
- *Unrelated:* The different shared meanings have nothing in common or of relevance to the other.
- *Conflictual:* There may be contradictory shared meanings.
- *Similar* There may be same shared meanings between the two organizations.

These four types of cultural relationships will provide different abilities to overcome the barriers *(See* Table 8.1). Similar

Table 8.1: Barriers to Acculturation

Types of Differences	Barriers			
	Dilution	Socialization	Maintenance	Helplessness
Comple-mentary	Advantage	Positive	Low defence of own	Empower
Unrelated		Minor Clashes		
Conflictual		Lower Acculturation		
Similar	Advantage	Positive	Local	Low

organizations have advantages of less initial dilution and shared socialization mechanisms. However, they may face the problem of maintenance mechanisms due to their likely defence of their cultures. The complementary cultures will have more initial dilution and have some positive interaction. They may tend to achieve more acculturation. The unrelated cultures will have minor cultural clashes and there is no need for acculturation.

Integration

The integration process can be either 'hard' or a 'soft' approach. The hard approach tends to be quick, forceful and an asymmetric implementation. While the soft approach tends to be a protracted and leads to continuous reciprocal development, the hard approach may lead to reactive scenario. The total integration process suggests three approaches: Imposing, supportive and avoiding. The *imposing* approach is adopted by the dominant firm to break the cultural maintenance mechanisms as quickly as possible. This approach uses changes in name, formal structure, management systems, top managers, etc. This may result in resistance or helplessness by the acquired firm.

The *avoiding* approach tries to maintain the existing system. It may not be able to develop joint socialization mechanisms. These two approaches – imposing and avoiding – will be extreme approaches and are inadequate for integration management. They may not be able to overcome the acculturation barriers.

- The *supportive* approach starts with a positive interaction by selecting success the projects initially and creating positive reinforcement. This approach starts with programmes, training, cross-visits and joint social events.

Career Perspectives

Most of the studies on M&A deal with career related issues from an organizational perspective. The career plans of individuals get disintegrated due to mergers and acquisitions. There are four career concepts, viz.:

- *Steady State:* Career choice is made once for a lifetime commitment.
- *Linear:* Choice focuses on upward movement as determined by externals such as hierarchy.
- *Spiral:* A series of occupations, one linked to other, developing new skills.
- *Transitory:* Frequent changes of jobs with variety as the dominant force.

These individual differences in career concepts will affect employee perception of a situation against the backdrop of uncertainty involved in M&A.

- M&A integration processes will typically lead to increased non-routine work contributions that Linear, and especially, steady state employees will have the most difficulties in performing, and transitory, and especially, spiral the most ease.
- The intrinsic rewards from increased non-routine work in M&A integration phases will be negative for steady state and positive for transitory and spiral employees.
- M&A will typically lead to perceptions of decreased job security that will be viewed most negative by steady state employees.
- M&A will typically lead to reduced advancement opportunities for many employees that will be viewed most negative by those with linear career concepts.
- M&A will typically upset employees' career planning that will be viewed most negatively by those with spiral and linear career concepts.

- The overall career disruption and resulting desirability of movement in M&A will typically be the greatest for steady state and linear employees and the least for transitory and spiral.
- Ease of movement will be the greatest for transitory employees and the lowest for steady state employees.
- M&A will typically result in:
  - Few voluntary exits, many dissatisfied employees, and many layoffs among steady employees
  - Many voluntary exits among linear employees
  - Many somewhat satisfied long-term employees among spiral employees
  - Many short-term employees among transitory employees.
- More the overlapping corporate combination, more the non-routine integration work, more will be the negative career disruption for steady state employees and the more positive for spiral, and *vice versa.*
- Rescue combinations typically result in overall positive career disruptions the strongest for steady, state employees and the most negligible for transitory.
- The careers of 'acquired' employees will be more adversely affected by the combination than those of the 'acquiring' firm.
- The joint organizations formed by M&A will typically experience drains in:
  - managerial drive from voluntary exits of linear employees together with increased turnover of Linear and surviving transitory employees.
  - experience due to layoffs for steady state employees with increased turnover of linear and surviving Transitory employees.
  - Commitment from withdrawal by and exits of steady state and Linear employees.
  - Competence from voluntary exits of the most marketable employees within each career concept.

These propositions focus on individual differences in career concepts. These are different from viewing employees just as employees. The classification of different employees provides some suggestions in the rescue plan during the combination of companies.

It is essential to *energize* Spiral employees who can revitalize the joining organization through their creativity and participation.

TYPES OF INTEGRATION

Internationalization in recent years has proceeded through acquisitions of foreign firms. Most of the time, companies consider financial, operational, strategic and other technical aspects in their decision making. However, there are several problems that result subsequently. The problems are mostly due to *softer* aspects. They are due to different languages, laws, values and traditions. These effect integration plans, and participation by top management is necessitated.

In the US, Federal Trade Commission classifies the different combinations of companies into horizontal, vertical and conglomerate mergers and acquisitions. The horizontal combination is due to joining together of the companies in the same product line and in the same markets. Partially related are the vertical type whereas those unrelated are treated as conglomerate M&As.

He considers two dimensions of production and market. This gives the distinction as to whether there is overlapping, complementary or unrelated competence between the firms. It is considered that unrelated competence has a very low strategic potential.

The classification of these companies according to categories is as follows:

- Prototype-Werke and ATB Technische are overlapping acquisitions
- Jacob AG is a complementary acquisition

All three are important strategically. However, the integration process differs in overlapping versus complementary competence acquisitions.

The three SKF acquisitions do not fit into hard or soft mode. Prototype-Werke was softer than others but not laisser-faire driven. SKF's visions and objectives got through the CEO of the company. ATB integration was harder than PrototypeWerke but not a control driven approach. SKF played a supportive role. While the Jacob AG integration included all the three types of integration modes, it was left alone initially to the original entrepreneurial management. As it realized the poor financial management, SKF initiated a supportive approach with training, participative management, etc. When the employees showed resistance, SKF adopted the harder, control driven approach to deal with the situation.

The success of Prototype-Werke and ATB were due to high strategic potential and supportive integration approach. There was initial failure of integration atJacob AG. This was due to a soft approach and unwillingness of the employees to cooperate. From these examples, it shows that the supportive approach will be valuable in acquisitions of high complementary firms. In cases of high overlapping competence, there will be less wastage of competence by control or equality driven integration modes. In cases of lower strategic potential, the wastage can be reduced by the laisser-faire mode.

INTEGRATION: CASES

Emerson Electric

- Emerson Electric has never made a hostile bid, but it tries to acquire a good company. It has acquired European companies such as:
- Leroy-Somer (LS), France's largest producer of electric drives and motors.
- Switched Reluctance Drives (SRD) of Leeds, developer of an innovative type of drive.
- Control Techniques, the Welsh-based drives producer acquired in January 1995.
- Emerson is known by its brands:
- Rosemount and Fisher Controls in process control
- Copeland in compressors in refrigeration
- Buehler International in sample preparation equipment

Emerson had a sales revenue of $10 billion in 1995 and was staffed by 78,900 employees. Management is decentralized and corporate staff is small. Emerson Europe only has a 10-member team at its

London headquarters. On acquiring, Emerson keeps the business intact and retains top management.

There are few changes for a company in the initial aftermath of an Emerson takeover. However, it introduces its financial reporting system quickly. Emerson uses a system of contingency planning called ABC budgeting, where the A budget applies to the most likely scenario, the B budget to a lower level activity, and so on. It tries to culture synergies, broaden the product range on sale at the centres which enable it to expand (Andrew Baxter, 1996).

In 1989, the founder of 15' grand daughter wanted to sell her stake of 30 per cent. LS had a big US distribution company for Emerson products while Emerson was looking for ways to become more international. Emerson's US Electric Motors business had a position in North America but no presence outside. Emerson acquired LS for FFr 2.9 billion.

- In 1990, it acquired McGill, the US bearings producer.
- In 1991, Emerson sold 80 per cent of its I CD Drives business to CT in return for a 29.9 per cent stake. It had a three-year standstill agreement and later bid for the UK company for £204 million.
- Emerson acquired F.G.Wilson, the privately owned, Northern Ireland-based producer of standby diesel generating sets.

Glaxo-Wellcome

Glaxo acquired Wellcome for £9.1 billion in 1995. This was a hostile takeover and created a company with a turnover of more than £ 10 billion. Table 8.5 gives the comparative position before and after the merger of the two units.

- The integration led to the announcement of 7,500 job cuts.
- It is also closing WeGcome's research centre in Beckenham, Kent.
- A joint venture in non-prescription drugs was sold for $1 billion to its partner, Warner-Lambert.
- The US manufacturing plant at Greenville, North Carolina was up for sale in April 1996.
- Manufacturing and research sites have been sold in France, Italy and Spain.

Table 8.2: Glaxo-Wellcome Comparative Position

ITEMS	Before	AFTER
Employees R&D	6150	5500
Spending R&D	£ 1.2 billion	£ 1.2 billion
Sites	12	46
Production (Primary sites)	9	8
Production (Secondary sites)	3*	38**

* Manufacture of drugs active ingredient
** Manufacture of pills, liquids and packaging

Merger planning began much before the bid on January 23, 1995. Boston Consulting group was involved. The salient features:

- Each layer of management to make proposals about which subordinates were to go or stay (and their areas of responsibility).
- Many task forces to suggest a series of cost-cutting strategies according to local markets, law and customs.
- Sir Richard Sykes, chief executive, was the head of a steering committee.

There was a timetable:

- April: Information gathering
- May and June: Preparation of plans of action
- June 23: Presentation by the task forces to the executive committee,

The two companies' perception of each other regarding their culture is shown in Table 8.3.

Table 8.3: Differences in Cultures

Glaxo	Wellcome
Overly-commercial company enthusiastic for hightech research gadgetry; refuse to study tropical diseases	• Over-centralized organization unrealistic in their expectations of financial success • Tie up with academia

The management declared that a new company was being built in the place of the two old companies. This means a change. For instance, in research all projects are put together and rival evaluation teams, each with members from the old companies, assessed every project on success and commercial potential. The overlapping projects were retained and projects with the least promise were scrapped.

The new company had two secondary manufacturing sites in each market with the primary manufacturing duplicated in the UK and the US. Managers at each site had to provide rationale for their existence. There were some compromises such as:

- Sophia Antipolis plant in the south of France. This was sold to management on the understanding that Glaxo-Wellcome would use it as a supplier.
- The choice between Greenville in the US and Dartford, east of London, two main manufacturing sites. Greenville was subsequently closed.
- The scheme offered/allowed employees to choose either Wellcome's or Glaxo's redundancy terms.
- In France, it established Competence plus comprising redundant employees who were guaranteed up to 15 months on full salary and given training courses to acquire new skills.
- Existing employees got the benefit of reduced hours. Glaxo had 39 hours a week while Wellcome had 37 hours a week, the latter was adopted by the new company.
- Wellcome people took the lead in the combined company in France (Daniel Green, 1996).

FordMazda

In June 1996, Ford paid $481 million to raise its stake to 33.4 per cent and effectively took control of the Mazda. This was considered bold, the objectives of buying are:

- Reduce cost by reducing personnel and suppliers
- Integrate Japanese partner into a global 'Ford 2000' strategy
- Benefit from Mazda's technical and engineering abilities
- Six months on, the scenario is different.
- Idle and unadaptable Hofu factory

- Faithful engineers, with a sentimental attachment to the gas-guzzling rotary engine
- Rigid corporate culture and a parochial mindset.

This has led to doubt whether Ford will be able to integrate Mazda into its fold.

It may not be able to achieve economies of scale.

Sumitomo Bank is Mazda's second largest shareholder. It persuaded for almost a year to get Ford to sign on the deal without complete access to Mazda's inner workings.

Late 1996 witnessed Ford trying to find ways to use Mazda's core competence in small-car design know-how and engineering excellence. It is also trying to find ways to rebuild the market share in japan. They are trying to combine Mazda components and auto 'platforms' to cut development costs.

Manufacturing: Mazda has two plants: Hofu, new and efficient but inflexible, and the Ujina plant in Hiroshima which is old with an ageing workforce. Closing the latter plant may create a backlash. So Ford is concentrating on building up sales. Ford has shifted some production from its US plants to japan to utilize Mazda factories. Mazda is reluctant to discontinue business of making taxis.

Sales: It has been successful in selling the Demio model. Ford has started researching consumer needs and communicating them to Mazda design teams.

Management: Though Ford has financial control of Mazda,japanese executives are resisting to change their ways. Tactics aimed at changing Mazda's culture include recruiting more new employees with foreign-language abilities. Ford is also trying'to include non-Japanese and mid-career workers.

Design: Earlier, the two companies had teamed up for design, e.g., Ford Probe which is Mazda's 626, whereas Mazda's 121 was a rebadged Ford Fiesta. Mazda has engineering strengths. Its designs of the Miata and Millenia have been in the top ranking in *Automobile* for seven years. The two companies have not yet decided the role of Mazda in Ford's global design operations.

Procurement: Mazda's suppliers have been loyal in the Hiroshima area. Ford is trying to have joint world-wide purchasing. This is a threat to Mazda's suppliers. Mazda is trying to minimize the dislocation by helping its parts makers to meet the challenge (Updike, *et al., 1996).*

BMW and Rover

BMW acquired Rover for £800 million from British Aerospace in early 1994. There are two views:

- Optimists feel that the German company's financial, engineering and marketing skills have helped Rover. Rover has been able to introduce new vehicles such as the Range Rover, the MGF and the Rover 200. Thus, nascent talent has been exploited.
- Pessimists have taken the same examples and note their poor building quality, brakes and restricted interior space.

BMW has raised Rover's investment to 7 per cent of sales per annum compared with half that a year under BAe. However, Rover lost £ 158 million in 1995.

- Recently, there has been replacement of a number of senior staff members by BMW staff. These appointments are viewed as an indicator of BMW's failure to appreciate the depth of Rover's problems at the beginning. BMW started by running Rover at an arm's length, and is now assuming overall control.
- The acquisition was mainly to gain control of the Land Rover off-road subsidiary and to expand BMW's volume car business. Land Rover is a leader in four-wheel drive vehicles. BMW was successful in high-priced medium-sized and large rear-wheel drive vehicles. It broadened coverage of the mass car market with Rover.

BMW was slow in formulating its plans for Rover.

- The British company was treated as a collection of brands and not a homogeneous unit. It was thought necessary to treat Land Rover, MG and Mini as distinct brands. It is now introducing a fourth model to compete with smaller, cheaper sports-utility vehicles such as Toyota's Rav4 and Honda's CR-V. BMW changed the MG brand into MGF convertible. Mini has become a brand. The new version of Mini will be an upmarket 'lifestyle' product rather than a utilitarian vehicle.

- It is now planned to rationalize Rover's range to three models based on two platforms compared with the earlier five models based on five platforms. The new cars will be 'British' in their design. The problem is to bridge the gap in BMW and Rover standards. Rover dealers are focusing on Rover 600 mid-sized Saloon and Land Rovers. This selectivity has increased sales in Italy.
- BMW plans to raise sales of Rovers from 500,000 units a year to between 700,000 and 800,000 units by the early years of the coming up century.
- BMW has a marketing problem of keeping Rover and BMW brands as distinct. However, to get economies of scale, the future BMWs and Rovers have to have common parts in terms of engines and electronics. It is the marketing department's job to emphasize the differences.
- BMW is trying to integrate Rover. The former has a tradition of having only two chairmen in the previous two decades. Whereas Rover had many chairmen (six). So far, co-operation has been limited to small groups of engineers and senior managers.

Sony

In October 1996, the Sony President, Nobuyuki Idei, named John Calley as president of Sony Pictures Entertainment. Sony has invested about $10 billion in Columbia and TriStar Pictures. Calley is supposed to restore morale, confidence and stability at the studio which has been in deep trouble during Peter Guber's regime.

Sony started with the $200-million deal to get Peter Guber and Jon Peters to run the company in 1989. Besides, Sony paid $700 million to release the pair from their Warner Bros contract. They made millions of dollars in paychecks and bonuses. However, Peters was removed in 1991 and Guber in 1994. Sony, thus, wrote-off a $3.2

billion. It was a costly flop. Mike Medavoy chief of TriStar was removed and later Marc Platt. Finally, the movie chairman Mark Canton was removed by President Alan Levine, in September 1996 (Brown, 1996).

Calley became president of United Artists in 1993 and was able to turn around the ailing company with small staff and cost-consciousness. This success helped Kirk Kerkorian to sell MGM/ UA studios for $1.3 billion.

Ted Ashley, Frank Wells and Calley controlled Warner Brothers from 1969 to 1980. This was considered to be a very successful production team. After that Calley retired. It was then that Michael Ovitz, the president of Disney, had pushed Calley to come out of retirement and take the UA assignment.

Sony started discussions with Calley in the summer of 1996. The new team comprising Sony executive, J.F. Sagansky will report to Calley as co-president responsible for management. Masayuki Nozoe will join the team from the parent company.

Sony Picture Entertainment may offer an initial public offering of shares. This is to increase pressure to perform on its operating divisions and give the company added financing flexibility.

Seven years after Sony's acquisition of Columbia from Coca-Cola for $3.4 billion, and after two years of Nobuyuki Idei becoming President of Sony, order seems to be restored.

Conventionally, the entertainment business is successful when there is an integration of production with distribution such as in Walt Disney, Time Warner and News Corp. Even though SPE owns a cinema chain. Federal regulations prevent foreign entities from owning television stations. This meftps it has to have an alliance with television network companies. Besides, a full-fledged merger between Sony's entertainment business and a US TV network is not allowed under US law because Sony is Japanese. This means only an alliance. However, it is felt it is better to sell out as was done by Matsushita after its disaster ·

SUMMARY

Management integration is of critical importance for successful M&As. Major cultural aspects such as systems, values and dimensions are described. This is followed by the nature of synergy expected for smooth operation of the venture. Under this aspect, several issues like response to cultural shocks, acculturation, integration and career perspectives are considered. Different alternatives are possible in the integration process. For illustrative purpose, SKF, a Swedish company's three acquisitions and management integration efforts involved is given. Subsequently, six different cases are given to highlight their efforts in management integration and success/failure of such attempts.

Chapters 1–3 have dealt with the conceptual framework necessary to understand M&As. The last chapter takes up industry-wise presentation of M&As in the global context. Some cases which involve mergers within the national boundary but come under legal system of other countries are also included.

9

Strategies for Creating Value Through M&A

It is widely accepted that most acquisitions fail to create shareholder value. This occurs for one or more of the following four reasons:

- Wrong Strategy
- Wrong Information
- Wrong Price
- Wrong Implementation Plan

Fortunately, the shareholder value approach enables companies to **avoid all of these pitfalls.** The shareholder value approach is the

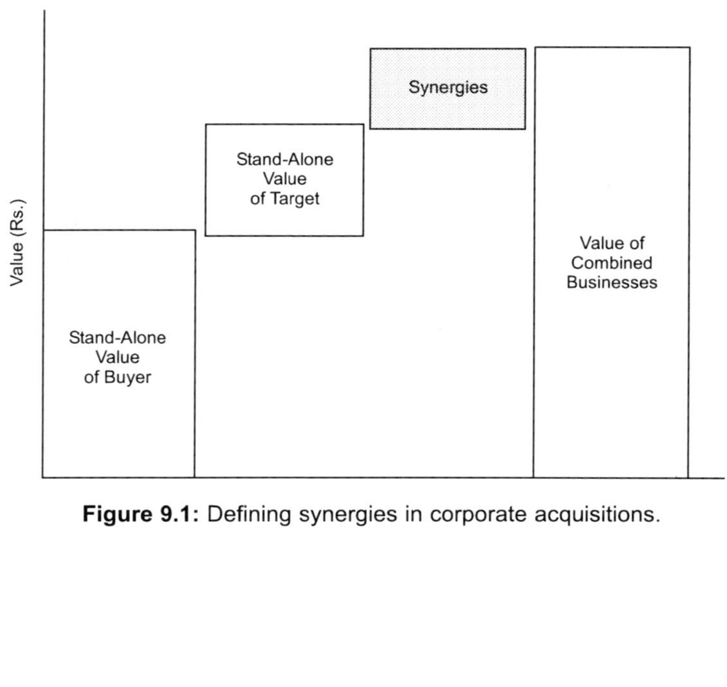

Figure 9.1: Defining synergies in corporate acquisitions.

most effective method for both the buyer and the seller to determine the value of a company, as well as the value created by a potential transaction. In addition, it clarifies whether or not the transaction is strategically sound and dictates what information is required to make an informed choice.

The shareholder value approach determines the likely price range during negotiations, where the price might settle, and the value captured by each party. With this information, both the buyer and the seller enter negotiations with a richer understanding of an appropriate deal price, and conduct negotiations with a better chance of creating value for their shareholders. Acquisitions create value when the value of the businesses combined is greater than the sum of their stand-alone values. **The amount by which the combined value exceeds the individual values is commonly referred to as the value of synergies, or simply "synergies."**If synergies are not significant, there is a good chance that the parties involved are employing the wrong strategy, the first pitfall. Synergies represent increases in value to both the target and the buyer, and arise from many sources including:

- Access to new markets, production capacity, distribution channels, knowledge or technologies
- Economies of scale
- Elimination of duplicate costs
- Defensive synergies (the value associated with not allowing a competitor to complete the transaction).

Whenever synergies exist, the target company is worth more to a potential bidder than to its current shareholders. This creates an opportunity for both the buyer and seller to create value by striking a deal at a price somewhere between the values to each party. The range of prices is referred to here as the *negotiating range*. The stand-alone value of the target represents the lower end of the negotiating range. This value also represents the seller's "walk-away" price since no board would consider selling their company for less than its worth to its shareholders. The stand-alone value of the target plus the anticipated synergies to both the buyer and target set the upper end of the negotiating range. This represents the buyer's "walk-away" price; above this price the buyer is paying more for the target than it

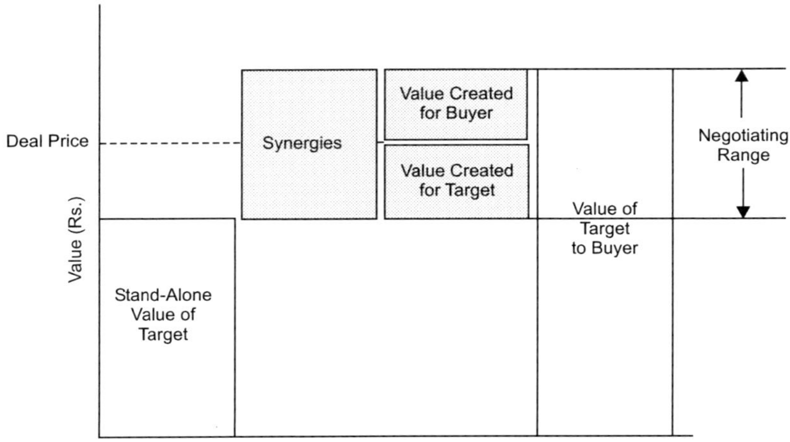

Figure 9.2: The "Negotiating Range" for Corporate Acquisitions

is worth to his shareholders, and therefore, is destroying shareholder value.

Therefore, determining the correct acquisition price involves using the shareholder value approach to define the negotiating range and to estimate the division of synergy values between the buyer's and seller's shareholders. This avoids the third pitfall, *wrong price*, provides a road map for achieving synergies, and aids in preventing the fourth pitfall—*wrong implementation plan.*

DEFINING THE NEGOTIATING RANGE

The target's value as a standalone entity determines the low end of the negotiating range. For public companies, this can be estimated by multiplying the target's current stock price by the number of outstanding shares, and then adding the value of debt. This calculation results in a value that incorporates the market's expectations of the target's future performance. If the market expects that the company will continue to operate as a stand-alone entity, this is a quick and economically reliable way to estimate the target's stand-alone value. However, if the market expects that the company will be acquired, there may be an "acquisition premium" built into its price. This premium reflects the market's assessment of both the probability of a deal and the potential synergies that the deal will create. Adding estimated synergies to this over-stated stand-alone value can result in double counting synergies and overpaying for the target. To avoid this, a recent date must be identified when the market first became aware of the potential for a transaction (e.g., the date information about a potential deal leaked to the market),and the target's stock price just before that date should be used to estimate its stand-alone value.

An even more effective method to estimate the stand-alone value of a target is to use shareholder value. This involves estimating the target company's value drivers and cash flows, and employing the generally accepted and well proven discounted cash flow approach to calculate value. High quality value driver analysis prevents companies from the second pitfall of acquisitions — *wrong information.* To estimate the upper end of the negotiating range, the value of synergies has to be added to the target's stand-alone value. Synergy values can be estimated by analyzing each synergy's impact on a firm's value drivers, and re-running the shareholder value calculation.

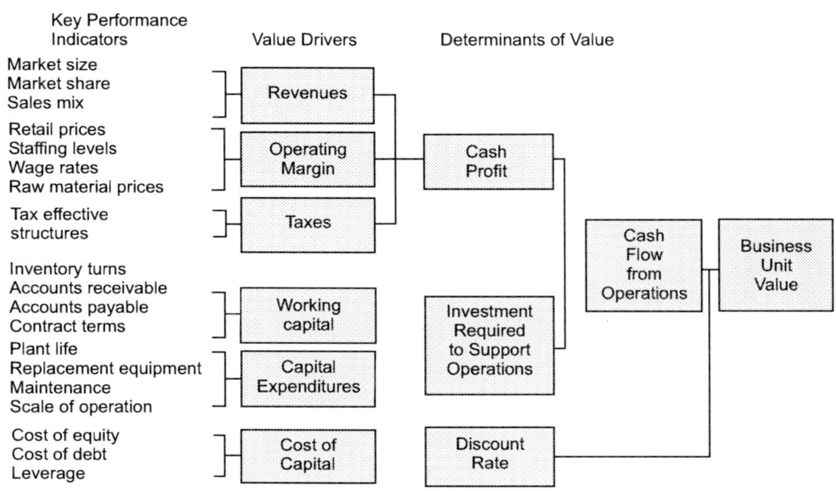

Figure 9.3: Estimating value through value drivers

Once synergies are estimated, their expected values are summed to estimate the total value of synergies arising from a transaction. While this is easily said, identifying and quantifying synergies often requires extensive interviews with key managers, analysis of company and peer group data, and comprehensive financial modeling. However, buyers often are too optimistic about the timing and magnitude of synergies to consider these factors, resulting in an inappropriately high walk-away price. This can be avoided by contacting the people actually involved in the creation of each synergy and reaffirming that they are truly able and motivated. Affirming key managers' "buy in" to achieve the synergies *before the transaction* and linking their compensation to the results is the best way to ensure that synergies will actually be realized.

Finally, it is important to estimate the costs associated with, and timing required to, realize each synergy. All synergies are not created equally. Typically it is easier to achieve cost synergies (head count reductions, supplier consolidation) than revenue synergies (cross-selling, bundling).

UTILIZING SCENARIO ANALYSIS

Another useful tool in defining the negotiating range is scenario analysis. To apply scenario analysis, possible events that could favourably or unfavourably impact the target's value must be identified (a competitor enters or leaves the industry), and then the probability of their occurrence must be assessed. Key managers and industry experts are often good sources for this information. Next, the impact of each scenario on the target and synergy value drivers must be estimated, and shareholder values associated with each scenario must be calculated.

As more and more scenario values are calculated, one develops what is known as a "value probability distribution," which reflects the best understanding of the uncertainty in the target's value. This value probability distribution illustrates the range of values the target could achieve, and the estimated probability that it will assume each value. Considering this range in negotiations is far better than hoping that all possible conditions were taken into account and captured in a single final target price.

This analysis helps buyers avoid over-bidding, allowing them to set their walk-away prices according to the probability of actually creating value at that price. For example, these distributions can answer questions such as, "If we pay $X for Target Y, what is the probability that we will end up creating value?" In addition, this analysis serves as a road map or prioritization for the post-acquisition integration process. While many companies take a "wait and see" approach to integration, the best method is a "full speed ahead" approach in order to capture synergies. The scenarios or sensitivities that create the most value must be the highest priority in the 90 days post-acquisition. If most of the value is in cross-selling products to the target company's customers, the focus must be on marketing and sales, while the synchronization of the information systems departments can wait.

The combination of scenario analysis and the shareholder value approach has two other important applications. First, the above question can be turned around to ask, "If the seller wants a price of $X, what do we have to believe in terms of synergies in order to create value?" The question can then be answered in concrete, value driver terms (revenue growth rates of 10% and/or operating margin improvements of 5%). This tool is particularly useful when constructing contingency based deals such as those in which drivers form the payout formula. Management can then more easily assess the probability of these operating improvements actually occurring. Unless the proposed acquisition is a blockbuster, buyers must be leery of value driver forecasts that have never been achieved in the history of the industry by any competitor-industry dynamics limit business performance.

ESTIMATING HOW SYNERGY VALUES WILL BE DIVIDED BETWEEN THE BUYER'S AND SELLER'S SHAREHOLDERS

The empirical research on the issue of dividing synergies between the buyer's and seller's shareholders is not reassuring to buyers. On an average, much of the synergy value ends up going to the seller's

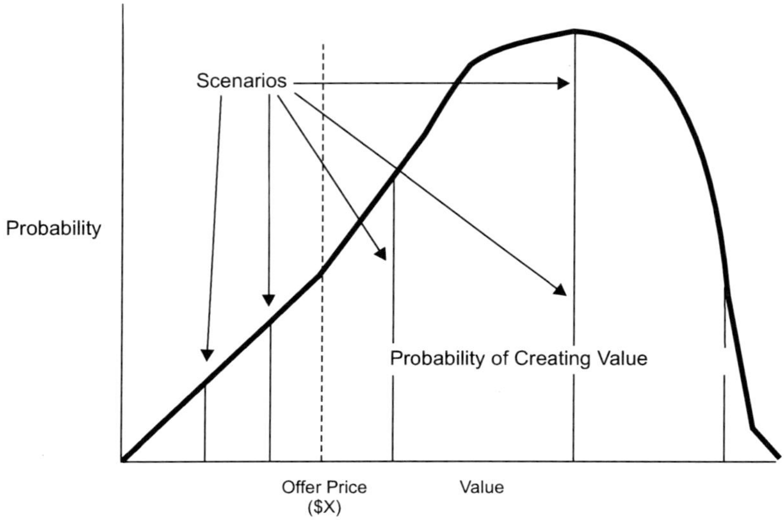

Figure 9.4: Sample value probability distribution for target Y.

shareholders. This result is especially ironic since buyers usually initiate acquisition transactions and shoulder the burden of achieving the synergies. The figures are even more stark for multiple bidder transactions, in which the same study finds average returns to target shareholders approached 45%. To understand why this happens, one must examine the bidding environment.

If there is only one bidder for a target company, allocation of synergies is usually based on the amount of synergy creation "due" to each party, their options for achieving similar synergies outside of the transaction, and each party's negotiation skills.

However, when there is more than one bidder, the negotiation dynamics often shift to the favour of the seller. For example, assume that we have two bidders for a target company, and Bidder B can achieve slightly greater synergies with the target than Bidder A. If Bidder A offers a price anywhere below its "walk-away" price, it will be to Bidder B's advantage to place a higher bid. Assuming both bidders are rational, the bidding will continue until Bidder B bids a price that is slightly higher than Bidder A's walk-away price. At that price, Bidder A ceases bidding and the deal is struck.

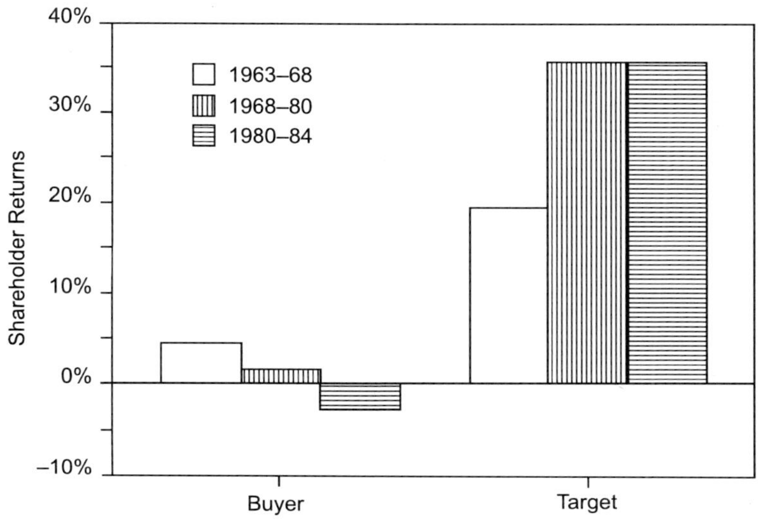

Figure 9.5: Average returns from acquisitions.

Notice that the only synergies that Bidder B can retain for its shareholders are the ***unique*** synergies that it can create with the target company. All of the synergies that are common to both Bidder A and B end up going to the target's shareholders. Thus, the majority of synergy value ends up going to targets because most acquisition synergies can be realized by more than one bidder. This reflects the basic shareholder value principle of finding the highest valued use for all assets. If the buyer cannot answer the question, "Why is this target worth more to us than to any other bidder?" then, in a competitive bidding environment, he will either be outbid by someone who can answer the question, or pay a price that transfers most of the synergy value to the seller. Therefore, the best way to estimate how synergy values will be divided between the buyer's and seller's shareholders is to identify and value the ***unique*** synergies that the buyer can create with the target using the shareholder value approach.

DOING THE DEAL

- **Start with an Offer:** When the CEO and top managers of a company decide that they want to do a merger or acquisition,

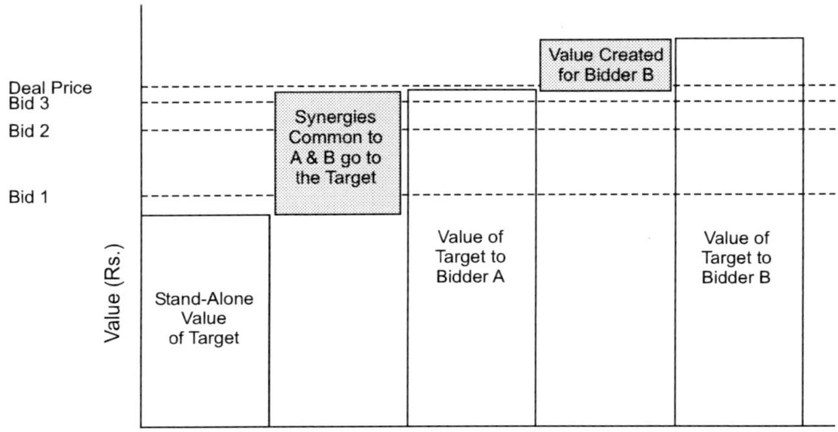

Figure 9.6: Creating value in a two-bidder environment.

they start with a tender offer. The process typically begins with the acquiring company carefully and discreetly buying up shares in the target company, or building a position. Once the acquiring company starts to purchase shares in the open market, it is restricted to buying 5% of the total outstanding shares before it must file with the SEC. In the filing, the company must formally declare how many shares it owns and whether it intends to buy the company or keep the shares purely as an investment. Working with financial advisors and investment bankers, the acquiring company will arrive at an overall price that it's willing to pay for its target in cash, shares or both. The tender offer is then frequently advertised in the business press, stating the offer price and the deadline by which the shareholders in the target company must accept (or reject) it.

- **The Target's Response:** Once the tender offer has been made, the target company can do one of several things:
  - **Accept the Terms of the Offer:** If the target firm's top managers and shareholders are happy with the terms of the transaction, they will go ahead with the deal.
  - **Attempt to Negotiate:** The tender offer price may not be high enough for the target company's shareholders to accept, or the specific terms of the deal may not be

attractive. In a merger, there may be much at stake for the management of the target - their jobs, in particular. If they're not satisfied with the terms laid out in the tender offer, the target's management may try to work out more agreeable terms that let them keep their jobs or, even better, send them off with a nice, big compensation package. Not surprisingly, highly sought-after target companies that are the object of several bidders will have greater latitude for negotiation. Furthermore, managers have more negotiating power if they can show that they are crucial to the merger's future success.

- **Execute a Poison Pill or Some Other Hostile Takeover Defence:** A poison pill scheme can be triggered by a target company when a hostile suitor acquires a predetermined percentage of company stock. To execute its defence, the target company grants all shareholders - except the acquiring company - options to buy additional stock at a dramatic discount. This dilutes the acquiring company's share and intercepts its control of the company.
- **Find a White Knight:** As an alternative, the target company's management may seek out a friendlier potential acquiring company, or white knight. If a white knight is found, it will offer an equal or higher price for the shares than the hostile bidder.

Mergers and acquisitions can face scrutiny from regulatory bodies. For example, If the two biggest long-distance companies in the U.S., AT&T and Sprint, wanted to merge, the deal would require approval from the Federal Communications Commission (FCC). The FCC would probably regard a merger of the two giants as the creation of a monopoly or, at the very least, a threat to competition in the industry.

- **Closing the Deal:** Finally, once the target company agrees to the tender offer and regulatory requirements are met, the merger deal will be executed by means of some transaction. In a merger in which one company buys another, the acquiring company will pay for the target company's shares with cash, stock or both. A cash-for-stock transaction is fairly straightforward:

Target company shareholders receive a cash payment for each share purchased. This transaction is treated as a taxable sale of the shares of the target company. If the transaction is made with stock instead of cash, then it's not taxable. There is simply an exchange of share certificates. The desire to steer clear of the tax man explains why so many M&A deals are carried out as stock-for-stock transactions. When a company is purchased with stock, new shares from the acquiring company's stock are issued directly to the target company's shareholders, or the new shares are sent to a broker who manages them for target company shareholders. The shareholders of the target company are only taxed when they sell their new shares. When the deal is closed, investors usually receive a new stock in their portfolios - the acquiring company's expanded stock. Sometimes investors will get new stock identifying a new corporate entity that is created by the M&A deal.

MAJOR M&A IN THE 1990s

Table 9.1: Top 10 M&A deals worldwide by value (in mil. USD) from 1990 to 1999:

Rank	Year	Purchaser	Purchased	Transaction value (in mil. USD)
1	1999	Vodafone Air touch PLC[1]	Mannesmann	183,000
2	1999	Pfizer[2]	Warner-Lambert	90,000
3	1998	Exxon[3][4]	Mobil	77,200
4	1999	Citicorp	Travellers Group	73,000
5	1999	SBC Communications	Ameritech Corporation	63,000
6	1999	Vodafone Group	Air Touch Communications	60,000
7	1998	Bell Atlantic[5]	GTE	53,360
8	1998	BP[6]	Amoco	53,000
9	1999	Qwest Communications	US WEST	48,000
10	1997	WorldCom	MCI Communications	42,000

Table 9.2: Top 9 M&A deals worldwide by value (in mil. USD) since 2000

Rank	Year	Purchaser	Purchased	Transaction value (in mil. USD)
1	2000	Fusion: America Online Inc. (AOL)	Time Warner	164,747
2	2000	Glaxo Wellcome Plc.	Smith Kline Beecham Plc.	75,961
3	2004	Royal Dutch Petroleum Co.	Shell Transport & Trading Co	74,559
4	2006	AT&T Inc.	BellSouth Corporation	72,671
5	2001	Comcast Corporation	AT&T Broadband & Internet Svcs	72,041
6	2004	Sanofi-Synthelabo SA	Aventis SA	60,243
7	2000	Spin-off: Nortel Networks Corporation		59,974
8	2002	Pfizer Inc.	Pharmacia Corporation	59,515
9	2004	JP Morgan Chase & Co	Bank One Corp	58,761

CROSS-BORDER MERGERS AND ACQUISITIONS

Companies have followed their customers—who are going global themselves - as they respond to the pressures of obtaining scale in a rapidly consolidating global economy. In combination with other trends, such as increased deregulation, privatization, and corporate restructuring, globalization has spurred an unprecedented surge in cross-border merger and acquisition activity.

According to Securities Data Corporation, there were more than 2000 announced cross-border acquisitions in 1996 worth over $252 billion. While this represents 54% more acquisitions than in 1991, the increase in dollar value has been even more remarkable, tripling during this time period. Clearly cross border M& as have become a fundamental characteristic of the global business landscape. Even mergers of companies with headquarters in the same country - while usually not "counted" as cross-border are very much of this type. When Boeing acquires McDonnell Douglas, the two American companies must integrate operations in dozens of countries around the world. This is just as true for other supposedly "single country" mergers, such as the $27 billion dollar merger of Swiss drug makers Sandoz and Ciba-Geigy (now Novartis). Hence, understanding the problems and opportunities of cross-border mergers and acquisitions is an essential element in understanding most M& as, and indeed in understanding the nature of global strategy.

In spite of the huge volume of activity in the cross-border M&A marketplace, an inescapable fact emerges when these deals are examined more closely – the majority of cross border M&As are not successful. For example, economists David J. Ravenscraft and William F. Long found that most of the 89 acquisitions of American companies by foreign buyers between 1977 and 1990 they studied did not improve operational performance one year after the acquisition. Numerous anecdotal accounts corroborate these results. For example, the acquisition of Columbia Pictures by Sony Corp in 1989. After paying a significant premium for the company and keeping a hands-off attitude toward their senior executives in Hollywood – who were busy overspending on office renovations, company perks, and unsuccessful movies – Sony was forced to take an unprecedented $3.2 billion write-down in 1994. This merger is now a classic case study of what not to do in cross-border deals. Some of the problems encountered by Sony include legal problems stemming from their recruitment of senior management who were under contract at Time Warner, lack of internal controls over budgeting, weak understanding of the fundamentals of the acquired business, and an overly optimistic belief in "synergies" arising from vertical integration and from applying Sony's technological competencies to the movie and television business. Of course, these are mistakes that can arise in any merger or acquisition; what makes them particularly troublesome in cross-border deals are the inherently greater challenges of melding country cultures, communicating across long distances, dealing with misunderstandings arising from different business norms, and even fundamental differences in management style.

In sum, there are two fundamental imperatives that must be underscored in any discussion of cross-border mergers and acquisitions. First, companies engage in a merger or acquisition to create value and that value creation comes about through a combination of synergy realization to cut costs and competitive strategy repositioning to increase revenues and growth. And second, both the synergy realization and competitive strategy goals cannot be achieved without significant attention to the challenge of acquisition integration. If cross-border M&A strategies are to fulfill their potential, and justify the premium companies typically pay to engage in them, managers will need to fully understand, and embrace, these two imperatives.

INDIAN MERGERS AND ACQUISITIONS

Until upto a couple of year's back, the news that *Indian companies having acquired* American-European entities was very rare. However, this scenario has taken a sudden U turn. Nowadays, news of *Indian Companies acquiring foreign businesses* is more common than other way round. *Buoyant Indian Economy, extra cash with Indian corporate,*

Table 9.3: The top 10 acquisitions made by Indian companies worldwide are as follows

Acquirer	Target Company	Country targeted	Deal value ($ ml)	Industry
Tata Steel	Corus Group plc	UK	12,000	Steel
Hindalco	Novelis	Canada	5,982	Steel
Videocon	Daewoo Electronics Corp.	Korea	729	Electronics
Dr. Reddy's Labs	Betapharm	Germany	597	Pharmaceutical
Suzlon Energy	Hansen Group	Belgium	565	Energy
HPCL	Kenya Petroleum Refinery Ltd.	Kenya	500	Oil and Gas
Ranbaxy Labs	Terapia SA	Romania	324	Pharmaceutical
Tata Steel	Nat steel	Singapore	293	Steel
Videocon	Thomson SA	France	290	Electronics
VSNL	Teleglobe	Canada	239	Telecom

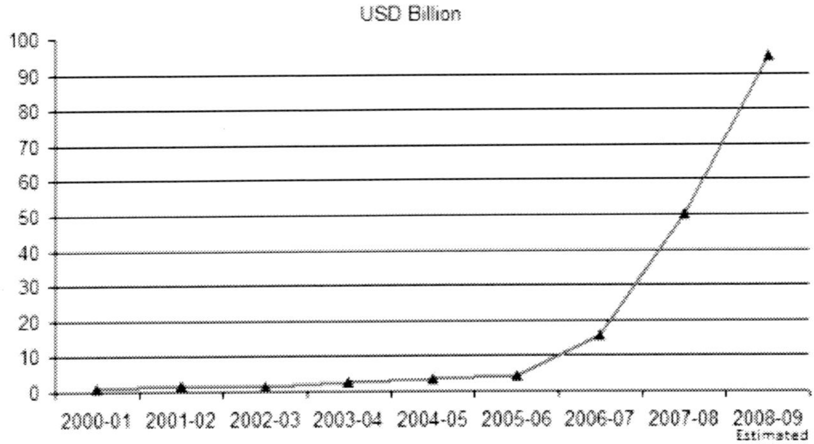

Government policies and newly found *dynamism in Indian businessmen* have all contributed to this new *acquisition trend*. Indian companies are now aggressively looking at North American and European markets to spread their wings and become the global players.

The Indian IT and ITES companies already have a strong presence in foreign markets; however, other sectors are also now growing rapidly. The increasing engagement of the Indian companies in the world markets, and particularly in the US, is not only an indication of the maturity reached by Indian Industry but also the extent of their participation in the overall globalization process.

If you calculate top 10 deals it account for nearly US $ 21,500 million. This is more than double the amount involved in US companies' acquisition of Indian counterparts.

Graphical representation of Indian M&A deals since 2000.

SUMMARY

Employing the shareholder value approach will enable companies involved in M&A to execute transactions with the following characteristics:

- Right Strategy
- Right Information
- Right Price
- Right Implementation Plan

This, in turn, will ensure that the deal will create value for shareholders.

10

Merger and Acquisitions: Why They Fail and How to Make these Successful

It's no secret that plenty of mergers don't work. Those who advocate mergers will argue that the merger will cut costs or boost revenues by more than enough to justify the price premium. It can sound so simple: just combine computer systems, merge a few departments, use sheer size to force down the price of supplies and the merged giant should be more profitable than its parts. In theory, 1 + 1 = 3 sounds great, but in practice, things can go awry.

It's no secret that plenty of mergers don't work. In theory, 1+1 = 3 sounds great, but in practice, things can go awry.

Historical trends show that roughly two-thirds of big mergers will disappoint on their own terms, which means they will lose value on the stock market. The motivations that drive mergers can be flawed and efficiencies from economies of scale may prove elusive. In many cases, the problems associated with trying to make merged companies work are all too concrete.

FLAWED INTENTIONS

For starters, a booming stock market encourages mergers, which can spell trouble. Deals done with highly rated stock as currency are easy and cheap, but the strategic thinking behind them may be easy and cheap too. Also, **mergers are often attempt to imitate**: somebody else has done a big merger, which prompts other top executives to follow suit. A merger may often have more to do with glory-seeking than business strategy. The executive ego, which is boosted by buying the competition, is a major force in M&A, especially when combined with the influence from the bankers, lawyers and other assorted advisers who can earn big fees from clients engaged in mergers. Most CEOs get to where they are because they want to be the biggest and the best, and many top executives get a big bonus for merger deals, no matter what happens to the share price later. On the other side of the coin, mergers can be driven by generalized fear. Globalization, the arrival of new technological developments or a fast-changing economic landscape that makes the outlook uncertain are all factors that can create a strong incentive for defensive mergers. Sometimes the management team feels they have no choice and must acquire a rival before being acquired. The idea is that only big players will survive a more competitive world.

The Obstacles to Make it Work

Coping with a merger can make top managers spread their time too thinly and neglect their core business, spelling doom. The chances for success are further hampered if the **corporate cultures** of the companies are very different. When a company is acquired, the decision is typically based on product or market synergies, but cultural differences are often ignored. It's a mistake to assume that personnel issues are easily overcome. For example, employees at target company might be accustomed to easy access to top management, flexible work schedules or even a relaxed dress code. These aspects of a working environment may not seem significant, but if new management removes them, the result can be resentment and shrinking productivity. More insight into the failure of mergers is found in the highly acclaimed study from McKinsey, a global consultancy. The study concludes that companies often focus too intently on cutting costs following mergers, while revenues, and ultimately, profits, suffer. Merging companies can focus on integration and cost-cutting so much that they neglect day-to-day business, thereby prompting nervous customers to flee. This loss of revenue momentum is one reason why so many mergers fail to create value for shareholders. But remember, not all mergers fail.

Size and global reach can be advantageous, and strong managers can often squeeze greater efficiency out of badly run rivals. Nevertheless, the promises made by deal makers demand the careful scrutiny of investors. The success of mergers depends on how realistic the deal makers are and how well they can integrate two companies while maintaining day-to-day operations.

MERGER MANAGEMENT

Risks in mergers and acquisitions

A combination of factors—increased global competition, regulatory changes, fast changing technology, need for faster growth and industry excess capacity—has fuelled mergers and acquisitions (M&A) in recent times. The M&A phenomenon has been noticeable not only in developed markets like the US, Europe and Japan but also in emerging markets like India. In 1998, worldwide mergers and acquisitions were valued at $2.4 trillion. In 1999, this figure increased to $3.4 trillion. In 2000, the pace seemed to slow down, with only the Glaxo Wellcome - SmithKline Beecham merger valued at over $50 billion. However, the total value of the deals worldwide crossed $3.5 trillion. Much of this activity took place in the first half of 2000.Like capacity expansion, vertical integration and diversification, a large merger or an acquisition is a strategic move since it can make or break a company. However, mergers and acquisitions involve unique challenges such as the valuation of the

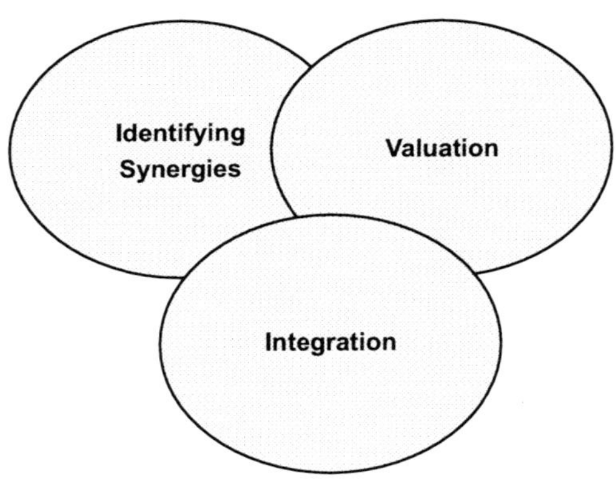

Figure 10.1: Strategic issues in mergers and acquisitions

company being acquired and integration of the pre-merger entities. Valuation is a subjective matter, involving several assumptions. Integration of the pre-merger entities is a demanding task and has to be managed skillfully.

Quite clearly, mergers and acquisitions involve heavy risks. In their excitement and enthusiasm to close the deal fast, managers throw caution to the winds. Later, there is a gap between expectations and actual performance and shareholder's wealth is eroded.

Why Mergers are Risky?

Major acquisitions have to be handled carefully because they leave little scope for trial and error and are difficult to reverse. The risks involved are not merely financial ones. A failed merger can disrupt work processes, diminish customer confidence, damage the company's reputation, cause employees to leave and result in poor employee motivation levels. So the old saying, discretion is the better part of valour, is well and truly applicable here. A comprehensive assessment of the various risks involved is a must before striking an M&A deal. Circumstances, under which the acquisition may fail, including the worst case scenarios, should be carefully considered. Even if the probability of a failure is very low, but the consequences of the failure are significant, one should think carefully before hastening to complete the deal.

There are two main reasons for the failure of an acquisition. One is the ***tendency to lay too much stress on the strategic, unquantifiable benefits of the deal***. This results in over-valuation of the acquired company. *The second reason is the use of wrong integration strategies.* As a result, actually realised synergies turn out to be well short of the projected ones.

Many companies are confident about generating cost savings before the merger. But they are unaware of the practical difficulties involved in realising them. For example, a job may be eliminated, but the person currently on that job may simply be shifted to another department. As a result, the head count remains intact and there is no cost reduction.

Many firms enter a merger hoping that efficiency can be improved by combining the best practices and core competencies of the acquiring and acquired companies. Cultural factors may however, prevent such knowledge sharing. The 1998 merger of Daimler Benz and Chrysler is a good example. Also, it may take much longer to generate cost savings than anticipated. The longer it takes to cut costs, the lesser the value of the synergies generated.

There are two main reasons for the failure of an acquisition. One is the ***tendency to lay too much stress on the strategic, unquantifiable benefits of the deal****. This results in over-valuation of the acquired company. The second reason is the use of wrong integration strategies. As a result, actually realised synergies turn out to be well short of the projected ones.*

Revenue growth, the reason given to justify many mergers, is in general more difficult to achieve than cost cutting. In fact, growth may be adversely affected after a merger if customer or competitor reactions are hostile. When Lockheed Martin acquired Loral, it lost business from important customers such as McDonnell Douglas, who were Lockheed's competitors. So, companies must also look at the acquisition in terms of the impact it makes on competitors. The acquisition should minimise the possibility of retaliation by competitors. Some M&A experts look at revenue enhancement as a soft synergy and discount it heavily while calculating synergy value.

The strategic implications of a merger should be understood carefully. Otherwise, the shareholders' wealth will be eroded. As one school of thought puts it neatly, "When you make a bid for the equity of another company, you are issuing cash or claims to the shareholders of that company. If you issue claims or cash in an amount greater than the economic value of the assets you purchase, you have merely transferred value from the shareholders of your firm to the shareholders of the target – right from the beginning."

Tata Tea: Tetley acquisition runs into problems

In mid-2000, India's largest tea company, Tata Tea announced it was buying the UK-based Tetley for £271 million in a leveraged buyout. Tetley, which earned a net profit of £35 million in 1998 on sales of £280 million was the third largest brand in the global $600 million packaged tea market—behind Unilever's Brook Bond and Lipton. Tata Tea viewed the acquisition as a quick way to gain access to markets in the US, Canada, Europe and Australia. It also looked at the opportunities created by Tetley's estimated weekly purchase of three million kg of tea from 10,000 estates in 35 different countries. Besides, Tata Tea hoped to gain packaging expertise from Tetley.

Tata Tea did not pay cash upfront. Instead, it pumped £70 million of equity into a special purpose vehicle. Then it leveraged the equity to borrow £235 million from the market. Tata Tea hoped that cash flows from Tetley would be adequate to pay off the debt. At the time of finalising the deal, there were press reports that Tata Tea was probably overpaying—it had offered £100 million more than the second highest bidder.

To service the debt, Tetley needed to generate cash flows of at least £48 million per year, whereas it generated only £29 million in 1999. Tata Tea had hoped for a quantum jump in cash flows after the acquisition. But unfortunately for Tata Tea, retail tea prices in the UK market fell. Moreover, the popularity of tea continued to decline in the UK while the market share for natural juices and coffee went up.

By September 2001, the deal was running into short-term financial problems. The Tatas announced they would bring in an additional £60 million as equity. This would facilitate retirement of expensive debt and reduce interest charges by about £8 million per year. If cash flows touch £40 million, the risk of not being able to service the debt will be eliminated. This will however, not be an easy task. Tata Tea Managing Director, R.K. Krishna Kumar recently admitted that additional investments will be needed to revive demand.

Companies making an acquisition not only have to meet the performance targets the market already expects, but also the higher targets implied by the acquisition premium. When they pay the acquisition premium, managers are essentially committing themselves to delivering more than what the market expects on the basis of current projections. This is a point which is often forgotten.

Even when the numbers do not justify an acquisition, executives may insist on going ahead for strategic benefits that cannot be quantified. In the heat of finalizing the deal, what is conveniently overlooked is that most strategic benefits ultimately should be reflected in some form of cost reduction or revenue growth. Similarly, rushing ahead to finalise a deal before a competitor does so, is not always a wise move. In many cases, it makes sense to allow the competitor to pay a higher price and weaken its competitive position rather than rush into the deal.

Acquisitions involve changes and often have a destabilising effect. During the integration of the pre-merger entities, stress, tension, uncertainty and an exodus of employees are likely. To avoid this, building a climate of trust among the employees of the merging entities is extremely important. Most companies underestimate the difficulties involved in integrating the pre-merger entities. A recent example is the ICICI – ICICI bank merger.

International paper:
Aggressive acquisitions strategy creates problems

The paper industry has been known to go through boom and bust cycles. Size and market share are critical in the paper industry, whose products look more like commodities than brands. John Dillon, the CEO of International Paper (IP) the world's largest paper company looks at acquisitions as a way to control prices. After paying $7.1 billion to acquire office paper company Union Camp in early 1999, IP purchased its rival, Champion Paper Corp for $9.6 billion in June 2000. These expensive acquisitions left IP with a debt of $15.5 billion, (50% of capital and four times cash flows) towards the end of 2000.

Dillon has been divesting non-core businesses such as petroleum and minerals to pay for the acquisitions. The markets however, remain cynical about IP's moves.

IP is yet to prove it can integrate its acquisitions and realise the synergies it has projected before its acquisitions. It has been slow to close down factories, an important step in reducing industry capacity and consequently improving prices. In October 2000, Dillon announced that he would be shutting 1.2 million tonnes of capacity or 5% of total production.

Much more however, needs to be done. Reaction to the Champion deal has been lukewarm. The company's stock price has fallen during the period 1995-2000. IP's growth-by-acquisitions strategy may well turn out to be risky, especially at a time when the US economy has gone into a recession.

Porter[1] argues that acquisitions make sense only when three conditions hold good:

- The acquired company's management is more keen on withdrawing, than continuing to run the operations. So, the minimum price, it expects, is quite low.
- The market for companies is imperfect and does not eliminate above-average returns through the bidding process.
- The buyer has unique abilities and competencies which it can use to manage the acquired company's business far more efficiently and effectively.

IDENTIFYING THE SYNERGIES

The aim of an acquisition is to make the merged entity more valuable than the sum of the values of the pre-merger entities. As mentioned earlier, synergies can add value only if the merged entity registers a performance that is better than what is already reflected in the market prices of the pre-merger entities.

In almost two out of three acquisitions, the acquirer's stock price falls after the deal is announced. This is a clear indication that the

[1] Michel Porter's 'Competitive strategy'.

markets tend to be cynical about the realization of the synergies projected. One reason could be that the markets have already discounted the expectation of an improvement in the operating performance of the acquired company. In extreme cases, the markets may even feel that by diverting resources from stronger divisions, for the purpose of realizing synergies, value may be subtracted, rather than added. At a more strategic level, acquisitions, by engaging the top management in the integration process may allow competitors to leap ahead. Boeing faced a major crisis in its production line in the late 1990s, when its attention was entirely focused on its integration with McDonnel Douglas.

The Boeing - Mc Donnell Douglas Merger

In 1993, the US government announced that its military procurement budget was being cut by 50% and informed defence contractors that they must consolidate. One company which looked at the turn of events with concern was Mc Donnell Douglas (MD), a leading manufacturer of military aircraft. Meanwhile, the much stronger Boeing realised that its excessive dependence on the cyclical market for civil aircraft was risky. To address this concern, it acquired a major stake in Rockwell International, a defence supplier.

When MD realised its competitive position was deteriorating rapidly, it even considered acquiring the defence businesses of Hughes Electronics and Texas Instruments. At this point, Boeing CEO, Phil Condit and MD CEO, Hary Storecipher felt that the time had come to revive merger talks which had failed in 1995. Boeing knew that if MD went ahead with other acquisitions, it would be priced beyond its own reach. So, it rushed to close the deal. The merger was announced in December 1996 and received approvals from competition authorities in the US and Europe by August, 1997.

After the merger, Boeing ran into problems on account of a factor it had totally failed to anticipate. In the wake of competition from Airbus, it had aggressively booked orders by slashing prices. When demand rose sharply, Boeing's production system was thrown out of gear. Due to a parts shortage, much work had to be done outside the normal production system. By September 1998, Boeing was in big trouble. It had to take a charge of $4 billion. Quite clearly, the task of implementing the merger had distracted the attention of the top management from operational issues.

In February 1999, Boeing's share price reached a low. Condit warned his top management that the company was a potential takeover target. There were rumours that GE had its eyes on Boeing, but GE denied them. Boeing made some changes in senior management and put in place a new organisation structure with different businesses focussed on different customer needs. It decided to tap new businesses such as broad-band communications, satellite navigation for air traffic controllers and services such as running airforce bases. Boeing also realised the importance of sharing knowledge and leveraging its research capabilities across the organisation. Phantom Works, the R&D centre of MD became the focal point for new initiatives to improve manufacturing processes across the group. The idea was to integrate the expertise of Boeing, MD and Rockwell, through both short-run and long-run programmes.

Looking back, it is quite evident that the Boeing-MD merger was not really well planned. The integration process was faulty and consumed a lot of precious management time. Core functional areas did not receive the attention they needed. Most of the synergies realised came by sheer chance than by any great planning. An important lesson from the Boeing - MD merger seems to be that synergies often come in areas where they are least expected.

Source: "Building a new Boeing," The Economist, August 10, 2000.

Much of the risk in an M&A deal arises from the acquiring company's inability to identify and quantify synergies accurately. Often, the synergies which are highlighted, do not materialise, while those which may have been completely overlooked become very important. Usually, it is years after the acquisition that it becomes clear whether the price paid for the acquisition was the right one or not.

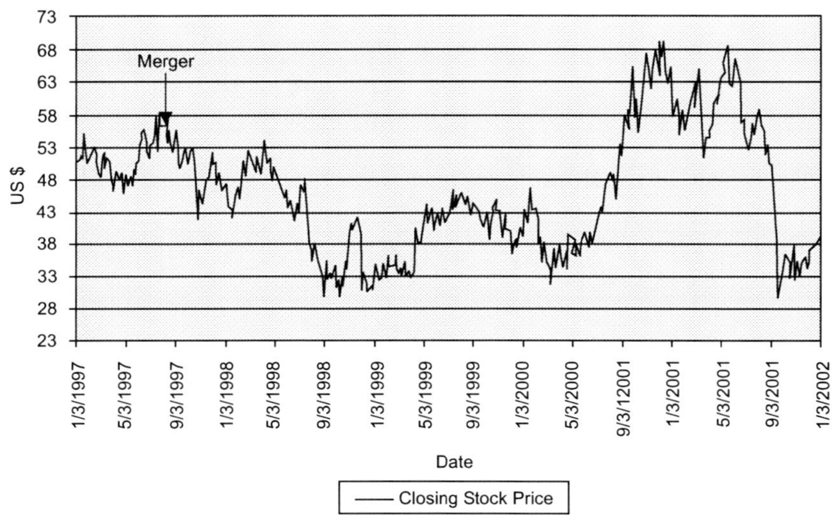

Figure 10.2: Boeing.

STOCK VS CASH DEALS

The way the deal is financed determines how risk is shared between the buyer and the seller. In general, there are two types of financial risk faced during an acquisition – the fall in the share price of the acquiring company from the time of announcement of the deal to its closing, and the possibility of synergies not being realized after the deal is closed. In a cash deal, the acquiring company assumes both the risks completely. In a stock swap, where a fixed value of the acquiring company's shares is offered to the acquired company, the first risk remains with the acquiring company, but the second risk is shared by the two companies. In a stock swap where a fixed number of shares is offered to the acquired company, both the risks are shared between the two companies.

The method of financing the deal is influenced by several factors. If the acquirer feels its shares are undervalued, it prefers a cash deal as any fresh issue of shares would further erode the wealth of existing shareholders. If the acquirer is very confident about actually realising the projected synergies, a cash deal makes sense. Where such confidence is lacking, a stock deal allows the risk to be at least partially hedged. In general, a fixed value offer is an indication of greater confidence on the part of the acquirer than a fixed number of shares and tends to be better received by the market. A fixed share offer, ironically enough, by minimising the pre-closing market risk for the acquirer, acts as a kind of self-fulfilling prophecy and drives the share price downwards.

INTEGRATION

Many mergers fail at the integration stage. So, it is important to understand the risks involved in integration and the ways to manage these risks. All acquisitions must begin with a strategic vision, which should serve as a guide for the integration process. There should also be an operating strategy which addresses the issue of how the value chain performance can be improved, whether competitors will react aggressively, and if they do, how they can be dealt with. Vision and operating strategy must be backed by proper systems and processes to align the behavior of managers with corporate objectives. Some operations should be tightly integrated while others should be left alone.

The AOL Time Warner Merger

On January 10, 2000, America Online (AOL) and Time Warner (TW) announced that they were merging. For all practical purposes, the deal was a reverse takeover by AOL. While the icon of the internet world had just 20% of TW's revenues and 15% of its workforce, its large market cap made it the senior partner. AOL shareholders received one share in the merged entity while TW shareholders got 1.5 shares for each of their existing shares. AOL shareholders owned 55% and TW shareholders 45% of the new company. Effectively, AOL paid a premium of 71% over the market value of TW. The combined entity was valued at $350 billion.

Though the two companies were confident of boosting revenues, many analysts expressed concerns that the merger would slow down AOL and rob it of its entrepreneurial drive. AOL however, remained confident that TW's cable network and content would generate new growth opportunities.

Before the announcement of the deal, TW shares traded at a multiple of 14 times EBITDA (Earnings Before Interest Tax depreciation and Amortisation) while AOL shares traded at a multiple of 55. The immediate reaction to the deal was negative. By January 12, the combined market capitalisation was actually lower at $260 billion, compared to $270 billion before the announcement. The market value of AOL shares fell by 19% while that of TW shares went up by $22 billion.

AOL which had a strong brand and enjoyed a large customer base was clearly one of the pioneers in the new economy. However, anticipating the rapid commoditisation of the Internet access business, AOL realised it needed the 'pipes' of cable television to carry Internet content. Moreover, AOL did not really have much content of its own. It decided to move fast and make full use of its high market capitalisation. In October 1999, Steve Case, CEO of AOL called TW CEO, Gerald Levin to discuss the merger, Levin sensed an opportunity as his company's stock was not doing particularly well in the market. In December 1998, TW had been worth more than AOL. But by December 1999, AOL's worth was 2.5 times that of TW. Quite clearly, TW was on the decline. Case also sweetened the deal for TW by inviting Levin to be the merged entity's CEO.

After the merger was announced, the Federal Trade Commission (FTC) began to interrogate the senior executives of the two companies to determine whether the merger would come under the purview of anti-trust legislation. Case and Levin refused to accept a demand by FTC to regulate the placement of AOL-TW content. However, they agreed to report any complaints from competitors if they were denied AOL-TW content.

"Low hanging fruit" synergies were quickly identified. CNN.com programmes could be featured on AOL, while AOL discs would be bundled with TW product shipments. Warner movies could be promoted on AOL-owned Moviefone. The merged entity could offer books, movies, magazines and music to customers on TV, paper, PC, cell phone or any of the other wireless devices.

Even as the FTC was in the process of approving the merger, integration efforts began. Inter-divisional committees were set up to facilitate the integration. Efforts to generate cross-selling opportunities in the areas of subscriptions, advertising and promotions began. An attempt to sell TIME's magazines through AOL was very successful.

A year later, the merger was showing signs of trouble. The projected revenue growth of 12-15% and $1 billion in cost savings looked way off target. According to Merrill Lynch estimates, growth would only be 11%, while losses would cross $5 billion due to merger write-offs. A slowing US economy and a sharp cutback on ad spending by companies was hitting growth. By early 2001, AOL's stock had dropped by 48% to $37.50. (See graph showing the stock price movement).

One positive feature of the merger is that the transition at the highest level of management has been smooth. Levin has been clearly in charge of both day-to-day operations and key strategic and personnel moves. Case has disengaged from day-to-day operations to concentrate on macro level issues. In an email to *Fortune,*[1] Case said that the management set-up kept him informed about what was happening and allowed him to provide his perspective where required, without in any way meddling with the day-to-day operations.

It is now clear that the fortunes of AOL-TW are closely tied to the erstwhile AOL group. Many of the top executive positions have gone to AOL. Most of its senior executives are still around, 18 months after the merger was announced. While AOL's performance in the first quarter of 2001 was good, TW has continued to struggle due to falling advertising revenues. Moreover, making Hollywood movies remains an unpredictable, low margin business.

The markets perceive the integration to be still incomplete. In response to the 2001 second quarter results, the share price declined by 9% even though EDITDA jumped by 20% over the previous year. Cultural differences continue to be a formidable barrier to the integration process. As the *Economist*[2] recently reported: "There is a wide cultural gap between the restless 20 – somethings from AOL and New York institutions such as the 78 year old Time Inc... There is much grumbling among

[1] July 23, 2001.
[2] July 21, 2001.

journalists (at Time Warner)... about a new tightness with money and the fears, this has prompted for editorial quality."

AOL feels things are moving in the right direction. As an example of the synergies being generated, it cites a recent Madonna world tour arranged by Warner Brother Records, in which AOL subscribers can buy advance tickets and see unreleased photos and videos. AOL remains confident that its community can be persuaded to buy a range of entertainment products.

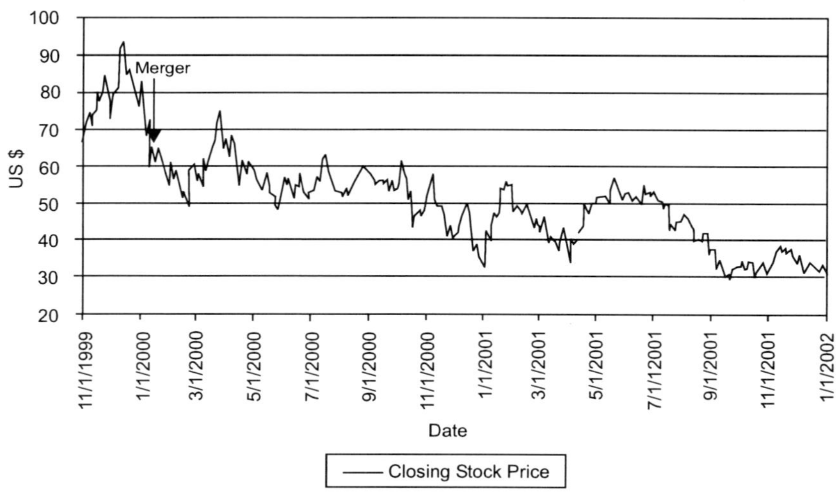

Figure 10.3: AOL Time Warner

Personal chemistry, especially at the top, matters a lot during the integration of the pre-merger entities. In general, it is advisable not to have two bosses. Decisive leadership is best provided by a single individual, not by a two-man team or a committee. Indeed, if two co-CEOs are named after the merger, there will ensue a period of uncertainty during which people wait to see who finally gains the upper hand. In the Citicorp-Travellers Group merger, Sandy Weill of Travellers has taken control, ousting Citicorp's John Reed and in the Daimler Chrysler merger, Jurgen Schrempp has gained ascendancy over Chrysler's Bob Eaton. In both cases, until a clear leader emerged, things were in a state of flux and employees remained confused.

HOW TO MAKE M&A SUCESSFUL

Understanding the Role of Communication

Communication plays an important role during the integration of the pre-merger entities. Genuine communication increases the perceived benevolence of the management and consequently promotes trust. It minimises the negative reactions of employees in the acquired company. As a popular saying goes, the certainty of misery is better than the misery of uncertainty. Lack of communication increases uncertainty and weakens the confidence of employees in the management. A good communication strategy is necessary to ensure that rumours are not allowed to fill the information gap. Employees must be informed about the acquiring company, the proposed changes and the impact of these changes on the employees. All efforts should be made to reassure the employees of the acquired firm and make them understand the intentions and philosophy of the acquiring company. In the case of cross-border acquisitions, the role of communication is even more critical.

Immediately after the acquisition, employees need to know what will happen to their job, their colleagues and their company. It is only through honest communication that their anxieties can be set at rest. Here, the quality of communication is the overriding factor. Later, when employees have to adjust to the changes, frequency of communication becomes important. Frequent communication however does not mean that all details must be communicated, especially when the management itself is not clear about what will happen. A high level of transparency will send the right signals to the employees even if all the information cannot be shared with them. When IBM acquired telecommunication equipment maker Rolm in 1984, it made the mistake of dictating terms to the acquired company's employees. Some key technical employees left. The takeover was not effective and IBM sold Rolm to Siemens.

Understanding the Importance of Cultural Differences

More often than not, significant cultural differences exist between the pre-merger entities. Managing these cultural differences is the strategic challenge during integration. Consider the following examples:

- The merger of UK-based Beecham and the US based SmithKline involved not only two national cultures but also two business cultures—one very scientific and academic and the other more commercially oriented.
- The American pharmaceutical company, Upjohn's centralized and aggressive culture clashed with Swedish major Pharmacia's decentralized laid back management style.
- After the merger between Daimler Benz and Chrysler, the Germans and Americans have struggled to understand each other and their ways of working. Daimler's bureaucratic engineering culture in which different departments work separately has clashed with Chrysler's free-wheeling, cross-functional product development approach.
- Cultural clashes can be significant in industries such as the media, where egos tend to be big. This was so in the case of the 1989 merger between Time and Warner.
- Cultural differences became an important issue when Aetna, a tradition-bound, stodgy and slow-moving organization merged with US Healthcare, generally considered to be a brash, aggressive and entrepreneurial Health Maintenance Organization (HMO).
- Citicorp's staid buttoned-down world of traditional commercial banking has had to take on Traveller group's freewheeling, deal making, investment banking culture. One pressing issue in this merger has been the overbearing attitude of investment bankers who are typically paid much higher salaries than their counterparts in commercial banking.
- The Exxon-Mobil merger has also seen the coming together of two contrasting cultures. Exxon is generally considered to be independent and not particularly good at managing the media. Mobil on the other hand, is more accessible, accepts new ideas and is good at public relations. Exxon's slow decision-making processes focus on cutting costs, while Mobil has been known to take big risks. It moved into central Asia

in the aftermath of the break-up of the Soviet Union, ahead of many other oil companies.

Different cultures exhibit differences based on these dimensions. International business management has to take cognizance of these differences in management functions. This would enable the generation of synergies from the interface of different cultures.

CULTURAL COMPETENCE

From the outside, a tree grown in California would probably look just like a tree grown in Japan. However, the growth of each tree is largely dependent upon the soil that the roots of the tree have to "interact" with in order to grow. The strength of the roots is also dependent on the environment the tree is exposed to, from sunshine to thunderstorm.

Imagine the values of a particular culture are represented by the roots of the tree. These roots are the source of strength needed by the tree in order to survive in the surrounding environment (society). The type of fertilizer and water fed to the tree contributes significantly to its growth.

Also, you cannot transplant a tree unless you prepare the roots for a new soil.

Source: Elashmawi, et al. (1993), p. 65

Guide to a happy merger

Question the logic: Ask how exactly the combination will generate synergies.

Specify roles clearly: Arrive at an agreement over the degree of integration and define clearly the roles of top leaders.

Design the integration process carefully: Combine the pre-merger entities in ways that preserve the anticipated sources of strategic leverage.

Don't escalate commitment carelessly: Avoid making additional acquisitions to justify the deal. If one deal does not click, cut losses and withdraw, instead of throwing good money after bad.

Don't give autonomy without a clear logic: In some cases, the acquired company must be allowed to operate with a great degree of independence. In other cases, this should not be so. Autonomy should be given based on the merits of the situation, not just because the acquired company demands it.

Apply what has worked in the past: Core practices that have contributed to past success, must be applied to the new business.

Don't be carried away by favourable short-term results: In many cases, it makes sense to grant autonomy to the acquired company's managers only after a period of sustained excellence.

Don't give key jobs to top executives who missed out on promotions earlier: Such a move often creates problems. These executives may be upset at having been overlooked for the top job. As a result, trust may become a problem over time.

Don't compromise on values: No matter how good the numbers look, if the core values of the merging entities clash, the merger is heading for big trouble.

Source: David A Wadler, The New York Times, 1998.

Dilemmas/paradoxes in mergers and acquisitions

Slow vs quick change: Some advocate rapid change within the first 100 days of the merger. Others suggest a slower process that carries people along. More than speed however, compassion and goal congruence are the more important factors.

Information sharing: Though all efforts should be made to share as much information as possible, it must be kept in mind that people caught in the process of integration will still tend to perceive that they are not being kept fully informed.

Managing vs coping: It is important to have a plan, but also to keep in mind that all factors may not be fully within the control of managers. People's fears and tensions will always disrupt organisational processes to some extent.

Strategic significance: Studies indicate that the more significant, the target is to the acquirer, the greater the likelihood that the acquiring company will step in and take control of the situation, especially when progress is below expectations. (Daimler Benz certainly seems to be doing that to Chrysler). This creates antagonism among various employee groups and prevents a more iterative, evolutionary process that seems to characterise many successful mergers.

Long-term and short-term focus: Sometimes, integration efforts tend to have an overly long-term focus. However, it is often the handling of short-term people-related issues that tend to have the biggest impact on the integration process.

It takes time: Mergers and acquisitions result in severe disruptions and impose a tremendous strain on those involved. It may take up to five years for the change process to be fully completed. Expectations on both sides must be adjusted accordingly.

Source: AON Risk Services, Edition 3, 1998.

Overall, it can be seen that successful M&A depend on a successful strategy and a due diligence. Bad mergers are always done in haste and without any long term vision. Sometimes economic downturn takes a toll on companies and they suddenly find that what they perceived to be a good merger does not work well in the contemporary economic environment. Looking at the examples given above, companies can work towards very happy mergers with sustainable strategies and people-centric approaches.

11

Cases in Mergers and Acquisitions

CASE 1: TATA & CORUS: A CASE OF ACQUISITION

"There are not many opportunities for producers in emerging low-cost markets to gain access to the markets of Europe other than by acquiring a company like Corus," John Quigley (Editor, Industry Publication Steel week). Finance Minister P. Chidambaram offered unspecified help, if needed, to close the deal; fellow steel magnate Lakshmi Niwas Mittal cheered the acquisition, and excited TV newsreaders gushed. India's first Fortune 500 MNC was born.

Tata acquired Corus, which is four times larger than its size and the largest steel producer in the U.K. The deal, which creates the world's fifth-largest steelmaker, is India's largest ever foreign takeover and follows Mittal Steel's $31 billion acquisition of rival Arcelor in the same year. Over the past five years, Indian companies had made global acquisitions for over $10 billion. The Tata bid almost equals this amount. Most of them have averaged $100 to 200 million.

"It is a two-way street now," Kamal Nath (Commerce Minister, India) said. "Not only India is seeking foreign investment, but Indian companies are emerging investors in other countries."

Until the 1990s, not many Indian companies had contemplated spreading their wings abroad. An Indian corporate or group company acquiring a business in Europe or the U.K. seemed possible only in the realm of fantasy. Recent reports of United Nations Conference on Trade and Development (UNCTAD) and other organizations have recorded the fact that nowadays Foreign Direct Investment (FDI) is more likely to flow in through cross-border mergers (and not through Greenfield Projects). Though Corus is four times bigger than Tata but in the year 2006 the operating profit for Tata was $840 million, whereas in case of Corus it was $860 million. There are some major inputs, which leads Tata towards this huge profit.

On October 20, 2006, the boards of Tata Steel and Corus announced their agreement on the terms of the recommended acquisition of the entire issued and to be issued share capital of Corus at a price of 455 pence in cash for each Corus Share, valuing Corus at £4.3 billion. Tata Steel said its 455-pence-a-share offer for Corus represents on an enterprise value, a price earning ratio of 7.9 times Corus' '06 earnings and includes a premium of approximately 26.2% to the average closing mid-market price of 360.5 pence. Details of the merger were likely to be decided by a strategic and integration committee that would develop and execute the integration and growth plans for the combined entity. Corus is much larger than Tata Steel, both in volumes and sales figures. Globally, it is ranked ninth in terms of volume. Tata Steel, in comparison, is ranked 58.

Ratan Tata, Chairman of Tata Steel, said: "This proposed acquisition represents a defining moment for Tata Steel and is entirely consistent with our strategy of growth through international expansion. Corus and Tata Steel are companies with long, proud histories. We have compatible cultures of commitment to stakeholders and complementary strengths in technology, efficiency, product mix and geographical spread. Together we will be even better equipped to remain at the leading edge of the fast changing steel industry."

Tata and Indian Steel Industry

Tata Steel was established by Indian Parsi Businessman Jamsetji Tata in 1907, exactly in the year when British-American Tobacco (BAT) has started its first factory in India. But it started operating in the year 1912. Tata Steel holds a very vital place in Indian business history, because it has introduced some of the unique concepts like 8-hour working days, leave with pay and pension system for the first time in India and the first player to start rapid industrialization process. In the later part the concepts invented and implemented by Tata became lawful and compulsory practice for the Indian employees. From Tata Steel, Tata started investing in various other businesses like; Oil mills, Airlines, Publishing, Motors, Consultancy services, etc. in a short span of 30 years. In the year 1945, Tata entered into tea business by the name of Tata Tea, which was known as Tata Finlay earlier. Tata also entered into exports as Tata Exports, which is the most successful and the largest export house in India. During the entire business in India Tata has seen many ups and downs, in different fields of business.

SWOT Analysis

Strengths

- Lowest Cost Producer in world
- Experience of TATA group in doing global acquisitions
- Stable balance sheet (Low debt to equity ratio)

Opportunities

- Consolidation trend in Steel Industry
- CSN's tarnished image after failure of 2002 negotiations
- To get exposed to the global steel market (will save time and learning space for them)

Weaknesses

- Corus was triple the size of TATA steels in terms of production

Threats

- Brazilian player CSN
- Russian player Severstal
- No committed financiers to support the possible deal

Corus and Steel Production in the U.K.

Corus Group plc was formed on 6th October, 1999, through the merger of two companies, British Steel and Koninklijke Hoogovens, following the privatization of many steelworks companies by the U.K. government. The company consists of four divisions which include: Strip Products, Long Products, Aluminum and Distribution and Building Systems. With headquarters in London, Corus operates as an international company, satisfying the demand of many steel customers worldwide. Its core business comprises manufacturing, development and allocation of steel and aluminum products and services. The company has a wide variety of products and services which comprise the manufacturing of electrical steel, narrow strip, plates, packaging steel, plated steel strip, semi-finished steel, tube products, wire rod and rail products and services. However, the company is also engaged in providing a variety of services including design, technology and consultancy services.

Corus' products and services are acquired by customers from diverse fields such as commercial and military aerospace ventures, the automotive, construction, engineering, defense and security, as well as the rail and shipbuilding industry. In terms of performance, the company is regarded as the largest steel producer in the UK with £10,142 million of annual revenue (for 2005) and a workforce of 50000 employees. In order to sustain and run its global steel making, processing and distribution operations the company makes annual investments of over £6 million for the purchase of various goods and services, such as iron ore and coal, alloys, refractory, rolls and paint. Looking at the financial status of the company from 1996-2005, a degree of fluctuation between the years can be seen. But irrespective of all these factors Corus continue the business as it was continuing.

In 1990, the Hoogovens group had five divisions; Steel, Aluminum, Technical Services, Subcontracting, and the newly formed Steel Processing and trading. In 1999, the trend towards greater rationalization in the European steel industry led to the merger discussions with British Steel. At that time Hoogovens had 17 business units with a turnover of 4.9 b Euro.

The British Steel Corporation was formed from the UK's 14 main steel producing companies. In 1987, the UK government formally announced its intention to privatize the British Steel Corporation. The British Steel Act 1988 transferred the assets of the corporation to British Steel, a company registered under the Companies Act. The early 1990s saw reduced demand and it was not until 1993 that growth in the UK economy gradually gathered pace and was reflected in a partial recovery in steel demand and prices. The trend continued into 1994 and helped by continuing efficiency and productivity gains, British Steel returned to profit. On October 6, 1999, the merger of Hoogovens with British steel to form Corus came into effect.

Corus has manufacturing operations in many countries with major plants located in the UK, the Netherlands, Germany, France, Norway and Belgium. The company produced around 18 million tonnes of crude steel in 2005, which represented approximately 10 per cent of total EU production and positioned the company as the 9th largest steel producer in the world and the 2nd largest producer in Europe. Corus produces carbon steel by the basic oxygen steel making method in the UK at Port Talbot, Teesside and Scunthorpe and in the Netherlands at IJ muiden. In addition, carbon steel is produced by the electric arc furnace method in the UK at Rotherham. Corus has approximately 50 per cent of the UK carbon steels market and around 11 per cent of the European (including UK) carbon steels market.

In 2005, Corus generated turnover of £9.1 billion and produced 19 million tonnes of steel and delivered over 0.6 mt of aluminum. At the end of December 2005 Corus had 47,300 employees. From October 2003 Corus has been structured into four main divisions: Strip Products, Long Products, Aluminium and Distribution and Building Systems. Corus has a strategy focused around carbon steel, with the intention of ensuring upstream steel making facilities are optimized and that the leading position of its I J muiden site is maintained. Pursuing selective growth of downstream businesses and seeking opportunities to participate in the ongoing consolidation of the world's steel industry were the part of long term strategy of Corus. Following his appointment as Chief Executive of Corus with effect from 1 May, 2003, Philippe Varin carried out an intensive and detailed review of the Group's activities. As a result a number of key initiatives were launched, known as the 'Restoring Success' initiatives. These focus on introducing new leadership and instilling a new corporate culture across the Group, aligning the financial resources available to the Group with its future strategic needs, and returning all parts of the Group to acceptable levels of profitability. The latter will be done by building on our 'Restoring Success' initiatives existing cost reduction programmes, implementing restructuring proposals for the UK asset base and initiating group-wide efficiency measures.

Deal

The deal (between Tata and Corus) was officially announced on April 2nd, 2007 at a price of 608 pence per ordinary share in cash. This deal is a 100 per cent acquisition and the new entity will be run by one of Tata's steel subsidiaries. As stated by Tata, the initial motive behind the completion of the deal was not Corus' revenue size, but rather its market value. Even though Corus is larger in size compared to Tata, the company was valued less than Tata (at approximately $6 billion) at the time when the deal negotiations started. But from Corus' point of view, as the management has stated that the basic reason for supporting this deal were the expected synergies between the two entities. Corus has supported the Tata acquisition due to different motives. However, with the Tata acquisition Corus has gained a great and profitable opportunity to make an exit as the company has been looking out for a potential buyer for quite some time.

The total value of this acquisition amounted to £6.2 billion (US$12 billion). Tata Steel the winner of the auction for Corus declares a bid of 608 pence per share surpassed the final bid from Brazilian Steel maker Companhia Siderurgica Nacional (CSN) of 603 pence per share. Prior to the beginning of the deal negotiations, both Tata Steel and Corus were interested in entering into an M&A deal due to several reasons. The official press release issued by both the company states that the combined entity will have a pro forma crude steel production of 27 million tonnes in 2007, with 84,000 employees across four continents and a joint presence in 45 countries, which makes it a serious rival to other steel giants.

The official declaration of the completed transaction between the two companies was announced to be effective by Court of Justice in England and Wales and consistent with the Scheme of Arrangement of the Tata Steel Scheme on April 2, 2007. According the Scheme regulations, Tata Steel is required to deliver a consideration not later than 2 weeks following the official date of the completion of the transaction. The process has started on September 20, 2006 and completed on July 2, 2007. In the process both the companies have faced many ups and downs.

The details of this process has described below:

September 20, 2006	Corus Steel has decided to acquire a strategic partnership with a Company that is a low cost producer
October 5, 2006	The Indian steel giant, Tata Steel wants to fulfill its ambition to expand its business further.
October 6, 2006	The initial offer from Tata Steel is considered to be too low both by Corus and analysts.
October 17, 2006	Tata Steel has kept its offer to 455p per share.
October 18, 2006	Tata still doesn't react to Corus and its bid price remains same.
October 20, 2006	Corus accepts terms of £ 4.3 billion takeover bid from Tata Steel
October 23, 2006	The Brazilian Steel Group CSN recruits a leading investment bank to offer advice on possible counter-offer to Tata Steel's bid.
October 27, 2006	Corus is criticized by the chairman of JCB, Sir Anthony Bamford, for its decision to accept an offer from Tata.
November 3, 2006	The Russian steel giant Severstal announces officially that it will not make a bid for Corus.
November 18, 2006	The battle over Corus intensifies when Brazilian group CSN approached board of the company with a bid of 475p per share.
November 27, 2006	The board of Corus decides that it is in the best interest of its will shareholders to give more time to CSN to satisfy the preconditions and decide whether it issues forward a formal offer
December 18, 2006	Within hours of Tata Steel increasing its original bid for Corus to 500 pence per share, Brazil's CSN made its formal counter bid for Corus at 515 pence per share in cash, 3% more than Tata's offer

January 31, 2007	Britain's Takeover Panel announces in an e-mailed statement that after an auction Tata Steel had agreed to offer Corus investors 608 pence per share in cash
April 2, 2007	Tata Steel manages to win the acquisition to CSN and has the full voting support form Corus' shareholders

Post-Acquisition Tata

Tata Steel has formed a seven-member integration committee to spearhead its union with Corus group. While Ratan Tata, chairman of the Tata group, heads the committee, three of the members are from Tata Steel and the other three are from Corus group. Members of the integration committee from Tata Steel include managing director B Muthuraman, deputy managing director (steel) T. Mukherjee, and chief financial officer Kaushik Chatterjee. The Corus group is represented in the committee by CEO Phillipe Varin, executive director (finance) David Lloyd, and division director (strip products) Rauke Henstra.

The acquisition by Tata amounted to a total of 608 pence per ordinary share or £6.2 billion (US $12 billion) which was paid in cash. First of all, the general assumption is that the acquisition was not cheap for Tata. The price that they paid represents a very high 49% premium over the closing mid-market share price of Corus on 4 October, 2006 and a premium of over 68% over the average closing market share price over the twelve-month period. Moreover, since the deal was paid for in cash automatically makes it more expensive, implying a cash outflow from Tata Steel in the amount of £1.84 billion.

Tata has reportedly financed only $4 billion of the Corus purchase from internal company resources, meaning that more than two-thirds of the deal has had to be financed through loans from major banks. The day after the acquisition was officially announced, Tata Steel's share fell by 10.7 per cent on the Bombay stock market. Despite its four times smaller size and smaller capacity, Tata Steel's operating profit for 2006, earning $840 million on sales of 5.3 million tonnes, were very close in amount to those generated by Corus ($860 million in profits on sales of 18.6 million tons).

Tata's new debt amounting to $8 billion due to the acquisition, financed with Corus' cash flows, is expected to generate up to $640 million in annual interest charges (8 per cent annual interest cost). This amount combined with Corus' existing interest debt charges of $400 million on an annual basis implies that the combined entity's interest obligation will amount to approximately $725 million after the acquisition.

The debate whether Tata Steel has overpaid for acquiring Corus is most likely to be certain, since just based on the numbers alone it turns out that at the end of the bidding conflict with CSN Tata ended up paying approximately 68 per cent above the average price of Corus' shares. Another pressing issue resulting for this deal that has created a dilemma between experts and analysts opinions is whether this acquisition for the right move for Tata Steel in the first place. The fact that Tata has managed to acquire a British steel maker that has been a symbol of Britain's industrial power and at the same time its dominion over India has been perceived as quite ironic. Only time will show whether Tata will be able to truly benefit from the many expected synergies for the deal and not make the typical mistakes made in many large M&A deal during this beginning period.

"I believe this will be the first step in showing that Indian industry can in fact step outside the shores of India in an international marketplace and acquit itself as a global player." — Ratan Tata

Table 11.1

Corus Group (in UK)	19
Tata Steel - Jamshedpur	10
Tata Steel - Jharkhan	12
Tata Steel - Orissa	6
Tata Steel - Chattisgarh	5
Nat Steel - Singapore	2
Millennium Steel - Thailand	1.7
Aggregate projected capacity	55.7

Table 11.2: Global steel ranking

Company	Capacity in (million tonnes)
Arcelor - Mittal	110.0
Pippon Steel	32.0
POSCO	30.5
JEF Steel	30.0
Tata Steel - Corus	27.7
Bao Steel China	23.0
US Steel	19.0
Nucor	18.5
Riva	17.5
Thyssen Krupp	16.5

Tata Steel-Corus Integration

"One enterprise – two entities" has been the driving philosophy of the integration process which has been designed at two levels: one at a strategic level and the other to maximise synergy benefits in various functions of the business.

A joint team was mandated to identify where the two entities needed to work together or work in a coordinated manner and also the processes which would be managed separately by the entities. The teams study and recommendations have resulted in the implementation of a governance structure in January 2008 to bring alive the 'Operating Model' designed.

To oversee the progress on the strategy and integration plans and ensure that key milestones are met, a Strategy & Integration Committee (SIC) has been constituted under Chairmanship of Group Chairman. A structured approach has been followed for the synergy and integration in various functional areas. Joint integration teams formed for key areas have identified synergies worth USD 450 million and action plans drawn up will ensure that these targets are realised by end March 2010.

Site specific workshops and knowledge sharing sessions have been conducted at various plant locations for identifying breakthrough improvements in the area of throughput increase and cost reduction.

During the year, synergy benefits of USD 76 million have been realised. Tata Steel has derived the benefits in the area of manufacturing, whereas in Corus, the benefits are from reduction in taxation and in shared services in the area of legal, investor relations, etc. in the Corporate Centre.

Details of Financing of Corus Deal

- The Net Funding Requirement of Corus is Rs. 56,150 crore (USD 12.90 billion).
- Tata Steel gave a loan to Tata Steel Asia Holdings (TSAH) of Rs. 11,750 crore.
- TSAH raised bridge loans of Rs. 10,900 crore.

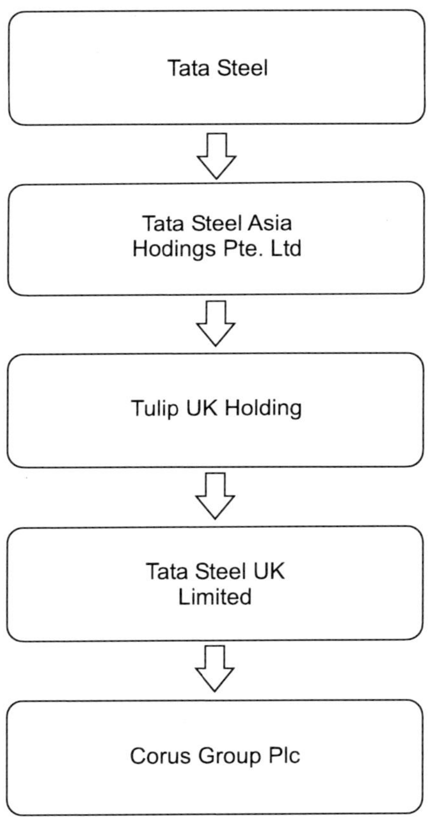

Figure 11.1

- Tulip UK Holding raised a mezzanine loan of Rs. 2,600 crore.
- Thus a total of Rs. 25,250 crore were infused into Tata Steel UK Limited by way of Equity.
- Tata Steel UK Limited raised senior debts and mezzanine loans of 30,900 crore. The total of Rs. 56,150 crores was used to pay for the Corus Acquisition.

Head I Win, Tail You Lose....

Tata Steel acquisition of Corus, one of the most startling US$ 12bn leveraged buy out (LBO) by the Indian company so far, received lukewarm response from investing fraternity. The initial excitement was overpowered by extreme nervousness on fear of its burden on Tata Steel balance sheet immediately. The other concern was impact of failure of such a large acquisition, in case it falls through, on Tata Steel's existence. It was like small fish that is trying to gulp the bigger one felt investors – local as well as foreign. In this background, Ideas 1st Research initiated coverage with objective to gauge the impact of Corus Zero on Tata Steel. To ascertain this we looked into the financing structure, which shows that Tata Steel has put in place a process before aggressively bidding for Corus. The finances are raised in such a manner that Tata Steel balance sheet will have to bear bare minimum load on one hand and it ensures that funds required for its future growth is not hampered. We initiate this coverage with "buy" recommendation with minimum price target of Rs. 670 Ex-right with a further up side target of Rs. 1,000. We expect Tata Steel to surpass our price target once Corus integration is complete.

Investment Positives

The Corus is not expected to hurt, the way market fears

Assuming that Tata Steel is not able to manage the mega buyout of Corus and end up with chaos, the investor fraternity has excessively discounted Tata Steel's stock price. Counterfeiting the fact, our examination says, even if we consider corus acquisition a dud investment, the extremely strong cash flows of Tata Steel will not let this issue influence its future growth and expansions.

Deprived of the rally, all other stell stocks gained while the index mover lost the impetus

Tata Steel being the most efficient and totally integrated player carrying capative reserves of iron ore and coal both, missed the bandwagon, whereas the peer stocks gained in line because of the investor's changed insight on the steel industry. We believe removing Corus out of picture, Tata Steel would have maintained lead among the steel stocks.

The fine art of financing the deal

Tata management has adopted the prudent fund raising model for Corus acquisition, in which Tata Steel will put up US$ 4.1 bn, rest from Tata Singapore and non-recourse loan on corus to the tune of US$ 6.14 bn, limiting the risk factor. Thus, impact on Tata Steel balance sheet will be at most US$ 4.1 bn of the total acquisition of Corus of US$ 12.9 bn.

What if synergy materialized

Without considering any synergistic gains from Corus, Tata Steel's stock price should have made its lifetime high. With everything working smoothly the way Tata Steel envisage we envisage Tata Steel to be in the top league, hitherto elusive, for any Indian steel company. Some of the combined benefits are technology edge for Tata Steel, entry into high margin European market and backward integration for Corus (who owns number of high end value added product patents) with steady and cost effective steel slabs.

Unconventional Way of Looking at the Tata

Tata Steel, a totally integrated private sector steel company is all set to prove its mettle. Corus acquisition that has unnerved the market as well as investors fraternity is not expected to hurt the interests of Tata Steel shareholders as feared. **First** we will look at the **plausible scenario of the Tata Steel market performance if it would not have gone for the LBO of corus. Second, impact Tata Steel investors will have to bear** if the total investment in corus goes down to tubes.

Tata Steel Price Sans Corus?

While conventional reports churns numbers and try to forecast years hence in terms of company's growth prospects vis-a-vis market capitalization (stock price performance), we would start with hypothetical example of what could have been Tata Steel price sans Corus.

Tata steel was quoted between Rs. 640/680 when the metal stocks were in limelight. At the same point in time price of other steel stocks such as SAIL, JSW and JSPL were quoted around Rs. 95, Rs. 360 and Rs. 2000 respectively. Since then, all these stocks after riding a roller coaster have gone up by around 40 per cent to 50 per cent thanks to change of perception of Indian steel companies.

Hence, we can safely assume that Tata Steel would have gone up least by 50 per cent if not more from its lower band of Rs. 640/ 680 to about Rs. 1000. the assumption is based on the fact that Tata Steel is most efficient totally integrated steel plant and should have benefited more as compared to peers group. Not to mention the fact that they are sitting on a huge pile of reserve of two of the most important raw materials—iron ore and coal.

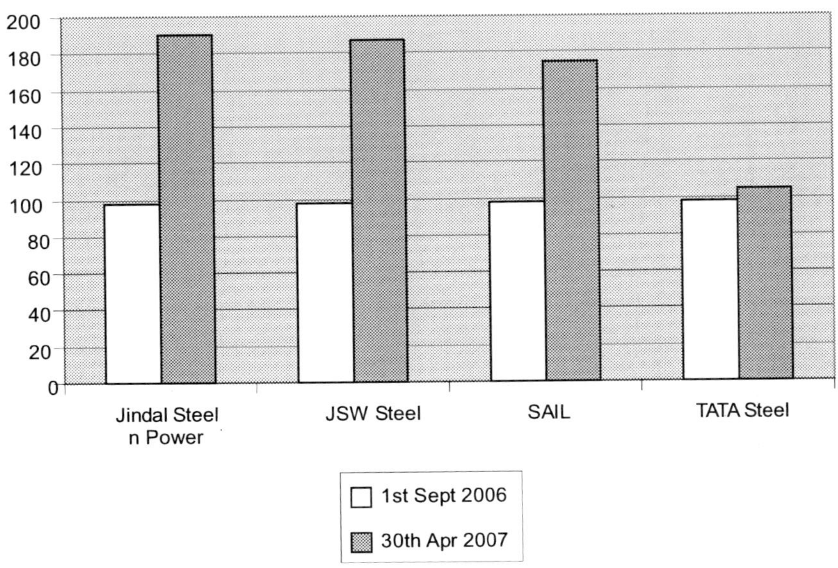

Figure 11.2: Price movement of Tata Steel vis-a-vis other steel stocks.

Fear Factor

Failure to handle the LBO
The real fear as everybody sees is Tata Steel **failure to handle leverage route** that it has chosen to bid for Corus - which was considered one of the largest LBO by any Indian company so far. Besides integration – cultural or in terms of working also contributed to nervousness. The critics argue that without overhauling the Corus and making it trim and fit, it would not be possible for Tata steel to smoothly run the Anglo-Dutch giant. They further argue that Tata Steel itself has blotted workforce with cost per tonne per worker is about Rs. 3000, considered fairly high when compared with some of the peers such as Jindal Steel as well as other private sector companies.

Of course, the worst fear is the price of US$ 12.9 bn it would raise to complete the acquisition of corus. The fact of the LBO and its financing pattern has soothing impact on the investment fraternity and Tata Steel share price recovered from low of around Rs. 420 to about Rs. 550. However, all does not seem to be as questions that still worry investors at large are possibility of Corus becoming a dud investment.

First the Fine Art of Funding

Total funding plan

Total Amount Required to Finance the Acquisition	: **$12.9 billion**
Tata Steel's committed equity contribution	: $ **4.1 billion**
Out of its share of $4.1 billion Tata Steel invested	: $ **1.8 billion**

This $ 1.8 billion (Rs. 7900 crore), which was made through **internal generation** of **$700 million (Rs. 3000 crore), external commercial borrowings** of **$500 million (Rs. 2170 crore)** and funds from **preferential issue of equity shares** to Tata Sons at an average price of 499.7 per share that fetched **$640 million (Rs. 2770 crore).**

Tata Steel approved two rights issues and one foreign issue to raise remaining: **$ 2.3 billion** of its committed contribution. The remaining: **$8.8 billion** was financed through a non-recourse **debt** arranged by a consortium of banks for **$ 6.14 billion** at **Tata Steel**

UK and the balance **$2.66 billion** raised in the form of bridge finance by its subsidiary **Tata Steel Asia Singapore.**

The trick is that Tata is taking bulk of long term debt to the tune of about US$ 6.14 bn that is non-recourse on Tata steel assets or shareholders. Out of the above financing, total of US$ 8.8 bn would be raised on Corus assets. The direct debt burden of Tata Steel will rise by about Rs. 20,000 million, which is insignificant by any standard for its balance sheet size. The picture is clearer as despite the Corus takeover being considered LBO, the gearing as well as interest outgo remains extremely manageable.

CORUS ZERO

In the above scenario even if the Corus becomes totally dud investment and things do not work out as expected, Tata Steel shareholders will not have to be deprived of its future growth. Tata Steel has strong cash flow to take care of its future expansion without being worried about Corus impact. In the year ended march 2006 its cash flow including differed tax was around Rs. 40,000 million and it is expected to throw equivalent or more cash at least for next couple of years. Hence, the maximum punishment Tata Steel should have received is **by 1/3rd of the assumed price of Rs. 1000** (based on the assumption of sans Corus). Hence, we strongly believe that Tata Steel should be at least around **Rs. 670** ex-rights even if Corus becomes zero.

What about Corus

Corus stand-alone would have been quoted at around 550 p taking into rise of stock prices of all the international steel giants. During the period under the review, prices of all the international steel stocks such as US steel, POSCO, Nippon and Arcelor Mittal holdings went up by 30 per cent to 80 per cent due to re-rating and consolidation buzz. With steady and cost effective steel supply being available to Corus from Tata steel, its valuation should increase, as the company will have to be re-rated in line with those with assured linkages.

In the changed scenario we can safely assume that investment of Tata Steel into the Corus will not be eroded if not improved. Total

Table 11.3: Company and the consolidated and stand-alone financial accounts for the year ended 31st March, 2008.

	Tata Steel Group		Tata Steel Stand-alone	
	2007-08	2006-07	2007-08	2006-07
Net Sales / Income	131,535.88	25,212.38	19,693.28	17,551.09
Total Expenditure (net of expenditure transferred to capital)	113,542.76	17,762.23	11,469.74	10,577.82
Operating Profit	17,993.12	7,450.15	8,223.54	6,973.27
Add: Dividend and other income	574.21	438.07	335.00	433.67
Profit before Interest, Depreciation, Exceptional items and Taxes	18,567.33	7,888.22	8,558.54	7,406.94
Less: Interest	4,183.76	411.19	878.70	173.90
Profit before Depreciation, Exceptional items and Taxes	14,383.57	7,477.03	7,679.84	7,233.04
Less: Depreciation	4,136.95	1,010.98	834.61	819.29
Profit before Exceptional items and Taxes	10,246.62	6,466.05	6,845.23	6,413.75
Add/(Less): Exceptional items	6,124.44	(153.03)	221.13	(152.10)
Profit before taxes	16,371.06	6,313.02	7,066.36	6,261.65
Less: Provision for current taxation	3,353.73	2,145.52	2,252.00	2,076.01
Less: Provision for deferred taxation	674.58	(15.52)	108.33	(52.51)
Less: Provision for Fringe Benefits tax	20.99	17.41	19.00	16.00
Profit after taxes	12,321.76	4,165.61	4,687.03	4,222.15
Less: Minority Interest	139.94	67.52		
Add: Share of profit of Associates	168.16	79.18		
Profit after minority interest and share of profit of Associates	12,349.98	4,177.27	4,687.03	4,222.15
Add: Balance brought forward from the previous year	4,840.39	3,298.06	4,593.98	2,976.16
Balance	17,190.37	7,475.33	9,281.01	7,198.31
Which the Directors have appropriated as under to				
(i) Proposed Dividend	1,167.86	942.87	1,168.93	943.91
(ii) Dividend on Compulsorily Convertible Preference Shares	22.19		22.19	
(iii) Tax on dividend	207.75	163.42	202.43	160.42
(iv) Special reserve	5,913.16	3.95	—	—
(v) Statutory reserve	96.30	—	—	—
(vi) General reserve	1,549.08	1,524.70	1,500.00	1,500.00
Total	**8,956.34**	**2,634.94**	**2,893.55**	**2,604.33**
Leaving a Balance to be carried forward	8,234.03	4,840.39	6,387.46	4,593.98

investment of Tata Steel into the Corus is approx. to the tune of Rs. 180,000 mn which is approx. Rs. 200 ex- rights taking into account Rs. 180,000 mn investments divided by increased capital of Rs. 900 crore approx., (Rs. **180,000 mn / 9,000 mn = Rs. 200 per share)**

Immediate Synergy Benefit to Tata Steel

We believe that Tata Steel in turn will have stable customer in form of Corus. Besides, Tata Steel will also benefit in terms of technology transfer. It is almost impossible to put exact numbers to benefit of synergies on the valuation of Tata Steel stock, but we believe that it should be at **least Rs. 150 per share**. Our assumption is based on the announcement of Tata Steel management that immediate synergy benefit will be to the tune of US$ 350 mn p.a (Rs. 14000 mn). We value this saving at about Rs. 14000 mn (10 times) on the valuation of Tata Steel. This works out to be approx. Rs. 155/160 (Rs. 14000 mn/9000 mn approx post dilution).

Business Results

Tata Steel Group, on a consolidated basis had a net sales of Rs. 131,536 crore in the FY 2007-08 against Rs. 25,212 crore in the FY 2006-07. The total operating expenditure (before interest expenses and depreciation) was at Rs. 113,543 crore in FY 2007-08 against Rs. 17,762 crore in FY 2006-07. The major components of the expenditure in FY 2007-08 were purchase of finished and semi-finished steel, raw materials consumed, staff cost, freight and handling and other expenditure. The interest charges were at Rs. 4,184 crore in the current financial year against Rs. 411 crore in the last financial year. The exceptional items , a gain of Rs. 6,124 crore include the actuarial gain of Rs. 5,907 crore in Corus on funds for employee benefits. The gain is on account of recovery of bond yields used to discount scheme liabilities and recovery in asset values of the scheme funds. These gains are required to be accounted for through the Profit & Loss Account under Indian GAAP.

Pursuant to the Accounting Standard AS 21 issued by the Institute of Chartered Accountants of India, consolidated financial statements presented by the Company include financial information of its subsidiaries. The Company has received the approval from the Ministry of Corporate Affairs vide its Letter No. 47/337/2008-CL-

III dated 4th June, 2008, exempting the Company from attaching the balance sheet, profit and loss account and other documents of the subsidiary companies to the balance sheet of the company.

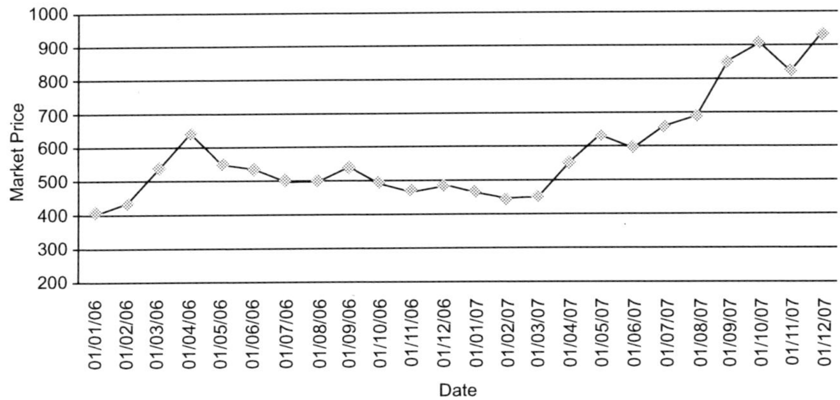

Figure 11.3: Tata Steel

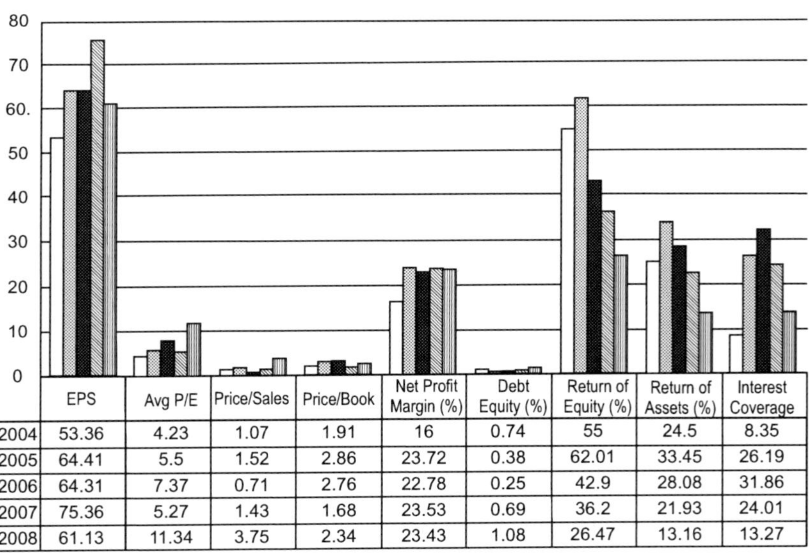

	EPS	Avg P/E	Price/Sales	Price/Book	Net Profit Margin (%)	Debt Equity (%)	Return of Equity (%)	Return of Assets (%)	Interest Coverage
2004	53.36	4.23	1.07	1.91	16	0.74	55	24.5	8.35
2005	64.41	5.5	1.52	2.86	23.72	0.38	62.01	33.45	26.19
2006	64.31	7.37	0.71	2.76	22.78	0.25	42.9	28.08	31.86
2007	75.36	5.27	1.43	1.68	23.53	0.69	36.2	21.93	24.01
2008	61.13	11.34	3.75	2.34	23.43	1.08	26.47	13.16	13.27

Figure 11.4: Tata Steel

As per the terms of the approval letter, a statement containing brief financial details of the Company's subsidiaries for the year ended 31st March, 2008 is included in the annual report. The annual accounts of these subsidiaries and the related detailed information will be made available to any member of the Company / its subsidiaries seeking such information at any point of time and are also available for inspection by any member of the Company / its subsidiaries at the Company's Registered Office. The annual accounts of the said subsidiaries will also be available for inspection as above at the Head Office of the respective subsidiary companies.

On 2nd April, 2007, Tata Steel UK Limited ('TSUK'), a subsidiary of Tulip UK Holding No. 1 which in turn is a subsidiary of Tata Steel completed the acquisition of Corus Group plc ('Corus'). The consolidated results include the financial statements of Corus from 2nd April, 2007. Consequently, the data of the previous year is not comparable.

In an overall analysis, it can be observed that the Tata-Corus deal was perceived to be a dream acquisition, given the long term strategy and positioning of Tata in the European markets at that critical juncture. For some time later, due to the economic downturn, the Corus factory remained closed. It remains to be seen how successfully Tata would make the best of the deal and profit from the same in the long term.

CASE - 2: ARCELOR MITTAL—CASE OF HOSTILE TAKEOVER

History of Arcelor

Arcelor was created through the merger of

- Arbed (Luxembourg)
- Aceralia (Spain)
- Usinor (France)

The three European groups were determined to mobilise their technical, industrial, and commercial resources in order to create a global leader in the steel industry.

The merger was officially launched on 19 February 2001 and the choice of the Arcelor name was announced on 12 December 2001. The merger became effective on 18 February 2002 when Arcelor shares were listed on several stock exchanges.

Arcelor is the largest steel producer in Europe and Latin America, and the second largest steel producer worldwide, with carbon and stainless steel shipments of 46.8 million tons and revenues of over 32.6 billion Euros, approximately CAD$46 billion, in 2005. Arcelor was created in February 2002 through the merger of three European steelmakers: Aceralia from Spain, Arbed from Luxembourg and Usinor from France. Control of Dofasco Inc., a Canadian-based integrated steel producer, was acquired by Arcelor in February 2006. Dofasco represents Arcelor's steelmaking facilities in North America.

History of Mittal Steel

Mittal, a Dutch company, is the world's largest steel company, with annual steel shipments of 49.2 million tons, accounting for approximately 4.0 per cent of world steel production (estimated to be 1,219 million tons in 2005) and revenues of over CAD$32.6 billion in 2005. It has steel operations in 16 countries throughout four continents and sales and marketing offices in 11 other countries. Mittal's operations are located principally in North America (including Mexico), Central and Eastern Europe, Africa, and Kazakhstan.

CEO Lakshmi Mittal's family owned 88 per cent of the company and its headquarter was in Rotterdam, Netherlands. The Company was the world's largest steel producer by volume and also the largest in turnover and is now a part of ArcelorMittal. It was the major player in *Steel*, Flat Steel products, Coated Steel, Tubes and Pipes.

Mittal was formed from the combination of Ispat International NV and LNM Holdings Group. This was followed by the 2005 merger between Mittal and the International Steel Group Inc. ("ISG") in the United States. Following the ISG merger, Mittal shipped approximately 19.7 million tons of steel (including inter-company shipments) in North America in 2005. This amount represents approximately 14 per cent of the 138.3 million tons of North

American steel production. Mittal generated sales of USD$12.5 billion in North America in 2005 (approximately CAD$14.3 billion.

Mittal's Strategy: Mittal Steel Perspective

L.N. Mittal has expanded his steel empire and enlarged his manufacturing capacity more than 10 times to 70 million tonnes over the last **10 years mostly by acquiring state-run steel mills in privatisation programmes across the globe.** These assets were acquired at throwaway prices as the steel price cycle had hit rock bottom during those years. He revived the plants through heavy cost cutting including massive layoffs. He did not face much opposition to such heavy restructuring as the companies were in pathetic shape and would have been anyway shut down if such measures had not been adopted.

Following are the Main points for Sustainable Competitive advantage in Steel Industry:

- A company in the commodity industry can have sustainable competitive advantages from two sources - superior management and enduring low cost position (which is also dependent on a superior management).
- Consolidation in a commodity industry improves the profitability of the top firms as it gives them better pricing power.

To bridge the gap with the top steel companies and emerge as the single-largest steel producer, Mittal courted an American, Wilbur Ross, who employed the same strategy as Mittal to build a steel empire in the US. The merger between Mittal Steel and Ross's International Steel Group created the top steel producer in the world.

But the gap between Mittal Steel and large competitors like Arcelor and Nippon Steel was not substantial. Arcelor was bigger in terms of total revenues and many others were more profitable as they produced more value added products.

Privatisation opportunities have dried up and even if one does arise in the future, the up trend in steel prices has pushed up the cost of acquiring manufacturing assets. Hence further inorganic growth acquisition of state owned companies has become less feasible.

Building new plants takes time. Mittal Steel has made not much progress after announcing a 10-million tonnes per annum steel plant in India last year. Even if the company finalise the agreement for mining lease this year, the plant would not be able to commence commercial production before 2010.

Mittal Steel had acquired a minority stake in a Chinese steel company. But a majority acquisition needs the blessings of the Chinese government, which may be difficult to come by. China has built up a huge domestic steel capacity, in excess of 350-million tonnes per annum, and hence setting up a new plant may not be attractive.

Merger of Arcelor with Mittal Steel

Mergers between any of the other top 5 steel producers would have toppled Mittal Steel from its perch as the top producer. Therefore in order to protect and secure its turf as the single most influential steel producer in the world, Mittal was forced to acquire a large competitor. Arcelor was the best fit in terms of geographical presence and product mix. Besides, Arcelor had a widely distributed shareholding structure which made an acquisition easier.

The company was the target of a takeover bid by its rival Mittal Steel on 27-01-2006. However, the bid resulted in substantial increase in Arcelor's share value. Two members of the board of Arcelor, Guillermo Ulacia and Jacques Chabanier also resigned suddenly. On May 26, 2006 Arcelor announced its intention to merge with Severstal. Since then several economists, media and shareholders have questioned the intentions of Arcelor in announcing its merger with Severstal due to a perceived opacity in the transaction. But on 25 June, 2006, the Arcelor board decided to go ahead with the merger with Mittal Steel and scrapped plans for Severstal merger. The new company is now called "Arcelor Mittal". Arcelor also paid Severstal €140 million as a "fine" for the fall-out of their failed talks. Lakshmi Mittal (owner of Mittal Steel) became the president and Joseph Kinsch (formerly Arcelor chairman) was appointed chairman of the new company till his retirement. Arcelor's merger with Mittal created the worldwide leader in the steel industry, increasing its bargaining power with suppliers and consumers. Mittal steel has agreed to pay 40.37 euros—a share to Arcelor, almost double the amount offered by Mittal last time.

Reaction to the Takeover

Arcelor's directors strongly opposed the takeover, with Arcelor's chief executive at that time, Guy Dollé, even dismissing Mittal as a "company of Indians". The French, Luxembourg and Spanish governments strongly opposed the takeover. The Belgian government on the other hand declared its stance as neutral and invited both parties to deliver a business plan with the future investments in research in the Belgian steel plants. The French opposition was initially very fierce and has been criticized in the British, American and Indian media as double standards and economic nationalism in Europe. Indian commerce minister Kamal Nath warned that any attempt by France to block the deal would lead to a trade war between India and France.

On June 20, the above claim by economists was confirmed when Severstal increased its valuation of Arcelor. Management of Arcelor had in fact undervalued the company itself. The capability of management which had openly supported the previous valuation of Arcelor came into question. Further the combined markets of France, Belgium, Luxembourg and Spain chided Arcelor management and suspended trading of its stock.

On June 26, the Board of Directors recommended the approval of the improved Mittal offer (49% improvement compared to the initial offer with 108% improvement of the cash component), proposed the creation of Arcelor-Mittal with industrial and corporate governance model based on Arcelor and scheduled a corporate meeting for June 30 to vote on this.

The Merger Process

2006 was a very exciting and challenging year for Arcelor Mittal. The new company was at the forefront of the consolidation process, leading the industry through mergers and acquisitions.

In January 2006, Mittal Steel launched a $22.7 billion hostile offer to Arcelor's shareholders. The deal was split between Mittal Shares (75 %) and cash (25 %).Under the offer, Arcelor shareholders would have received 4 Mittal Steel shares and 35 euros for every 5 Arcelor shares they held.

The Controversy

1. Arcelor Management

The management was extremely hostile to Mittal Steel's bid. It believed to have been doing the acquisitions and not the other way around. The CEO of Arcelor dismissed Mittal Steel as a "company of Indians".

2. European governments

The French Government and the government of Luxembourg was against the deal. The European Union approved of the deal in May 2006.

3. Moves by Arcelor to counter the bid

(i) **Declaration of dividend:** On February 16, Arcelor declared a dividend of 1.2 euros to convince the shareholders of a positive situation under current management.

(ii) **The Russian Angle:** To thwart the offer from Mittal Steel, Arcelor released a 13 billion euro merger plan with Severstal, a Russian company

(iii) **Role of Guy Dolle:** Analysts believe that Guy Dolle had issues with the personality and management of L.N. Mittal. Guy Dolle raised several issues about the safety record of Mittal. Guy Dolle is not a part of the new Arcelor-Mittal organization.

4. The stance of Indian government

Most Indians believed that the deal was not getting pushed because of Lakshmi Mittal's nationality. The Indian government raised the issue through commerce minister Kamal Nath. L.N. Mittal himself felt that there was no case of "racism" here as Mittal Steel was a European company and NOT an Indian one.

On 25th June, 2006 the deal finally clinched when the shareholders of Arcelor agreed to Mittal Steel's offer. Mittal had to considerably sweeten the initial offer-by raising its valuation of Arcelor to $32.9 billion. The Mittal family holds 43 per cent of the combined group.The combined company holds 10 per cent of the global market for steel.

Table 11.4

Parameters	Unit	Mittal Steel	Arcelor
Capacity	MT	63.0	46.7
Revenues	US$ bn	28.1	39.1
EBIDTA margins	%	20.6	17.3
PAT margins	%	12.0	11.8

After Subsequent Offering Period, Mittal Steel Holds 93.7% of Arcelor's Share Capital

Mittal Steel acquired the Arcelor shares tendered in its offer according to the following distribution:

- 7,473,725 Arcelor shares in the primary mixed cash and exchange offer;
- 1,630,315 Arcelor shares in the secondary cash offer; and
- 3,617,625 Arcelor shares in the secondary exchange offer.

As a result of the above, holders who tendered Arcelor shares (or Arcelor ADSs) in the secondary cash offer, in the aggregate, received the all-cash consideration of €40.40 per Arcelor share (or U.S. dollar equivalent) in respect of only 38.55% of the Arcelor shares that they tendered in the secondary cash offer and received the standard mixed consideration of €12.55 in cash and 13:12 Mittal Steel class A common share for each Arcelor share (or an amount in U.S. dollars equal to €12.55 in cash and 1.083 Mittal Steel class A common share in exchange for each Arcelor ADS) in respect of 61.45% of the Arcelor shares that they tendered in the secondary cash offer. It is, however, important to note that these figures do not take into account the full effect of fraction of shares or reflect the effect of rounding. The consideration that holders will receive in exchange for Arcelor shares (or Arcelor ADSs) that they tendered in the primary offer and in the secondary exchange offer will not be subject to any adjustment and will be paid in the amounts described in the offer prospectus, as supplemented.

Consideration

As a result, 13.8 million new Mittal Steel shares were issued as consideration for the offer and the cash portion of the total offer consideration was around €160.6 million. Once these new shares were issued on the settlement date, there were a total of

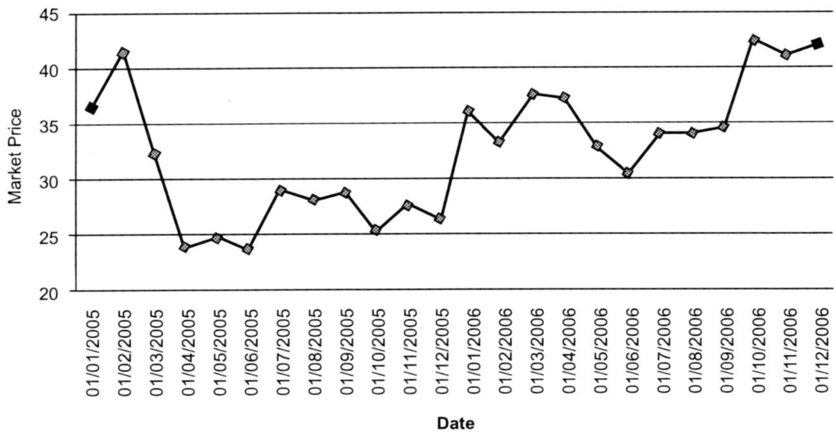

Figure 11.5: Arcelor Mittal

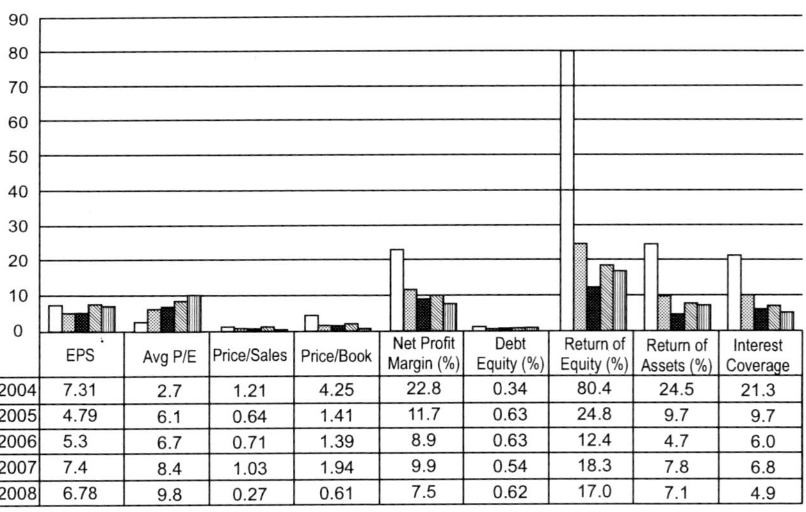

	EPS	Avg P/E	Price/Sales	Price/Book	Net Profit Margin (%)	Debt Equity (%)	Return of Equity (%)	Return of Assets (%)	Interest Coverage
2004	7.31	2.7	1.21	4.25	22.8	0.34	80.4	24.5	21.3
2005	4.79	6.1	0.64	1.41	11.7	0.63	24.8	9.7	9.7
2006	5.3	6.7	0.71	1.39	8.9	0.63	12.4	4.7	6.0
2007	7.4	8.4	1.03	1.94	9.9	0.54	18.3	7.8	6.8
2008	6.78	9.8	0.27	0.61	7.5	0.62	17.0	7.1	4.9

Figure 11.6: Arcelor Mittal

approximately 1,392.3 million Mittal Steel shares issued and the market capitalization of Mittal Steel was approximately €36.8 billion (US$47 billion) (based on the closing Mittal Steel share price on Euronext Paris of €26.42 and on the NYSE of US$33.76 on August 25, 2006), with a free float of approximately 769 million shares representing about 55.23% of the total market capitalization.

Arcelor Mittal

- Arcelor Mittal is now the largest steel company in the world.
- Arcelor Mittal is the leader in major global markets, including automotive, construction, household appliances and packaging.
- The company is headquartered in southern Luxembourg city, the former seat of Arcelor.
- Lakshmi Mittal (owner of Mittal Steel), a non-resident Indian is the Chairman and CEO
- It employs 310,000 employees in more than 60 countries.
- Arcelor Mittal key financials for 2007 show revenues of US$ 105.2 billion.
- A crude steel production of 116 million tonnes, representing around 10% of world steel output.
- As of May 17, 2008, the market capitalization of Arcelor Mittal was $144.37 billion.

End Result

The deal was finally clinched when the shareholders of Arcelor agreed to Mittal Steel's offer ending the transaction that had dragged on for months. Mittal had to however considerably sweeten the initial offer. Under severe pressure to counteract the Arcelor-Severstal merger, Mittal had to raise its valuation of Arcelor to $32.9 billion. The Mittal family holds 43 percent of the combined group. The combined company holds 10 percent of the global market for steel. The consolidation phase is well and truly underway. If Mittal Steel had succeeded in acquiring Arcelor as per the terms of its original bid announced in January, it would have been the end of Arcelor and its management. It would have created one giant Mittal Steel, double its original size, and LN Mittal would have remained the lord and master of a global steel empire. The deal as it is finally negotiated and recommended by the Arcelor board is vastly different. The price being offered by Mittal now is nearly 90 per cent higher than his original price, which means the Mittal family's stake in the merged entity would be just 43 per cent. Besides, Mittal Steel seems to be doing almost everything possible to meet Arcelor's demands.

The Arcelor chairman becomes the chairman of the merged entity and its CEO remains on the management board despite his known hostility to Mittal. Arcelor would nominate a majority of the directors and even the CEO is likely to be an Arcelor nominee. The Mittal family would also have to go by the board decisions and vote accordingly for a period of three years, unless LN Mittal uses his veto powers. The family cannot increase its stake beyond 45 per cent for a period of five years.

Worse still, the merged company would be registered and based in Luxembourg and would be called, not Mittal Steel and not even Mittal-Arcelor, but Arcelor-Mittal.

The Future

Even though Mittal was forced to concede a lot of ground to Arcelor, he still emerged as the single-largest shareholder in the merged entity. Arcelor-Mittal cannot be toppled from its position as the top producer in the foreseeable future, unless China decides to consolidate its steel industry under a couple of companies. The Arcelor-Mittal merger may trigger more consolidations in the steel industry much to the benefit of all steel producers. Cost savings would hopefully improve the cash flows of the merged entity and this would make Arcelor-Mittal financially stronger as well. The big task before Arcelor-Mittal is the process of integrating the two companies with diverse strategies and culture. Many high profile mergers have failed to deliver the anticipated results because of the inability to achieve smooth integration between the merging companies. L N Mittal has already stated that he would be spending the next few years to ensure that the merger goes ahead smoothly.

L.N. Mittal would become chairman of Arcelor-Mittal after Joseph Kinsch retires. The Mittal family can increase its stake beyond 45 per cent after five years and it will not take much of an effort to take the stake above 50 per cent. His son Aditya has reportedly refused to take up a senior management position in the merged entity at this juncture, though it is only a matter of time before he takes over from the professional managers from Arcelor.

When the next downturn in steel price cycle arrives, some of the steel producers are sure to face financial difficulties. Arcelor-Mittal, with stronger finances, can be expected to go out prowling for more acquisitions and, it is possible, that this time Aditya Mittal would be spearheading those buyouts.

ANALYSIS OF INCOME STATEMENT (AFTER THE MERGER)

Full Year and Fourth Quarter 2006 Results

Increase in Net Income and EPS

Net income for the twelve months ended December 31, 2006, was $5.2 billion, or $5.29 per share, as compared with net income of $3.4 billion, or $4.99 per share, for the twelve months ended December 31, 2005.

Increase in SALES and OPERATING INCOME

Consolidated sales and operating income for the three months ended December 31, 2006, were $23.2 billion and $2.6 billion, respectively, as compared with $18.0 billion and $2.6 billion, respectively, for the three months ended September 30, 2006. Consolidated sales and operating income for the twelve months ended December 31, 2006, were $58.9 billion and $7.5 billion, respectively, as compared with $28.1 billion and $4.7 billion, respectively, for the twelve months ended December 31, 2005.

Increase in SALES (VOLUME)

Total steel shipments for the three months ended December 31, 2006, were 26.7 million metric tonnes as compared with 22.9 million metric tonnes for the three months ended September 30, 2006. Total steel shipments for the twelve months ended December 31, 2006, were 78.1 million metric tonnes as compared with 44.6 million metric tonnes for the twelve months ended December 31, 2005.

Increase in NET INCOME
Net income for the three months ended December 31, 2006, was $1.9 billion, or $1.38 per share, as compared with net income of $1.8 billion, or $1.58 per share, for the three months ended September 30, 2006. Net income for the twelve months ended December 31, 2006, increased to $5.2 billion as compared with $3.4 billion for the twelve months ended December 31, 2005

Synergies of Merger

Steel shipments for the twelve months ended December 31, 2006, were 75% higher as compared with the twelve months ended December 31, 2005, primarily due to the inclusion of Arcelor, Mittal Steel Kryviy Rih and Mittal Steel ISG Inc. Excluding the impact of Arcelor, Mittal Steel Kryviy Rih and Mittal Steel ISG Inc., steel shipments for the twelve months ended December 31, 2006, were 7% higher as compared with the twelve months ended December 31, 2005, primarily due to increased shipments within the Long Carbon Americas and Europe and AACIS segments.

Operating income for the twelve months ended December 31, 2006, was $7.5 billion as compared with $4.7 billion for the twelve months ended December 31, 2005, primarily due to the inclusion of Arcelor, Mittal Steel Kryviy Rih and Mittal Steel ISG Inc. Excluding the impact of Arcelor, Mittal Steel Kryviy Rih and Mittal Steel ISG Inc., operating income for the twelve months ended December 31, 2006, was 11% lower at $4.1 billion as compared with $4.6 billion for the twelve months ended December 31, 2005.

Analysis of Cash Flow Statement (After the Merger)

The CASH FLOW increased after the Merger substantially

APPENDIX

Income Statement
All Numbers in thousands (USD)

PERIOD ENDING	Jun-07	Mar-07	Dec-06	Sep-06
Operating Revenue/Sales)	27,223,000	24,476,000	23,203,000	18,007,000
Total Revenues	27,223,000	24,476,000	23,203,000	18,007,000

Cost of Sales	21,897,000	20,130,000	16,748,000	14,566,000
Cost of Sales with Depreciation	21,897,000	20,130,000	19,044,000	14,717,000
Gross Margin	*	*	10,459,000	*
Gross Operating Profit	5,326,000	4,346,000	6,455,000	3,441,000
Selling, Gen. & Administrative Expense	*	*	2,960,000	*
Operating Income	4,232,000	3,455,000	2,630,000	2,558,000
Operating Income b/f Depreciation (EBITDA)	5,326,000	4,346,000	3,495,000	3,441,000
Depreciation	1,094,000	891,000	865,000	883,000
Depreciation Unrecognized	1,094,000	891,000	-1,431,000	732,000
Operating Income After Depreciation	4,232,000	3,455,000	2,630,000	2,558,000
Interest Income	*	*	251,000	*
Earnings from Equity Interest	195,000	154,000	163,000	100,000
Other Income, Net	62,000	21,000	265,000	2,000
Total Income Avail for Interest Expense (EBIT)	4,489,000	3,630,000	3,309,000	2,660,000
Interest Expense	182,000	10,000	649,000	280,000
Pre-tax Income (EBT)	4,307,000	3,620,000	2,660,000	2,380,000
Income Taxes	1,087,000	934,000	377,000	276,000
Minority Interest	497,000	436,000	366,000	302,000
Income before Income Taxes	4,307,000	3,620,000	2,660,000	2,380,000
Net Income from Continuing Operations	2,723,000	2,250,000	1,917,000	1,802,000
Net Income from Total Operations	2,723,000	2,250,000	1,917,000	1,802,000
Total Net Income	2,723,000	2,250,000	1,917,000	1,802,000
Normalized Income	2,723,000	2,250,000	1,917,000	1,802,000
Net Income Available for Common	2,723,000	2,250,000	1,917,000	1,802,000

CASH FLOW STATEMENT

All numbers in thousands(USD)

PERIOD ENDING	6 Month Jun-07	3 Month Mar-07	12 Month Dec-06	9 Month Sep-06
Cash Flow From Operating Activities				
Net Income (Loss)	4,973,000	2,250,000	6,086,000	3,309,000
Depreciation	1,985,000	891,000	2,296,000	1,431,000
Deferred Income Taxes	*	*	*	85,000

Operating (Gains) Losses	664,000	162,000	99,000	341,000
(Increase) Decrease in Receivables	*	*	-128,000	*
(Increase) Decrease in Inventories	*	*	-584,000	*
(Increase) Decrease in Payables	*	*	854,000	*
(Increase) Decrease in Other Working Capital	-1,240,000	-653,000	-768,000	-2,274,000
Other Non-Cash Items	*	*	-733,000	-37,000
Net Cash from Continuing Operations	6,382,000	2,650,000	7,122,000	2,855,000
Net Cash from Operating Activities	6,382,000	2,650,000	7,122,000	2,855,000
Sale of Property, Plant, Equipment	*	*	*	96,000
Sale of Long Term Investments	*	*	*	24,000
Purchase of Property, Plant, Equipment	-2,318,000	-988,000	-2,935,000	-1,302,000
Acquisitions	*	862,000	-5,842,000	-5,676,000
Other Investing Changes Net	-4,573,000	*	201,000	-42,000
Net Cash from Investing Activities	-6,891,000	-126,000	-8,576,000	-6,900,000
Issuance of Debt	2,708,000	15,000	30,869,000	8,434,000
Issuance of Capital Stock	*	*	8,000	*
Repayment of Debt	*	*	-24,726,000	*
Payment of Cash Dividends	-1,158,000	-514,000	-660,000	-450,000
Other Financing Charges, Net	-534,000	46,000	-46,000	5,000
Net Cash from Financing Activities	1,016,000	-453,000	5,445,000	7,989,000
Effect of Exchange Rate Changes	157,000	67,000	-6,000	-247,000
Net Change in Cash & Cash Equivalents	664,000	2,138,000	3,985,000	3,697,000
Cash at Beginning of Period	6,118,000	6,020,000	2,035,000	2,035,000
Cash at End of Period	6,782,000	8,158,000	6,020,000	5,732,000

Conclusion

One size doesn't fit all. Many companies find that the best way to get ahead is to expand ownership boundaries through mergers and acquisitions. For others, separating the public ownership of a subsidiary or business segment offers more advantages. At least in theory, mergers create synergies and economies of scale, expanding operations and cutting costs. Investors can take comfort in the idea that a merger will deliver enhanced market power. By contrast, de-merged companies often enjoy improved operating performance thanks to redesigned management incentives. Additional capital can fund growth organically or through acquisition. Meanwhile, investors benefit from the improved information flow from de-merged companies. M&A comes in all shapes and sizes, and investors need to consider the complex issues involved in M&A. The most beneficial form of equity structure involves a complete analysis of the costs and benefits associated with the deals. Let's re-cap what we learned in this tutorial:

- A merger can happen when two companies decide to combine into one entity or when one company buys another. An acquisition always involves the purchase of one company by another.
- The functions of synergy allow for the enhanced cost efficiency of a new entity made from two smaller ones - synergy is the logic behind mergers and acquisitions.
- Acquiring companies use various methods to value their targets. Some of these methods are based on comparative ratios - such as the P/E and P/S ratios - replacement cost or discounted cash flow analysis.
- An M&A deal can be executed by means of a cash transaction, stock-for-stock transaction or a combination of both. A transaction struck with stock is not taxable.
- Break up or de-merger strategies can provide companies with opportunities to raise additional equity funds unlock hidden shareholder value and sharpen management focus. De-mergers can occur by means of divestitures, carve-outs spin-offs or tracking stocks.

Mergers can fail for many reasons including a lack of management foresight, the inability to overcome practical challenges and loss of revenue momentum from a neglect of day-to-day operations.

CASE 3: HINDALCO NOVELIS ACQUISITION

> 'We look upon the aluminum business as a core business that has enormous growth potential in revenues and earnings,' 'Our vision is to be a premium metal major, global in size and reach....The acquisition of Novelis is a step in this direction.'
>
> – Kumar Mangalam Birla, Chairman, Hindalco Industries.

INTRODUCTION

Mergers and acquisitions have been the part of inorganic growth strategy of corporate worldwide. Post-1991 era witnessed growing appetite for takeovers by Indian corporate also across the world as a part of their growth strategy. This series of acquisitions in metal industry was initiated by acquisition of Arcelor by Mittal followed by Corus by Tata. Indian aluminium giant Hindalco extended this process by acquiring Atlanta based company Novelis Inc, a world leader in aluminium rolling and flat-rolled aluminium products. Hindalco Industries Ltd., acquired Novelis Inc. to gain sheet mills that it can supply to can makers and car companies. Strategically, the acquisition of Novelis takes Hindalco onto the global stage as the leader in downstream aluminium rolled products. The acquisition of Novelis by Hindalco bodes well for both the entities. Novelis processes primary aluminium to sell downstream high value added products what is exactly that Hindalco manufactures. This makes the marriage a perfect fit. Currently Hindalco, an integrated player, focuses largely on manufacturing alumina and primary aluminium. It has downstream rolling, extruding and foil making capacities as well, but they are far from global scale. Novelis processes around 3 million tonnes of aluminium a year and has sales centres all over the world. In fact, it commands a 19% global market share in the flat rolled products segment, making it a leader.

Hindalco has completed this acquisition through its wholly-owned subsidiary AV Metals Inc and has acquired 75.415 common shares of Novelis, representing 100 per cent of the issued and outstanding common shares AV Metals Inc transferred the common shares of Novelis to its wholly-owned subsidiary AV Aluminium Inc. The deal made Hindalco the world's largest aluminium rolling company and one of the biggest producers of primary aluminium in Asia, as well as being India's leading copper producer. Hindalco Industries Ltd has completed its acquisition of Novelis Inc under an agreement in which Novelis will operate as a subsidiary of Hindalco.

Company Overview

Hindalco Industries Limited

Hindalco Industries Limited, a flagship company of the Aditya Birla Group, is structured into two strategic businesses – aluminium and copper – with annual revenue of US $14 billion and a market capitalization in excess of US $ 23 billion. Hindalco commenced its operations in 1962 with an aluminium facility at Renukoot in Uttar Pradesh. Birla Copper, Hindalco's copper division is situated in Dahej in the Bharuch district of Gujarat. Established in 1958, Hindalco commissioned its aluminium facility at Renukoot in eastern U.P. in 1962 and has today grown to become the country's largest integrated aluminium producer and ranks among the top quartile of low cost producers in the world. The aluminium division's product range includes alumina chemicals, primary aluminium ingots, billets, wire rods, rolled products, extrusions, foils and alloy wheels. It enjoys a domestic market share of 42 per cent in primary aluminium, 63 per cent in rolled products, 20 per cent in extrusions, 44 per cent in foils and 31 per cent in wheels.

Hindalco has launched several brands in recent years, namely Aura for alloy wheels, Freshwrapp for kitchen foil and ever last for roofing sheets. The copper plant produces copper cathodes, continuous cast copper rods and precious metals like gold, silver and platinum group metal mix. Sulphuric acid, phosphoric acid, di-ammonium phosphate, other phosphatic fertilisers and Phosphor – gypsum are also produced at this plant. Hindalco Industries Limited has a 51.0% shareholding in Aditya Birla Minerals which has mining and exploration activities focused in Australia. The company has two R&D centres at Belgaum, Karnataka and Taloja, Maharashtra. They have been recognized by the Government of India's Department of Scientific and Industrial Research (DSIR). Year over year, Hindalco Industries Ltd. has been able to grow revenues from 121.2B to 193.2B. Most impressively, the company has been able to reduce the percentage of sales devoted to selling, general and administrative costs from 4.15% to 2.96%. This was a driver that led to a bottom line growth from 15.8B to 26.9B.

Company Overview: Novelis

Novelis is the world leader in aluminium rolling, producing an estimated 19 per cent of the world's flat-rolled aluminium products. Novelis is the world leader in the recycling of used aluminium beverage cans. The company recycles more than 35 billion used beverage cans annually. The company is No. 1 rolled products producer in Europe, South America and Asia, and the No. 2 producer in North America. With industry-leading assets and technology, the company produces the highest-quality aluminium sheet and foil products for customers in high-value markets including automotive, transportation, packaging, construction and printing. Its customers include major brands such as Agf a -Gevaert, Alcan, Anheuser-Busch, Ball, Coca-Cola, Crown Cork and Seal, Daching Holdings, Ford, General Motors, Lotte Aluminium, Kodak, Pactiv, Rexam, Ryerson Tull, Tetra Pak, Thyssen Krupp and others. Novelis represents a unique combination of the new and the old.

Novelis is a new company, formed in January 2005, with a new velocity, a new philosophy and a new attitude. Novelis is also a spin-off from Alcan and, as such, draws a rich 90 year history in the aluminium rolled product marketplace.

Important Facts about the Deal

Hindalco, the Aditya Birla Group's flagship company announced the completion of its acquisition of Novelis on June 1, 2007. The transaction made Hindalco the world's largest aluminium rolling company and one of the biggest producers of primary aluminium in Asia, as well as being India's leading copper producer.

On 10 February 2007, Hindalco entered into an agreement with Novelis to acquire the company in an all-cash transaction which values Novelis at approximately US$ 6.0 billion, including debt. Under the terms of the agreement, Novelis shareholders will receive US$ 44.93 in cash for each outstanding common share. Novelis shareholders approved the transaction by an overwhelming majority (99.8 per cent) in a special meeting on 10 May 2007.

Organic and inorganic both strategies have worked for the companies worldwide. But in the process of global expansions inorganic growth strategies have always been the first preference for the companies globally. As a part of its inorganic growth strategy of global expansion. The following points highlight the important points about this acquisition of Hindalco for this acquisition:

- The acquisition of Novelis by Hindalco was in an all-cash transaction, which values Novelis at enterprise value of approximately US$ 6.0 billion, including approximately US$ 2.4 billion of debt.
- This merger of Novelis into Hindalco will establish a global integrated aluminium producer with low cost alumina and aluminium production facilities combined with high-end aluminium rolled products.
- After the merger Hindalco will emerge as the biggest rolled aluminium products maker and fifth largest integrated aluminium manufacturer in the world.
- As Novelis is the global leader in aluminium rolled products and aluminium can recycling, with a global market share of about 19%. Hindalco has a 60% share in the currently small but future growth oriented Indian market for rolled products.
- Hindalco's position as one of the lowest cost producers of primary aluminium in the world is leverageable into becoming a globally strong player. The Novelis acquisition will give the company immediate scale and a strong global footprint.
- Novelis a globally positioned organization, operating in 11 countries with approx. 12,500 employees. In 2005, company reported net sales of US$8.4 billion and profit of US$ 90 million.
- The company reported net sales of US$7.4 billion and net loss of US$170 million in nine months during year 2006, on account of low contract prices.
- Novelis is expecting the full year loss to be US$263 million in 2006, however, the company is expecting to be in black with US$68 million profit in 2007. The total free cash flow is expected to be US$175 million in 2006.
- By January 1, 2010, all the sales contracts will get expired and profitability will increase substantially from then onwards.

- Novelis will work as a forward integration for Hindalco as the company is expected to ship primary aluminium to Novelis for downstream value addition.
- Novelis has a rolled product capacity of approx. 3 million tonnes while Hindalco at the moment is not having any surplus capacity of primary aluminium.
- Considering these factors, Hindalco's profitability is expected to remain under pressure and this will bounce back in 2009-10. The profitability will be accretive only in 2010-11.
- The debt component of Novelis stood at US$2.4 billion and additional US$2.8 billion will be taken by Hindalco to finance the deal. This will put tremendous pressure on profitability due to high interest burden.
- Hindalco's existing expansion will cost Rs. 25,000 crore and as a result debt and interest burden of the company will increase further.

Funding Structure for the Deal

Hindalco and Novelis have signed a definitive agreement for the acquisition, which values Novelis at around $6 billion. After excluding the $2.4 billion of debt, the equity component of the deal works out to $3.6 billion. Novelis shareholders would receive $44.93 per share in cash. This is a substantial value appreciation for Novelis shareholders as the stock has more than doubled in recent weeks, after the company confirmed the possible sale.

The funding structure of this deal is remarkably different from LBO that Tata Steel used to fund the Corus buy. The Tatas are to buy 100 per cent of Corus's Equity for US$ 12.9 billion. Only US$ 4.1 billion of this is being raised by Tatas. The remaining US$ 8 billion will be raised (as debt) and repaid on the strength of the Corus balance sheet. This was possible because Corus had relatively low debt on its balance sheet and was able to borrow more.

But that is not the case with Novelis. With a debt- equity ratio of 7.23:1, it can't borrow any more. So, the Birlas were unable to do a LBO. To buy the US$3.6 billion worth of Novelis equity, Hindalco borrowed almost US$2.85 billion (of the balance US$300 million is being raised as debt from group companies and US$ 450 million is being mobilized from its cash reseves).

That is almost one-third of Rs. 2,500 crore net profit Hindalco may post in 2006-07. (It has reported a net profit of Rs. 1,843 crore for the first three quarters of this year). The second part of the deal is the US$ 2.4 billion debt on Novelis Balance sheet. Hindalco will have to refinance these borrowings, though they will be repaid with the Novelis cash flows.

Table 11.5: The World of Novelis
It has spread its reach across these regions

	N. America	Europe	Asia	S. America
Assets	1,487	2,392	1,021	814
Net sales	2,841	2,688	1,235	626
Regional income	64	208	70	122
Descriptions of assets*	10 plants 2 recycling facilities	14 plants 1 recycling facility	3 plants	2 plants 2 smelters 1 refinery 2 bauxite mine

*Plants refer to aluminium rolled products facilities. All in figures in $ mn. Figures for nine months ended 30 September 2006.
Source: Company.

Valuation Concern

The second big concern is Novelis's valuation. Analysts believe the Birlas are paying too high a price for a company that incurred a loss of $170 million for the nine months ended 30 September, 2006. In its latest guidance, the Novelis management has indicated a loss of $240 million-285 million for the whole of 2006. Even in 2005, when Novelis had made a $90-million net profit, its share prices never crossed $30. So, why is Hindalco paying $44.93 a share for a loss-making company?

In its guidance, the Novelis management has indicated a pre-tax profit of $35 million-100 million for 2007. Going by the optimistic end of the guidance, the price Hindalco paid translates to a market capitalisation/profit before tax (PBT) multiple of 36 on Novelis's 2007 forecast. That appears to be high.

Table 11.6: In Numbers
Novelis' losses are a recent problem

	Jan-Sept 2006	Jan-Sept 2005	FY2005	FY2004	FY2003
Net sales	7,377	6,337	8,363	7,755	6,221
Operating expenses	7,224	5,938	7,962	7,145	5,737
EBITDA	153	399	401	610	484
Interest	149	148	194	48	33
Net income	–170	32	90	55	157

It is pertinent to make another comparison with Corus here. In March 2006, Corus sold its aluminium rolled products business to Aleris. The business, with revenues of $1.83 billion and a PBT of $55 million, was sold for $980 million. But Hindalco is paying double of that. (See 'The Value Equation'.)

Table 11.7: The Value Equation
How Novelis's valuation compares with a peer

	Novels 2005 actual	Novels 2007 guidance**	Corus aluminium 2005 actual
Assets	5,476	N.A.	1,427.84
Sales	8,363	N.A.	1,831.9
PBT	197	100	55.04
Market cap	3,,600	3,600	980*
Market cap/PBT	18.27	36	17.81

* Corus Aluminium was sold to Aleris for $980 million in March 2006.
**Guidance issued by the Corus management. All figures in $ million.
Figures for year ended December 2005.
Source: Corus, Novelis.

- Though no official comment is available, it is expected that the Birlas may have to infuse more equity (over and above the $6-billion acquisition plan) into Novelis to revive it.

- Moreover, **after the deal, Hindalco's consolidated debt-equity ratio may slip from about 0.5:1 to well over 2:1**. All these concerns make everyone wonder: Why did the Birlas choose to buy Novelis?
- The Hindalco management believes that the answer is clear as crystal. **Novelis will help the Aditya Birla Group double its turnover to over $20 billion**. "We had set this (group turnover of $20 billion) as a stretch target. We achieved it three years ahead of schedule. Now, we have to set ourselves fresh targets," Birla declared at the press conference.
- **Novelis will also give Hindalco an entry into the down-stream business of rolled aluminium products**. At the moment, Hindalco is limited to the upstream business of mining bauxite and converting it into alumina, and then smelting it into aluminium. Says managing director Debu Bhattacharya: "If we earn $10 for every $100 of aluminium we sell, we will now be able to earn another $10 for every $100 worth of aluminium that Novelis processes into rolled products."
- Globally, about 35 million tonnes of aluminium is consumed every year. About 40 per cent of this is rolled products, **a market Hindalco does not have a presence in**. But Novelis has a 19 per cent world share. Similarly in India, the rolled products market is expected to grow from 220,000 tonnes to a million tonnes in a few years. (China already consumes 2.5 million tonnes of rolled products.)
- **Novelis also brings technology.** For example, it has built a new fusion technology that increases the 'formability' of aluminium, making it more suitable for products like sheet metal that help build cars with more curves. Besides, the low weight of aluminium in relation to its strength is helping it find many new applications in the auto industry.
- **It would take 10 years for Hindalco to develop such technology on its own**, says Bhattacharya. It would also cost $12 billion to build assets that match Novelis's 29 plants in four continents with current production of 3.3 million tonnes (See Table 11.5). Says Donald Marleau, primary credit analyst, Standard and Poor's, Toronto: "This deal is high-level buying. Novelis is a strong acquisition because of the technology."

He says it is tough to develop such technology and even harder to get customer certification. (Standard and Poor's put Novelis on a rating watch soon after the deal was announced.)

There is another interesting link between the businesses of Hindalco and Novelis. Hindalco's finished product is aluminium that is, the raw material Novelis uses to make stock for cans, auto parts, etc. On the face of it, this seems like a perfect synergy.

- Hindalco's aluminium capacities are all committed to its existing customers. And Novelis has tied up its raw material supplies from sources with geographical proximity. Company officials say they wouldn't upset these contracts. **It is unlikely that the two will be able to do much business with each other till 2011.** That is when a big part of Hindalco's Rs. 12,500-crore expansion projects will go onstream. (It also has another Rs. 12,500-crore expansion planned.) "It is possible that some of our aluminium may find a home in Novelis. But that is only in the long term.
- **Novelis forms a natural hedge for Hindalco**. The latter's profits rise and fall with aluminium prices on the LME. But after Novelis's disastrous can contracts expire (by 2010), its business model and profitability will be LME independent. Then, aluminium will be a pass-through cost. Its raw material prices will be fully passed on to customers and Novelis's profits will be earned from the efficiency of its rolling operations. Says Marleau: "Novelis appears to be a weak company. But historically it had a steady record of cash flow. Only recently has it run into problems because of the ceiling on the price of its can products." So, when the ceilings go in 2010, as Hindalco's profits rise and fall with LME, Novelis will earn a steady cash flow. That's the perfect hedge, at least in theory.

What will Change After 2011?

- **Novelis's can pricing issues would have been resolved by then**. Its existing management believes Novelis can generate an annual cash flow of $400 million and earn a 12 per cent return on capital. It also believes that the debt to EBITDA ratio could be pared to the 2.5x and 3x band from the current 10x to 12x level.

- **After 2011, with more aluminium capacity at its disposal.** Hindalco may also find more synergies with Novelis. Most of its new capacities are coming up on the eastern seaboard with easy access to Novelis's plants in Malaysia and South Korea.
- But the real **big difference post-2011 could be in aluminium prices**. Many analysts expect aluminium prices to decline gradually from its current peak of over $2,800 a tonne (see 'Tracking Aluminium'). Standard Bank believes aluminium prices could come down to $2,400 a tonne. That could pull down Hindalco's profit margins. But Novelis, if revived successfully, may not be affected much. Bhattacharya believes that he has found the perfect antidote to hedge aluminium's volatility on the LME. That is why his team went in hot pursuit of Novelis.

Investment bankers close to the deal say that Hindalco made the first move. Novelis, for all its troubles, had not considered a sell out. In fact, when Hindalco made first contact, the Novelis management wasn't quite receptive. Sources say the parleys first began sometime in the first half of 2006. It took some time for the Novelis board to turn sellers. At that point, they roped in an investment bank and sounded out several other potential buyers. A competitive bidding process was kicked off. Unlike the dramatic and much publicised Tata-CSN shootout, the bidding was low profile. The identity of the other bidders and the price they offered are not known, though Birla says the bidding was 'very competitive'. Hindalco made only one bid — $44.93 per share. That won the deal.

FINANCIAL ANALYSIS

Presented below is a table which shows the past five year performance for Hindalco Industries on several key financial parameters. The financials are for the consolidated entity.

Hindalco has shown robust topline growth over the past 5 years. The growth in 2007-08 looks particularly impressive because of the acquisition of Novelis Inc., a foreign subsidiary, acquired by the company on 16.05.2007 through its wholly-owned overseas subsidiaries. With the acquisition of Novelis, Hindalco has also become the world's largest rolling company.

Table 11.8: Financial Analysis

Rs. In Million)	2007–08	2006–07	2005–06	2004–05	2003–04
Net Sales	600,128	193,161	121,197	101,053	82,233
% Growth	211%	59%	20%	23%	
Net Profit	23,873	26,858	15,796	12,848	9,935
% Growth	–11%	70%	23%	29%	
Net Margin (%)	3.98	13.90	13.03	12.71	12.08
Diluted EPS	20.34	26.73	16.02	13.03	10.11
Cash EPS	41.50	35.33	24.09	19.44	15.33
Return on Capital Employed	8.59	17.07	13.69	15.04	14.29
Return on Equity	13.76	20.96	16.85	16.79	14.13
Debt-Equity Ratio	1.87	0.66	0.67	0.64	0.53

Hindalco has leveraged itself significantly in the last fiscal but the debt-equity position is still comfortable. The company has also expanded its equity base, which has affected the EPS in the near term. But since it is for acquisition and growth related activities, it is not a concern for shareholders.

The company has been generating decent positive operating cash flows. This is a good thing for a company which has significantly leveraged itself. Positive operating cash flow ensures ample liquidity for working capital and other near term needs.

The return on equity and return on capital employed for Hindalco has been affected in the near term because of the acquisition and significant expansion of equity base. In my opinion it will improve in the future with higher commodity prices coupled with robust performance by the company.

CASE 4: HUTCH VODAFONE ACQUISITION

ABOUT HUTCH ESSAR

Hutch Essar is a leading Indian telecommunications mobile operator with 23.3 million customers at 31 December, 2006, representing a 16.4% national market share. Hutch Essar operates in 16 circles and has licences in an additional six circles. In the year to 31 December, 2005, Hutch Essar reported revenue of US$1282 million, EBITDA of US$415 million, and operating profit of US$313 million. In the six months to 30 June, 2006, Hutch Essar reported revenue of US$908 million, EBITDA of US$297 million, and operating profit of US$226 million.

Up until January 2006, Hutch Essar had licences in 13 circles, of which nine have 900 MHz spectrum. In January 2006, Hutch Essar acquired BPL, thereby adding three circles, each operating with 900 MHz spectrum. In October 2006, Hutch Essar acquired Spacetel, adding six further licences, with operations planned to be launched during 2007.

ABOUT VODAFONE

Vodafone is the world's leading international mobile communications group with operations in 25 countries across five continents and over 200 million proportionate customers by the end of January 2007, as well as 36 partner networks.

Acquisition of Hutch Essar by Vodafone

On February 12, 2007, Vodafone announced that it has agreed to acquire a controlling interest in Hutchison Essar Limited ('Hutch Essar'), a leading operator in the fast growing Indian mobile market, via its subsidiary Vodafone International Holdings B.V. Vodafone also announced that it has signed a memorandum of understanding ('MOU') with Bharti Airtel Limited ('Bharti') on infrastructure sharing and that it has granted an option to a Bharti group company to buy its 5.6% direct interest in Bharti.

Key highlights

By acquisition of a controlling interest in Hutch Essar, Vodafone announced that it has agreed to acquire companies that control a 67% interest in Hutch Essar from Hutchison Telecom International Limited ('HTIL') for a cash consideration of US$11.1 billion (£5.7 billion). For this, Vodafone will assume net debt of approximately US$2.0 billion (£1.0 billion). The transaction implies an enterprise value of US$18.8 billion (£9.6 billion) for Hutch Essar. The acquisition meets Vodafone's stated financial investment criteria— Infrastructure sharing MOU with Bharti. Whilst Hutch Essar and Bharti will continue to compete independently, Vodafone and Bharti have entered into a MOU relating to a comprehensive range of infrastructure sharing options in India between Hutch Essar and Bharti. Infrastructure sharing is expected to reduce the total cost of delivering telecommunication services, especially in rural areas, enabling both parties to expand network coverage more quickly and to offer more affordable services to a broader base of the Indian population.

Local partner 'Essar' Group currently holds a 33% interest in Hutch Essar and Vodafone will make an offer to buy this stake at the equivalent price per share it has agreed with HTIL. Vodafone's arrangements with the other existing minority partners will result in a shareholder structure post-acquisition that meets the requirements of India's foreign ownership rules.

Commenting on the transaction, Arun Sarin, the then Chief Executive of Vodafone, said: 'We are delighted to be deepening our involvement in the Indian mobile market with the full range of Vodafone's products, services and brand. This announcement is clear evidence of how we are executing our strategy of developing our presence in emerging markets. We have concluded this transaction within our stated financial investment criteria and we are confident that this will prove to be an excellent investment for our shareholders. Hutch Essar is an impressive, well run company that will fit well into the Vodafone Group.'

Operational plan for Hutch Essar

Vodafone executed an operational plan to build on the strengths of Hutch Essar in order to capture the Indian telecom growth opportunity.

Key Strategic Objectives

In the context of penetration that is expected to exceed 40% by FY2012, Vodafone is targeting a 20-25% market share within the same time frame. The operational plan focuses on the following objectives: Expanding distribution and network coverage, Lowering the total cost of network ownership, growing market share and driving a customer focused approach.

Site Sharing

The MOU outlines a process for achieving a more extensive level of site sharing and covers both new and existing sites. Around one-third of Hutch Essar's current sites are already shared with other Indian mobile operators and Vodafone is planning that around two-thirds of total sites will be shared in the longer term.

The MOU recognizes the potential for achieving further efficiencies by sharing infrastructure with other mobile operators in India. The MOU envisages the potential, subject to regulatory approval and commercial development, to extend the agreement to sharing of active infrastructure such as radio access network and access transmission.

Financial Assumptions

As part of the operational plan, Vodafone expects to increase capital investment, particularly in the first two to three years, with CAPEX as a percentage of revenues reducing to the low margin by FY2012. Cash tax rates of 11-14% for FY2008-12 are expected due to various tax incentives and will tend towards approximately 30-34% in the long term. As a result of this operational plan, the transaction meets Vodafone's stated financial investment criteria, with a ROI exceeding the local risk adjusted cost of capital in the fifth year and an IRR of around 14%.

Financial Impact on Vodafone

The transaction enhances Vodafone's growth profile on a proforma statutory basis, with Vodafone's revenue and EBITDA CAGR increasing by around one and a half percentage points over the three year period to 31 March 2010.

The transaction is expected to be broadly neutral to adjusted earnings per share in the first year post-acquisition and accretive thereafter excluding the impact of intangible asset amortisation for the transaction. Including this impact, the transaction is expected to be approximately seven percent dilutive to adjusted earnings per share in the first year post-acquisition and neutral by the fifth year.

The Board remains committed to its longer term targeted dividend payout of 60% of adjusted earnings per share. Furthermore, the Board expects the dividend per share to be at least maintained in the short term. The acquisition of HTIL's controlling interest in Hutch Essar was financed through debt and existing cash reserves and Vodafone expects proforma net debt of around £22.8-23.33 billion at 31 March, 2007 as a result of this transaction.

Further Transaction Details

HTIL's existing partners, who between them hold a 15% interest in Hutch Essar, have agreed to retain their holdings and become partners with Vodafone. Vodafone's interest will be 52% following completion and Vodafone will exercise full operational control over the business. If Essar decides to accept Vodafone's offer, these local minority partners between them will increase their combined interest in Hutch Essar to 26%.

In the event that the Bharti group company exercises its option over Vodafone's 5.6% direct interest in Bharti, consideration will be

Table 11.9: Enterprise Value Calculation

Hutch Essar 100% enterprise value	18.80
Hutch Essar 100% net debt[1]	(1.33)
Hutch Essar 100% equity value	17.47
Hutch Essar 67% equity value[2]	11.70
Holdco Net Debt[1.3]	(0.63)
Consideration paid by Vodafone to acquire 67% Hutch Essar	11.08
Hutch Essar net debt[1]	1.33
Holdco net debt[1]	0.63
Vodafone assumed net debt	1.96

1. Estimated as at 31st January, 2007.
2. Vodafone economic interest of 66.4% with remaining economic interests held by local partners.
3. Holdco refers to holding companies of HTIL owning shares in Hutch Essar.

received up to 18 months after completion of the Hutch Essar. Vodafone will continue to hold its 26% interest in Bharti Infotel Private Limited ('BIPL'), which is equivalent to an indirect 4.4% economic interest in Bharti. Vodafone will now account for its entire interest as an investment. UBS Investment Bank acted as financial adviser to Vodafone.

Financial Position and Resources for the years ended 31 March

Table 11.10: Consolidated balance sheet

	2008 £m	2007 £m
Non-current assets		
Intangible assets	70,331	56,272
Property, plant and equipment	16,735	13,444
Investments in associated undertakings	22,545	20,227
Other non-current assets	8,935	6,861
	118,546	**96,804**
Current assets	8,724	12,813
Total assets	**127,270**	**109,617**
Total equity shareholders funds	78,043	67,067
Total minority interests	(1,572)	226
Total equity	**76,471**	**67,293**
Liabilities		
Borrowings		
Long term	22,662	17,798
Short term	4,532	4,817
Taxation liabilities		
Deferred tax liabilities	5,109	4,626
Current taxation liabilities	5,123	5,088
Other non-current liabilities	1,055	954
Other current liabilities(2)	12,318	9,041
	50,799	**42,324**
Total equity and liabilities	**127,270**	**109,617**

Non-current Assets

Intangible assets

At 31 March, 2008, the Group's intangible assets were £70.3 billion, with goodwill comprising the largest element at £51.3 billion (2007: £40.6 billion). The increase in intangible assets was primarily as a result of £7.9 billion of favourable exchange rate movements and £7.6 billion arising on the acquisitions of Vodafone Essar and Tele 2, partially offset by amortisation of £2.5 billion.

Property, Plant and Equipment

Property, plant and equipment increased from £13.4 billion at 31 March 2007 to £16.7 billion at 31 March 2008, predominantly as a result of £4.1 billion of additions, a £1.2 billion increase due to acquisitions during the year and £1.6 billion of favourable foreign exchange movements, which more than offset the £3.4 billion of depreciation charges and £0.1 billion reduction due to disposals.

Investments in Associated Undertakings

The Group's investments in associated undertakings increased from £20.2 billion at 31 March, 2007 to £22.5 billion at 31 March, 2008, as a result of a £2.9 billion increase from the Group's share of the results of its associates, after the deductions of interest, tax and minority interest, mainly arising from the Group's investment in Verizon Wireless and favourable foreign exchange movements of £0.3 billion, partially offset by £0.9 billion of dividends received.

Other non-current assets

Other non-current assets mainly relates to other investments held by the Group, which totalled £7.4 billion at 31 March, 2008 compared to £5.9 billion at 31 March, 2007. The movement primarily represents an increase of £1.8 billion in the investment in China Mobile as a result of the increase in the listed share price, partially offset by the disposal of the Group's 5.60% stake in Bharti Airtel.

Current assets

Current assets decreased to £8.7 billion at 31 March, 2008 from £12.8 billion at 31 March, 2007, mainly as a result of decreased cash holdings following the completion of the Vodafone Essar acquisition.

Total Equity Shareholders' Funds

Total equity shareholders' funds increased from £67.1 billion at 31 March, 2007 to £78.0 billion at 31 March, 2008. The increase comprises primarily of the profit for the year of £6.8 billion less equity dividends of £3.7 billion, a £5.8 billion benefit from the impact of favourable exchange rate movements and the unrealised holding gains on other investments discussed above.

Borrowings

Long term borrowings and short term borrowings increased to £27.2 billion at 31 March, 2008 from £22.6 billion at 31 March, 2007, mainly as a result of foreign exchange movements and written put option liabilities assumed on the completion of the Vodafone Essar acquisition.

Taxation Liabilities

The deferred tax liability increased from £4.6 billion at 31 March 2007 to £5.1 billion at 31 March 2008, which arose mainly from £0.5 billion in relation to the acquisition of Vodafone Essar.

Other Current Liabilities

The increase in other current liabilities from £9.0 billion to £12.3 billion is primarily to due foreign exchange differences arising on translation and other current liabilities in the newly acquired Vodafone Essar.

Principal Benefits

The principal benefits to Vodafone of the transaction are:

- Accelerate Vodafone's move to a controlling position in a leading operator in the attractive and fast growing Indian mobile market. India is the world's 2nd most populated country with over 1.1 billion inhabitants. India is the fastest growing major mobile market in the world, with around 6.5 million monthly net adds in the last quarter. India benefits from strong economic fundamentals with expected real GDP growth in high single digits.

Table 11.11: Consolidated income statement

	2008 £m	2007 £m
Revenue	**35,478**	**31,104**
Cost of sales	(21,890)	(18,725)
Gross profit	**13,588**	**12,379**
Selling and distribution expenses	(2,511)	(2,136)
Administrative expenses	(3,878)	(3,437)
Share of result in associated undertakings	2,876	2,728
Impairment losses	–	(11,600)
Other income and expense	(28)	502
Operating profit/(loss)	**10,047**	**(1,564)**
Non-operating income and expense	254	4
Investment income	714	789
Financing costs	(2,014)	(1,612)
Profit/(loss) before taxation	**9,001**	**(2,383)**
Income tax expense	(2,245)	(2,423)
Profit/(loss) for the financial year from continuing operations	**6,756**	**(4,806)**
Loss for the financial year from discontinued operations	–	(491)
Profit/(loss) for the financial year	**6,756**	**(5,297)**
Attributable to:		
– Equity shareholders	6,660	(5,426)
– Minority interests	96	129
	6,756	**(5,297)**
Basic earnings/(loss) per share		
Profit/(loss) from continuing operations	12.56p	(8.94)p
Loss from discontinued operations	–	(0.90)p
Profit/(loss) for the financial year	**12.56p**	**(9.84)p**
Diluted earnings/(loss) per share		
Profit/(loss) from continuing operations	12.50p	(8.94)p
Loss from discontinued operations	–	(0.90)p
Profit/(loss) for the financial year	**12.50p**	**(9.84)p**

- Hutch Essar delivers a strong existing platform in India nation . wide presence with recent expansion to 22 out of 23 licence areas ('circles')23.3 million customers as at 31 December, 2006, equivalent to a 16.4% nationwide market share year-on-year revenue growth of 51% and an EBITDA margin of 33% in the six months.

- Experienced and highly respected management team driving additional value in Hutch Essar accelerated network investment and driving penetration and market share growth. Infrastructure sharing MOU with Bharti plans to reduce substantially network OPEX (operational expenditure) and CAPEX (capital expenditure) potential for Hutch Essar to bring Vodafone's innovative products and services to the Indian market, including Vodafone's focus on total communication solutions for customers.
- Vodafone and Hutch Essar both expected to benefit from increased purchasing power and the sharing of best practices Increases Vodafone's presence in higher growth emerging markets proportion of Group statutory EBITDA from the EMAPA region expected to increase from below20% in the financial year ending 31 March, 2007 (FY2007) to over a third by FY2012.

CASE STUDY 5: NTPC : ACQUISITION OF TANDA

TANDA, a small rural suburb, was acquired by NTPC (National Thermal Power Corporation) on January 15, 2000. It is located in eastern UP on the southern bank of the Ghaghra river. Through a UP Government Gazette Notification dated January 14, 2000 Tanda Thermal Power Station was to be handed over to the NTPC on January 15, 2000. So the team from NTPC rightfully took it over.

The TANDA generation undertaking along with the specified personnel was transferred to NTPC and all its properties, interests, rights and titles were revested in NTPC from the date of transfer. The plant inherited by NTPC had a fairly long history of its own. The Feasibility Report was made by M/s Desein in 1973. The UP Government sanctioned the Power Plant in 1979. The plant was to have a generation capacity of 440 MW from 4 units of 110 MW each. Provision was made in the design to augment the capacity to 840 MW. The foundation stone of this project was laid by the then Prime Minister Smt. Indira Gandhi on December 30, 1981. It took 17 years to complete the plant. Unit I was synchronized on 21/03/1988 and

Figure 11.7: The taken-over plant

became commercial on 01/01/1990. Unit 4 was the last, being synchronized on 20/02/98 and becoming commercial on 01/07/98. Units 2 & 3 became commercial in April, 1991 and January, 1993 respectively.

Tanda as a Consideration for Upseb Liablities to NTPC

The acquisition of TANDA by the NTPC was a transfer from UPSEB (Uttar Pradesh State Electricity Board) to NTPC **in consideration for** the obligations of the Board to NTPC. Board was having **outstanding liabilities of Rs. 1,000 crore** to NTPC. Now after the acquisition of TANDA plant by the NTPC these liabilities of the Board were discharged.

Few Special Aspects of the Acquisition

- UPPCL (Uttar Pradesh Power Corporation Limited), the successor entity of the Board, assumed the obligations of the board under the power purchase agreement dated on 10.01.2000 to purchase the electrical capacity or energy on terms contained therein.
- NTPC adjusted the outstanding liabilities of the Board to NTPC of Rs. 1000 crore. This was an integral part of the agreement between the Board, its successor UPPCL and NTPC.

- NTPC undertook the renovation and modernization of Tanda Generation Undertaking based on its technical assessment and as per guidelines and procedures followed by NTPC.
- The fixed charges payable by UPPCL to NTPC for the purchase of electrical capacity of Tanda Generation Undertaking were calculated on the basis of the above consideration amount of Rs.1,000 crore (plus any subsequent capital expenditure incurred by NTPC at the Tanda generating Station including that on renovation and modernization.
- A complete inventory of all the properties and assets, as on the date of transfer, pertaining to the Tanda Generation Undertaking was prepared jointly by UPRVUNL (Uttar Pradesh Rajya Vidhyut Utpadan Nigam Limited) and NTPC and for this purpose the State Government and UPRVUNL afford to the NTPC all reasonable facilities.

Changes Made By NTPC to the Financial System of TANDA

System adopted	Steps involved
Salary Payment	1. System changed from payment in cash to bank account.
	2. Annual IT return, form-16 computerized.
Auditing	1. Regular quarterly audits introduced.
Integrated system between F&A and C&M	The integrated system ensures indenting to withdrawal through the system only for better inventory control.

Before the acquisition by NTPC, the motivation and productivity levels of the staff of TANDA were very low and were in consonance with the poor baseline parameters and condition of the plant. The levels can also be judged from the fact that about 1200 level manpower was nearly halved, while the plant productivity actually increased. The Man/MW ratio which was 2.73 at the time of takeover has come down to 1.39 at present. Add to this the fact that better performance was achieved by the same UPSEB employees who were earlier functioning on a very low productivity as indicated by standard power generating parameters viz. PLF, availability etc.

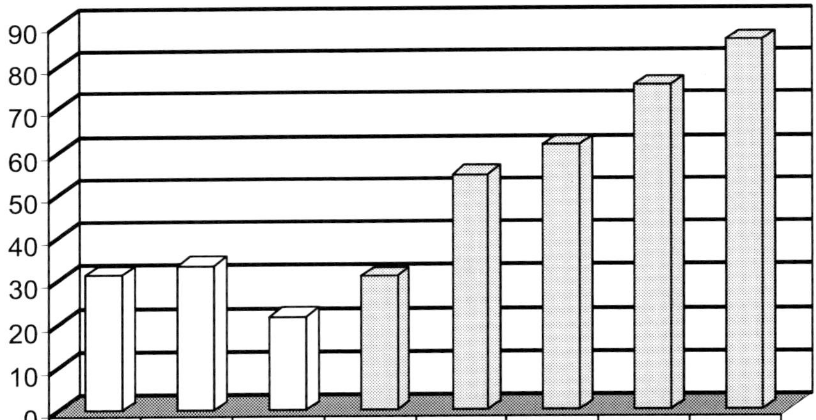

	97-98	98-99	99-00	00-01	01-02	02-03	03-04	04-05 (Till July)
PLF	31.21	33.49	21.59	30.87	54.52	61.39	75.32	85.86

Figure 11.8: Trend of Plant Load Factor (PLF)

It is clear that the accepted UPSEB manpower did absorb the NTPC culture by becoming part of a most professional outfit. Strong communication and development programmes helped to speed up the process. The NTPC culture of "hands-on" executives provided personal leadership examples to the newly absorbed staff, and aided the process of growth of their technical competence. Overall there were strong interfaces between the experience of the NTPC executives', the technological problems and solutions and the vitally important manpower and HR issues.

CRITICAL FINDINGS IN THE ABOVE CASES

It has been observed that in majority of the cases acquiring company's shareholder's gain due to M&A. There has been reported appreciation in share prices in majority of the cases. This is also consistent with the literature that Indian stock markets do take a positive view of M&A strategies being adopted by the Indian companies and acquiring company's shareholders benefited from majority of the cases. As has been mentioned in the research findings, the reasons for appreciation may be related to the anticipated value enhancement of the merged entity as a result of expected increase in cash flows from the M&S. This is in tandem with the findings that the shareholders might have taken into account the expected increase in performance due to better profitability, market leadership, new growth prospects and cost efficiency. It has also been found out that takeovers are motivated by expectations of improved performance due to realization of synergistic benefits which reflected in the share prices. This has been reflected in the motives of Indian M&As which might have caused the share prices appreciation. A strong R&D and strategic alignment has also emerged as important motive of Indian M&As which may have influenced the share price behaviour of the Indian enterprises.

- Empirical evidence has shown that upon announcement of a merger bid, on average:
  - Share price of the *targeted* company rise 16%
  - Share price of *acquiring* company are essentially unchanged (a fall of 0.7%)
  - Value of total package (buyer plus seller) rises on average by 1.8%
- Sellers earn higher returns because
  - Buyers are typically substantially much larger firms that the significant gains from the merger do not affect the firm's share price
  - More importantly, it is often the case that there is a competition among bidders, which increases the gains for the target firm.

Share price behaviour: It has also been observed in majority of the cases that there is heavy build up share prices during the period leading to mergers and acquisitions. This suggests that existence of Insider Trading in our stock exchanges. Here, SEBI needs to be more proactive as few persons privy to such information ought to benefit from such price sensitive information. The poor common members of the acquirer company may not get such advantage form this build up. In all these years SEBI has initiated probes of Insider Trading but only after media outcry. The regulators did catch up a few offenders in the recent past. But, they need to come up with more strict preventive measures.

Integration Aspects: The post integration issues are one of the most important areas in case of mergers and acquisitions. The issues which include cultural clashes, employee layoffs, wage structure and top management turnover are the critical areas having wide policy implications. The process of integration is substantially more complex to study empirically because of the lack of process level data typically available for a sufficiently large number of observations.

Data Deficiency: While pursuing the present book, there are lot of difficulties in collecting data on mergers and acquisitions in India. There is an acute deficiency of data with respect to mergers and acquisitions in particular. Only SEBI from 1997 maintains a limited database on mergers and acquisitions relating to companies registered on Indian stock exchanges.

To assess whether mergers work, it is necessary to examine the motives and reasons underlying the move before evaluating the results. Synergy or no synergy, in the ultimate analysis any strategic or financial decision must eventually add to shareholder value. Thus in conclusion, one can say that though synergistic motives drive most mergers, they are not always achieved, and even if achieved, they do not translate into improved shareholder returns.

However, there is a higher probability of shareholders benefitting from the mergers if the synergies are actually realized in the post-merger period. Therefore, pre-merger due diligence assumes greater significance from the perspective of accurately assessing the synergies possible otherwise it could end up eroding rather than adding to shareholder value.

CONCLUSION

One size doesn't fit all. Many companies find that the best way to get ahead is to expand ownership boundaries through mergers and acquisitions. For others, separating the public ownership of a subsidiary or business segment offers more advantages. At least in theory, mergers create synergies and economies of scale, expanding operations and cutting costs. Investors can take comfort in the idea that a merger will deliver enhanced market power.

By contrast, demerged companies often enjoy improved operating performance thanks to redesigned management incentives. Additional capital can fund growth organically or through acquisition. Meanwhile, investors benefit from the improved information flow from demerged companies.

M&A comes in all shapes and sizes, and investors need to consider the complex issues involved in M&A. The most beneficial form of equity structure involves a complete analysis of the costs and benefits associated with the deals.

Hence we can conclude that:

- A merger can happen when two companies decide to combine into one entity or when one company buys another. An acquisition always involves the purchase of one company by another.
- The functions of synergy allow for the enhanced cost efficiency of a new entity made from two smaller ones—synergy is the logic behind mergers and acquisitions.
- Acquiring companies use various methods to value their targets. Some of these methods are based on comparative ratios—such as the P/E and P/S ratios—replacement cost or discounted cash flow analysis.
- An M&A deal can be executed by means of a cash transaction, stock-for-stock transaction or a combination of both. A transaction struck with stock is not taxable.
- Break-up or demerger strategies can provide companies with opportunities to raise additional equity funds, unlock hidden shareholder value and sharpen management focus. Demergers can occur by means of divestitures, carve-outs spin-offs or tracking stocks.
- Mergers can fail for many reasons including a lack of management foresight, the inability to overcome practical challenges and loss of revenue momentum from a neglect of day-to-day operations.

References

- S Shiva Ramu, Cross Border Mergers and Acquisitions.
- Jonathan Reuvid, Mergers and Acquisitions: A Practical Guide for Private Companies and Their Advisors, pp. 201-206
- Bhide, A., 1989, The Causes and Consequences of Hostile Takeovers, Journal of Applied Corporate Finance, Vol. 2, 36-59.
- Trautwein, F, 1990, 'Merger Motives and Merger Prescriptions', Strategic Management Journal, Vol 11, o 4, p. 284.
- Lubatkin, M, 1983, 'Mergers and Performance of the Acquiring Firms', Academy of Management Review, Vol. 8, No. 2, pp. 218-225.
- Impact of M&As on Corporate Performance: A Case Study by Sanjiv Mittal and Sunil Gupta.
- Mergers, Acquisitions and Leverage Buyouts", by Robert Lawrence Kuhn.
- Srinivasan and Bibek Prasad Mishra, Why do Firms Merge/ Acquire.
- Pareek, U, 2002. Training Instruments in HRD and OD, 2nd Edition, New Delhi, TMH pp. 487-491
- Institute of Mergers, Acquisitions and Alliances Research, Thomson Financial.
- The Why and How of Mergers, Strategic Management Journal, Vol. 11, No 1, pp. 79-86

- Franks, J; Harris Titman, S (1991). "The Post Merger Share-Price Performance of Acquiring Firms," Journal of Financial Economics, 29(1), 81-96.
- Khanna, S (1999). "Financial Reforms and Industrial Sector in India,"
- Weston, J F; Chung, K.S. and Hoag, S.E. (2000). Mergers, Restructuring, and Corporate Control, New Delhi: Prentice Hall of India.
- Mergers and Acquisitions: A Valuation Handbook by Joseph H. Marren.
- Successful Mergers by Marion Devine.
- Guide to Value-Creating M&A, By Vikram Chakravarty Vinimaya, July-Sep, 2007 issue
- An Analysis of Mergers in the Private Corporate sector in India, P. L. Beena.
- Mergers *et al.*: Issues, Implications and Case Laws in Corporate Restructuring by S. Ramanujam.
- Sirower, M.L., 1996, The Synergy Trap, Simon & Schuster.
- Alexander Groner, The American Heritage History of American Business and Industry, American Heritage, 1972; Matthew Josephson, The Robber Barons: The Great American Capitalists, 1861–1901, Harcourt Brace, 1962; Ida Tarbell, History of the Standard Oil Company, Amereon Ltd, 1993; Joseph F. Wall, Andrew Carnegie, University of Pittsburgh Press, 1989.
- Causes and Consequences of Hostile Takeovers, Journal of Applied Corporate Finance, Vol. 2, 36-59.
- Healy, P.M., K.G. Palepu and R.S. Ruback, 1992, Does Corporate Performance Improve after Mergers?, Journal of Financial Economics, Vol. 31, 135-176.
- Bradley, M., A. Desai and E.H. Kim, 1988, Synergistic Gains from Corporate Acquisitions and their Division between the Stockholders of Target and Acquiring Firms, Journal of Economics, Vol. 21, 3-40.
- J. Fred Weston and Samuel C. Weaver, Mergers and Acquisitions.
- Matsusaka, John G. "Takeover Motives During the Conglomerate Merger Wave."

- Charles R. Geisst, Monopolies in America, Oxford University Press, 2000.
- Ckbo, B. Espen, "Horizontal Mergers, Collusion, and Stockholder Wealth," Journal of Financial Economics 11 (1983), 241-274.
- icfai University Journal on Mergers and Acquisitions, Vol. 1,2.
- Patrick A Gaughan, Mergers: What can go wrong and how to prevent it.
- Bernard Black, "Is this the first international merger wave?," The M&A Lawyer, July/August 2000.

INTERNET SOURCES

- www.vikalpa.com
- www.iimb.ac.in
- www.nibmindia
- www.nseindia.com
- www.money.redifff.com
- www.indiainfoline.com
- www.nyse.com
- www.bseindia.com
- www.idfisearch.com

Index

capital

capital